THE

AMERICAN SIBERIA

BY

J. C. POWELL

CAPTAIN OF THE FLORIDA CONVICT CAMP

———

A FACSIMILE REPRODUCTION
OF THE 1891 EDITION
WITH AN
INTRODUCTION AND INDEX
BY
WILLIAM WARREN ROGERS

BICENTENNIAL FLORIDIANA
FACSIMILE SERIES

A UNIVERSITY OF FLORIDA BOOK

THE UNIVERSITY PRESSES OF FLORIDA
GAINESVILLE 1976

THE BICENTENNIAL FLORIDIANA
FACSIMILE SERIES
published under the sponsorship of the
BICENTENNIAL COMMISSION OF FLORIDA
SAMUEL PROCTOR, *General Editor*

A FACSIMILE REPRODUCTION
OF THE 1891 EDITION
WITH PREFATORY MATERIAL, INTRODUCTION
AND INDEX ADDED

Library of Congress Cataloging in Publication Data

Powell, J   C
  The American Siberia.

  (Bicentennial Floridiana facsimile series)
  "A University of Florida book."
  Photoreprint ed. of the ed. published by H. J.
Smith, Philadelphia, which was issued as no. 1 of
The golden series.
  Includes bibliographical references and index.
  1. Convict labor—Florida. I. Title. II. Se-
ries. III. Series: The golden series ; no. 1
[HV8929.F7P823 1976]   365'.65'09759   76-44514
ISBN 0-8130-0372-5

GENERAL EDITOR'S PREFACE

Use the pruning knife with "a fearless and impartial hand" was the strong recommendation of George F. Drew, Florida's Redeemer governor, to the legislature in 1877. He deplored the $40,000 a year that it cost to maintain the state penitentiary, and he urged that convicts be leased to private employers who would care for them and also pay an annual fee to the state. The lease system was not new to Florida; it had been utilized in a limited way even before the Civil War. Florida, however, was the last southern state to adopt the system officially. The legislation in 1877 inaugurated a state convict leasing system and authorized a similar arrangement at the county level.

From an economic point of view, leasing of convicts made sense. In the first year of operation, the system saved Florida $4,600. But there were other problems, not the least of which were the safety and mortality of the prisoners. For an able-bodied man to be leased out for as long as seven years was the equivalent of capital punishment. Prison mortality figures were usually hidden, but an observer needed no document to substantiate the horrors of the system. The prisoners were worked from daylight to dark, and punishment was inflicted on the slightest provocation. According to one eyewitness: "Theirs is a grievous lot; a thousand times more grievous than the law ever contemplated."

Yet with all the cruelty, there were many apologists for the system. Some argued that the convicts benefited from being worked regularly, and that since most of them were accustomed to outdoor life, it was more humane and healthful than cooping them up within walls. The convicts were more reliable and productive than was free labor, and it was argued that they were needed on the railroads, in the turpentine camps, and in the mines that were so essential to the New South's economy. The biggest asset, however, in the minds of the Democratic Bourbons, was that Florida enjoyed a clear profit. There was little concern for the economic and political corruption which the system spurred, and neither the politicians nor the public cared too much about the fact that the prisoners all too often suffered from malnutrition, vermin, beatings, and from indescribable filth. Nevertheless, opinion slowly formed against leasing the convicts when experience showed that the abuses were virtually impossible to eliminate. The system began to be discarded around 1890 in state after state throughout the South, being replaced by the contractor public account systems. In 1904, only four southern states—Florida, Alabama, Georgia, and Virginia—still utilized the lease. Virginia moved to end it by legislative action in 1901, Georgia followed in 1908, and Florida in 1924. Alabama closed the door on this "relic of barbarism" in 1928.

The Progressive period saw many social changes occurring on the American scene. These included a much more enlightened attitude toward care and re-habilitation of convicts. It is ironic that Florida, which had participated so actively in the brutal convict lease system, established a model penitentiary at Raiford. J. S. Blitch, who had helped organize the political campaign which made Sidney J. Catts governor in 1917, became superintendent of the prison in 1918 after first serving as the governor's secretary. Catts took a genuine interest in prison conditions, frequently visiting the facilities at Raiford. He and Blitch made Raiford a national model of penal reform. One student of Florida prison reform concluded that the convicts there were "better cared for than they had ever been." Blitch was described as "one of the outstanding prison superinten-dents in the United States." There was, of course, an-other side to the story. The disappearance of "the American Siberia" from the Florida and southern scene did not eliminate the persistent evils that characterized it. Prisoners still suffered neglect and brutality, but in-creasingly in the twentieth century persistent efforts of public-spirited citizens, women's and civic clubs, and trained criminologists have sponsored reforms in the South and throughout the nation.

The story that John C. Powell tells in *The American Siberia*, the volume which Professor William Warren Rogers has edited in the Facsimile series, is a horrifying one. Based as it is upon Powell's own actual experiences in Florida, it calls for reflection as the state and nation celebrate the Bicentennial. It is a time to remember not only the great moments of our past, but to reveal the valleys of our history also, and to determine the progress that we have made in the direction of change and reform. The ultimate has not yet been achieved; continual support and concern are needed.

Powell's *The American Siberia or Fourteen Years' Experience in a Southern Convict Camp* is one of the volumes in the Bicentennial Floridiana Facsimile Series published by the University Presses of Florida for the American Revolution Bicentennial Commission of Florida. The full series includes twenty-five facsimile volumes of rare, out-of-print books which detail Florida's rich and exciting past. Each volume has been edited by a specialist, and in the case of *The American Siberia* by Professor Rogers. The editor has written a comprehensive introduction and has compiled an index.

William Warren Rogers, a native of Alabama, holds his degrees from Auburn University and the University of North Carolina at Chapel Hill. He has received a number of important research grants and has published widely in the areas of Southern, Florida, Georgia, and Alabama history. He is the author of a multi-volume history of Thomas County, Georgia, *Stephen S. Renfroe; Alabama's Outlaw Sheriff, The One Gallused Rebellion: Agrarianism in Alabama, 1865–1896,* and is co-author of *Labor Revolt in Alabama: The Great Strike of 1894.* He has also contributed articles to numerous scholarly journals. He is professor of history at the Florida State University.

University of Florida

SAMUEL PROCTOR
General Editor

INTRODUCTION

The American publishing house of H. J. Smith & Company produced an unusual book in 1891. The publication, printed in London at the same time by the firm of Gay and Bird, bore the lengthy but provocative title of *The American Siberia, or Fourteen Years' Experience in a Southern Convict Camp*. Authored by John C. Powell, the book contained fifteen illustrations by the artist, H. Mayer.

Powell, then a man of forty, did not look like a literary person. A full, slightly drooping mustache, a hairline that receded far back along his skull, and a gaunt look combined to give him the appearance of a clerk or perhaps a farmer. If his countenance was not that of a writer, it revealed even less his true occupation: captain of a Florida convict camp.

The details of Powell's biography, particularly his later life, are almost unknown. He was born and raised in south Georgia. He and his wife, Lizzie, also a native of south Georgia, had at least two children, both boys (another child was accidentally burned to death at the age of five months). During the period that Powell writes about, his family maintained residences at different times in Suwannee County, at Live Oak in Madison County, and at Monticello in Jefferson County.[1] Working with him from time to time as guards were his brother, W. F. Powell, and a brother-in-law, R. A. Mills.

Nothing is known about Powell's educational background, but it was singular, if not unprecedented, for a convict captain to write a book. No doubt his publishers had editors who aided Powell with his manuscript, but the writing has a certain style that must have been the author's own. Obviously, the book was published in the expectation of attracting readers and making money. In 1891 the muckraking era was still a long way from high tide and Progressivism had barely begun. Across the South the Bourbon Democrats were at war with the emerging Populists, and while the agrarians' program included a strong plea for penal reform, the main thrust of their demands was for economic and political reform. Still, there were a number of southern editors, politicians, writers, and critics who condemned the convict leasing system. In *The Silent South*, published in 1885, George W. Cable called convict leasing "a disgrace to civilization."[2] Mississippi had abolished the system in 1890, and Tennessee would do so in 1895.[3]

The publication of Powell's recollections was undoubtedly prompted in part by the success of George Kennan's recent book on Siberia. Kennan, an author, lecturer, and newspaperman, had shocked American readers with his revelations of crime and punishment, Russian style. A book similar to Kennan's *Siberia and the Exile System*, but based on conditions in America, seemed reasonably sure to attract readers.[4]

Whatever the motivations of Powell or his publishers, the captain's product was a unique and important work of lasting value. In his narrative Powell described from his own experiences what it was like to be a convict captain in the Florida penal system. In doing so, he detailed how the prisoners were housed, fed, and clothed, how they were cared for medically, how they were worked (his description of the brutal "turpentine process" is both excellent and excruciating), and how they were disciplined. The system, as Powell explained it, amounted in fact to an American Siberia. His convincing premise was that the only differences between the two regions were geographical and climatic.

Powell's story deals with the last half of the nineteenth century, but Florida's experience with the incarceration of human beings dates back to 1570 when Spanish soldiers built a prison at St. Augustine, the first one outside Mexico on the North American continent.[5] Much later, as a territory and a state, Florida lagged behind most of the other southern states in developing a prison system. For that matter, the South as a whole lay outside national efforts at prison reform. A large part of the explanation stemmed from the institution of slavery. Planters meted out private punishments, although there were also special slave courts. Even so, all of the southern states except Florida, North Carolina, and South Carolina had established state prisons by 1860. Florida and the Carolinas then relied on a system of county jails.[6]

The end of the Civil War saw an increase in crime by the whites. If this were not problem enough, the black population, now free, was no longer subject to private punishment. Such a situation heavily taxed the resources of the southern states. Seeking relief, the South turned to the convict lease system, an expedient that would become a national scandal before it was finally abandoned. As the system operated, the state leased to the highest bidder for a fixed sum all or many of its convicts. The lessee assumed total responsibility for the prisoners. Usually, the leases went to mining companies, planters, politicians, railroad companies, and lumber and turpentine industries. Not only was the state relieved of an economic burden, the prisoners became an actual source of income.[7] As George W. Cable acidly wrote, "the penitentiary whose annual report shows the largest cash balance paid into the State's treasury is the best." Cable saw the system as "a shameful and disastrous source of revenue."[8]

Convict leasing victimized both races, but was particularly harsh on blacks. Negroes were more frequently arrested than whites, and, once brought into court, were more likely to be convicted. Once the Bourbons had regained control of state governments, they enacted laws providing harsh penalties for petty crimes against property. Blacks were sure to be ensnared. Lessees were more interested in production than in the welfare of their prisoners, and one historian has written that in some ways "the lease system was harsher than slavery for blacks."[9]

Immediately after the war, the military and provisional governments in the South experimented with the lease system, and the Republican regimes that followed continued it. Florida had briefly tried leasing prisoners in the antebellum period, but was the last southern state to adopt the system officially.[10] Republican Governor Harrison Reed saw the need for a state prison in Florida, and after securing the use of Federal Arsenal property at Chattahoochee, he supported a bill establishing the system. Passed in 1868, the act organized the prison as a military post. It was not long before complaints were issued about the expenses of the prison. As a result, the Reed administration leased some of the prisoners to private contractors and so inaugurated in Florida the convict lease system.[11] In 1871 a law repealed the 1868 legislation and created a civil institution to replace the military organization, but the practice of leasing continued.[12]

Powell's story begins with the transferring of the reins of political power from the Republicans to the Democrats. Marcellus L. Stearns, the carpetbagger acting governor from Maine, departed Tallahassee and was succeeded by a conservative, George F. Drew of Ellaville, Madison County. Among the problems facing the Redeemer Democrats, who were committed to a policy of financial retrenchment and frugality in government, was that posed by the prison population.

Their solution was to continue, extend, and refine what the Republicans had begun. A law passed in 1877 legally established the state convict lease system. The same session enacted legislation creating a similar arrangement at the county level.[13]

Although Powell's book is not concerned with county prisoners, the system there was, if possible, worse than that of the state.[14] Besides the distinction between state and county convict leasing, a separate but related practice was that of peonage. Complex and confusing, peonage rested on debt. In some states a sharecropper unable to pay his debts could be forced to remain on the owner's plantation. Another form of peonage originated out of local jails. Inmates squared their debts by allowing an employer to pay their fines, and they, in turn, worked out their obligations.[15] Not publicized in Florida until the twentieth century, peonage was a direct outgrowth of convict leasing. Unscrupulous Florida contractors, especially at the county level, forced prisoners into debt and retained them as workers long after their sentences were completed.[16]

State implementation by putting the prisoners up for bids sets the stage for Powell's work. He describes how Green Chaires, a wealthy planter of Leon County, leased part of the prison force, while Major H. A. Wyse obtained the remainder. Wyse used the prisoners to construct a railroad in northeast Florida, and he hired Powell as his captain. The prisoners were also used to work in the endless tracts of pine forests that covered north Florida. Wyse agreed to supply the firm of Dutton, Ruff & Jones, headed by Charles K. Dutton of New York, with "gum." Dutton's firm dealt in turpentine, rosin, and naval stores, and it was up to Powell and the guards to see to it that the orders were filled. Soon turpentine camps and subcamps were established —they were moved from time to time amid much inefficiency—as bases. The main camp in the early years was near Live Oak and bore the melodic but hardly descriptive name of Sing Sing. The name was probably derived from the older state prison at Ossining, New York.

Some three years later the state put the convicts up for bids again. Major Wyse did not renew his contract, but Powell stayed on as captain for his new employer, the East Florida railroad. When in 1882, Charles K. Dutton became the lessee, Powell was retained once again. Powell's career was interrupted by a jurisdictional dispute with his superiors, and he resigned, without hard feelings, to engage briefly in farming and the mercantile business in Jefferson County. In 1890 E. B. Bailey of Monticello became the lessee. Bailey subleased some of the prisoners to four men who continued to use them in the turpentine camps. Those he employed in his own operations were put to work in the much less demanding business of farming. Yet it would be Bailey who shifted some of his prisoners to working in phosphate mines and added a new dimension of horrors to the system.[17] In need of an experienced captain to supervise the convicts, Bailey turned to the logical man, John C. Powell. At the time his book was written, Powell was a convict captain once again.

Relying almost exclusively on his own recall, Powell makes spelling errors—Governor Stearns becomes "Sterns," Major Wyse "Wise," Green Chaires "Cheers," and so on. There are examples of awkward punctuation, and many of the principals mentioned are not supplied with first names. Yet Powell writes clear, direct sentences, depending on the incredible stories he is relating to sustain reader interest. On occasion a sort of sensational, dime-novel construction and mood mar the prose, but such intrusions are rare. More than making up for such shortcomings are the book's strengths.

Certain colloquialisms keep cropping up with refreshing regularity. (This editor's favorite is Powell's penchant for declaring the inevitability of some event as "morally certain.") His descriptions of subtropical Florida are vivid, even haunting. Snakes, alligators, birds, maddening winged insects, and wild animals come to life in Powell's pages. Florida's relentless heat can be felt, and its swamps—tangled masses of jungle vines, luxuriant flowers, trees, treacherous bogs, bushes, and palmetto clumps—cut through by dark rivers are authentically portrayed. Powell is good at depicting the encompassing characteristics of the camps: their forlornness, how they looked, the materials they were made of, how they smelled. One can almost hear the chains rattle and the prisoners moan as they are locked in after a killing day of work and lie in the darkness waiting for the strange night sounds to begin. It is impossible to remain unmoved by Powell's accounts of prisoners inadequately clothed and fed and of sick men and women virtually untended (some camps were decimated by epidemics). Sadistic guards backed by the authority of gun and lash moved among the prisoners, always demanding more production.

The author's command of both cracker and black dialects and speech patterns is sometimes overdrawn but always believable. His brief but sharply etched portraits of the people he writes about—country folk, city rowdies, moonshiners, captains, guards, prisoners, trusties, employers—provide added authority. The approach is ruminative and basically chronological. Within this framework appear episodes and vignettes.

Powell's work is especially valuable for its compelling disclosures. The reader learns that the guards were usually young men recruited from the neighborhoods of the camps and poorly paid. One example is given of a prisoner who escaped and eventually became a guard himself in Georgia. Most of the prisoners were blacks, but there was little racial segregation. There were women prisoners, the vast majority of them Negroes, and there was little distinction made as to sex. The prisoners were lumped together regardless of the nature of their crimes. Hardened murderers worked and lived side by side with youths whose offenses were often so petty that they defy classification as crimes. If one goal of incarceration is to reform the prisoner, the opposite result was achieved in Florida's camps.

Quite possibly the book's main attraction for the reader of its time was the many accounts of prisoners who escaped and the subsequent efforts to recapture them. Powell observes that few prisoners attempted or committed suicide. Although no official records were kept of the escapes, many convicts tried to gain their freedom, and a few succeeded. Powell recounts the names, personalities, and physical descriptions of escapees and the circumstances of their flights. Most breakouts were desperate and unimaginative: a prisoner would sever his chains with a work instrument and dash madly into the woods, or failing that, hobble painfully away, hampered by the ever-present chains, an easy victim to recapture. Escape would be followed by an alarm and the quick pursuit by guards and their dogs (curiously, foxhounds proved to be more effective trackers than bloodhounds). Then came the tense moments of overtaking and recapturing the fugitive or fugitives. So many episodes of escape are treated that they become the book's major theme. Given the cruelties under which the typical prisoner lived and the frequently unfair severity of his punishment, the reader follows any given flight with the hope that the convict's escape will be successful.

Deviating from his story line to become philosophical, Powell speculated on what it was that drove a man to attempt escape. That some men condemned to life imprisonment had nothing to lose by taking off was easily comprehensible. Yet others, having almost completed their sentences, made impulsive, inexplicable attempts. Baffled by such behavior, Powell concluded that at some point life in a turpentine camp could become absolutely unbearable. A man would then become capable of any act, no matter how irrational.

There is no end to the incredible, unpredictable, and unsuspected information that emerges from the book. Lessee Green Chaires and his family lived upstairs in his home while the downstairs was used to house some thirty or so convicts; if it is not common knowledge that Lamont is a community in Jefferson County, it is even less widely circulated that the settlement was also known as Lickskillet; without detection one prisoner used his camp time to counterfeit coins so perfect that they easily passed for the real thing; few men ever lived so varied an existence as the prisoner Richard "Dick" Evans, formerly the sheriff and marshal of Pensacola; Taylor and Lafayette counties were such havens for escapees and desperadoes that law officials, fearing for their lives, refused to serve warrants in them—district judges would convene court in the counties on Monday and adjourn on Tuesday without a single case on the docket; Captain Powell's favorite dogs were named Loud and Music; and in the historic annals of bribing guards to insure successful escape, one of Powell's charges may have been unique in offering an orange grove in return for safe passage out.

Powell emerges as a conscientious but not a cruel man, certainly a man of personal courage. Although he often punished prisoners by whipping them or having them whipped, he did not engage in mindless torture. He records one example of having shot a man fatally, but even that was the result of a fusillade laid down by several guards. He writes of having shot one other man who later recovered. Without doubt he was unpopular with the inmates, and in 1879, he, along with several other men, was indicted for cruelty to prisoners. The case was dismissed.

The impression emerges from the book that Powell did not relish his job. At times he defended the system, but he comprehended that it was barbarous, inflicting savage physical punishment and laying open psychological wounds whose scars would never heal. Yet he was part of a system, and to the best of his abilities, which were considerable, he carried out his job. In ending his "desultory memoir," Powell accurately called it a "frank recital," but he was unhappily inaccurate in proclaiming convict leasing in Florida "an institution that is rapidly passing away."

How widely *The American Siberia* was circulated is unknown, but it had some impact. In England the London *Spectator*'s slightly incredulous reviewer praised it highly, and in 1893 the book was republished.[18] Powell's work may well have influenced Duncan U. Fletcher, a young state representative from Jacksonville. In 1893 Fletcher, later a United States senator, joined seventeen of his colleagues in an unsuccessful attempt to pass an act abolishing the lease system and creating a state prison.[19]

The process was a slow one, but as the twentieth century began, pressure mounted to rid the state of the inhuman and embarrassing system. More and more prominent Floridians voiced public opposition to an institution that would have dishonored the Middle Ages, and the first real progress came at the county level. In 1910 Hillsborough County voted to end leasing. Even so, the system died hard, and in 1911 Governor Albert W. Gilchrist vetoed a measure that would have abolished the leasing of state prisoners. Yet during the Gilchrist era lands were purchased for a state penitentiary at Raiford. Construction went forward, and in the next few years prisoners who were not leased were housed there. Elected governor in 1912, Park Trammell favored ending leasing and supported a bill to that effect. The administration-backed measure passed the Florida House but failed in the Senate.[20]

A legislative act of 1915 limited state leasing to black males, and finally, in 1919, the system was abolished, and the prisoners were shuttled into a state convict road force. Leasing at the county level and its by-product, peonage, continued.[21] Although delayed too many years, passage of the measure marked the culmination of a long reform campaign. Aware that humanitarian motives were prominent, a close student of Florida's prison system has suggested the presence of other impulses. At the time Florida, like other states, was undergoing a boom in highway expansion. The advantage of utilizing state convicts in the expensive process of laying down a network of roads was not lost on certain officials.[22]

The tragic and sensational case of Martin Tabert brought the lease system to its final end. Some counties had followed the lead of Hillsborough in abolishing leasing, but others, among them Leon, had not. In December 1921, Martin Tabert, a twenty-two-year-old North Dakotan who was exploring the South, was arrested for hopping a freight train in Tallahassee. Unable to pay his fine, Tabert was sentenced to sixty days in the Leon County jail and then leased to a lumber company. He was sent to a camp at Clara in Dixie County and died there in February 1922, flogged to death by a whipping boss. The young man's parents were informed that he had died of "fever and other complications," and more than a year passed before the real facts were revealed by a fellow convict who had witnessed the torture.

The *New York World* ran a series of articles exposing conditions in Florida's convict camps, and newspapers in Florida published irate editorials. Responding to a request from the North Dakota legislature, the Florida legislature established a joint House and Senate committee to investigate the Tabert matter and consider whether the leasing of county convicts should be abolished. Certain officials implicated in the case either lost their jobs or suffered humiliating publicity. The whipping boss was found guilty of second degree murder, but two years later was granted a new trial and acquitted. The principals in the Tabert affair got off light, but even so, the end result was the abolishment of leasing and of corporal punishment. In 1923 Governor Cary Hardee signed separate bills forbidding the whipping of prisoners and ending forever the lease system.[23]

In the decades that followed, Florida's prisons, like those in the rest of the country, would become increasingly overcrowded and inadequate. Yet the convict lease system, as described by John C. Powell in *The American Siberia* was no more. As one scholar has written, it was a system of "cruelty and brutality," one rarely "equalled in modern times."[24]

WILLIAM WARREN ROGERS

The Florida State University

NOTES

1. Manuscript Census, 1880, Population, Suwannee County, Florida, p. 115.

2. George W. Cable, *The Silent South* (New York, 1885), p. 172. Curiously, Cable analyzed convict leasing in all the southern states except Florida. Earlier in the 1880s Cable had spoken out against leasing both publicly and in the pages of *Century Magazine*.

3. Fletcher M. Green, "Some Aspects of the Convict Lease System in the Southern States," in *Essays in Southern History*, ed. Fletcher M. Green (Chapel Hill, N.C., 1949), p. 121.

4. Kennan, a long-time Associated Press reporter, had written widely for *Outlook*. His book on Siberia was published in 1891 by the Century Company.

5. James Bacchus, "Shackles in the Sunshine," Orlando (Fla.) *Sentinel Star Sunday Magazine*, June 17, 1973. The next two issues of the magazine, June 23 and June 30, 1973, continued the series by Bacchus. The prize-winning articles are pene-

trating and well written. They were the outgrowth of a seminar in race relations taken by Bacchus at Yale University and taught by Professor C. Vann Woodward.

6. Kathleen Falconer Pratt, "The Development of the Florida Prison System" (M.A. thesis, Florida State University, 1949), pp. 1–4; N. Gordon Carper, "The Convict-Lease System in Florida, 1866–1923" (Ph.D. diss., Florida State University, 1964), pp. 1–8.

7. For perceptive comments, see C. Vann Woodward, *Origins of the New South* (Baton Rouge, La., 1951), pp. 212–15; see also Hilda Zimmerman, "Penal Systems and Penal Reforms in the South since the Civil War" (Ph.D. diss., University of North Carolina, Chapel Hill, 1947), passim.

8. Cable, *The Silent South*, pp. 124, 126.

9. Bacchus, "Shackles in the Sunshine," June 17, 1973.

10. Carper, "Convict-Lease System in Florida," pp. 3, 10.

11. Florida *Acts and Resolutions*, 1868, c. 1635, pp. 35–43; Carper, "Convict-Lease System in Florida," pp. 14–15; see also Jerrell H. Shofner, *Nor Is It Over Yet: Florida in the Era of Reconstruction, 1863–1877* (Gainesville, Fla., 1974), p. 217.

12. Florida *Acts and Resolutions*, 1871, c. 1835, pp. 17–23; Carper, "Convict-Lease System in Florida," p. 27.

13. Florida *Acts and Resolutions*, 1877, c. 3034, pp. 92–95; c. 2090, p. 32; c. 2092, p. 38; for data on convict leasing in the mid-1880s, see U.S. Congress, House of Representatives, *House Executive Documents*, 49th Congress, 2d, sess., vol. 1, part 5, pp. 52, 381–93.

14. Carper, "Convict-Lease System in Florida," pp. 187–217.

15. Pete Daniel, *The Shadow of Slavery: Peonage in the South, 1901–1969* (Urbana, Ill., 1972), pp. 24–25; for demonstrating the difference between peonage and the convict lease system, Daniel gives substantial credit to Dan T. Carter, "Prison, Politics, and Business: The Convict Lease System in the Post-Civil War South" (M.A. thesis, University of Wisconsin, Madison, 1964).

16. Carper, "Convict-Lease System in Florida," pp. 204–329.

17. Ibid., pp. 97–98, 109.

18. London *Spectator*, January 30, 1892, pp. 143–44. The second publisher was the Chicago firm of W. B. Conkley Company. *The American Siberia* has been reprinted twice in recent years. In 1969 Arno Press and the *New York Times* reprinted the work without an introduction or an index. In 1970 Patterson-Smith of Montclair, N.J., brought it out in the

Reprint Series in Criminology, Law Enforcement, and Social Problems. The Patterson-Smith edition has an index and a brief but informative foreword by Blake McKelvey, an authority on American prisons.

19. Wayne, Flint, *Duncan Upshaw Fletcher: Dixie's Reluctant Progressive* (Tallahassee, Fla., 1971), p. 28.

20. Carper, "Convict-Lease System in Florida," pp. 273, 281–85; Pratt, "Development of the Florida Prison System," pp. 79–89.

21. Florida *Acts and Resolutions*, 1915, c. 6916, pp. 255–57; 1919, c. 7833, pp. 101–2; Carper, "Convict-Lease System in Florida," pp. 294–95, 301–3.

22. Bacchus, "Shackles in the Sunshine," June 17, 1973.

23. Florida *Acts and Resolutions*, 1923, c. 9332, pp. 413–14; c. 9202, pp. 231–35. Bacchus, Carper, and Pratt all cover the details of the Tabert case well. See also Carper, "Martin Tabert, Martyr of an Era," *Florida Historical Quarterly* 52 (October 1973): 115–31. For the case's larger setting, see George Brown Tindall, *The Emergence of the New South, 1913–1945* (Baton Rouge, La., 1967), pp. 213–14.

24. Green, "Aspects of the Convict Lease System," p. 115.

THE

AMERICAN SIBERIA

OR

Fourteen Years' Experience in a Southern Convict Camp

CAPT. J. C. POWELL.

THE

AMERICAN SIBERIA

OR

Fourteen Years' Experience in a Southern Convict Camp

BY

J. C. POWELL

CAPTAIN OF THE FLORIDA CONVICT CAMP

H. J. SMITH & CO
PHILADELPHIA—CHICAGO—KANSAS CITY
OAKLAND, CAL
1891

PUBLISHERS PREFACE.

The countless thousands who have read George Kennan's sketches of exile life in Siberia with awe and interest will be surprised and shocked to learn that the terrible cruelties he there depicts have their counterpart in the convict-lease system of one of our Southern States. Were it not for climatic and race conditions the reader could easily fancy that. "The American Siberia" is taken from Mr. Kennan's writings so far as working, feeding, sleeping, guarding, and punishing the prisoners are concerned.

To the horrors with which Mr. Kennan has made us acquainted Captain Powell has added the tracking of the fugitives with trained blood-hounds—a system compelled by the vast extent of uninhabitable forest and morass abounding in Florida—and has given us pen-pictures of the lawlessness which obtains not only among the desperadoes of that region but among the untutored backwoodsmen as well, which will prove a revelation to the reader.

Being an advocate of the convict-lease system as the one best suited to the present state of affairs in Florida, Captain Powell cannot be charged with exaggeration in his presentation of the actual workings of that system; his volume is, therefore, worthy of careful consideration.

Abounding in thrilling anecdotes of daring adventure, desperate deed, narrow escape, ludicrous situation, humorous repartee, pathetic incident, picturesque description of southern scenes and simple rustic life among a people, many of whom have never been beyond the confines of their own country, the "American Siberia" is offered to the public with the full conviction that it will prove an interesting and an instructive volume.

The Publishers.

Chicago, April 1, 1891.

PREFACE

Before inviting the attention of the readers to this little work, I beg to offer a few words of explanation. It is not a record, not a running history, but simply a narrative of those incidents in fourteen years experience which, by virtue of their unusual character, have retained a fixed place in my memory. My first object has been to present them in an entertaining form, and while I have adhered strictly to facts, I have largely omitted those dates and statistics which might give my work official weight at the cost of interest.

I have devoted the best years of my life to the management of the lease system of Florida, and my most earnest thought to its improvement. None know its defects better than I, and none are better aware that they spring from conditions alone. We have little material for skilled labor among the criminals of the South. The bulk of our convicts are negroes who could not by any possibility learn a trade, and how to employ them at anything save the simplest manual toil is a problem not yet solved. The camp system involves a discipline peculiar to itself. There are many things about it which may seem harsh, stringent and cruel, and would be, in a northern penitentiary, but are stern necessities here. Without them the prisoners could not be kept together for two consecutive days. There is a vast difference, in short, between stone walls and open fields, and what follows should be construed in that light.

I feel this much due not only to myself but to those lessees who have been my principals, and whose good faith I never had occasion to question.

J. C. POWELL.

THE AMERICAN SIBERIA

CHAPTER I

In the fall of 1876 a singular spectacle might have been observed at the little town of Live Oak, in Northern Florida. A train had just arrived, and from one of the cars some thirty odd men disembarked and formed in irregular procession by the road-side. The sun never shone upon a more abject picture of misery and dilapidation. They were gaunt, haggard, famished, wasted with disease, smeared with grime, and clad in filthy tatters. Chains clattered about their trembling limbs, and so inhuman was their aspect that the crowd of curiosity seekers who had assembled around the depot shrank back appalled.

These thirty starved and half-dying wretches were about half of the convicts of the State of Florida. They were those who had emerged alive from as awful an experience as men were ever fated to undergo. Florida had shortly before passed from radical rule. Governor Sterns had been superseded by George F. Drew, now a merchant in Jacksonville, and with the change of administration came a gen-

7

eral overhauling of state institutions, including the
penal system. Prior to that time a penitentiary
had been maintained in a very old building at Chattahoochee, since remodeled and used as an insane
asylum. The state was poor, largely unsettled,
torn with political strife, and as might have been
expected, the prison was run in a rather happy-go-
lucky fashion, and the history of its early years is
a story of experiments, expedients and make-shifts
of which little or no record was kept.

I do not pretend to say whose fault it was. A
man named Martin was warden, and the place was
horror's den. He had been placed in charge of the
building during the war, at a time when it was used
as an arsenal. The state got rid of its criminals
by turning them over bodily to him, and paid him
bonuses amounting to over $30,000 for accepting the
charge. He had vast vineyards and worked the convicts in them, manufacturing all kinds of wine, at
which he made a fortune. There were no restric-
tions whatever placed upon him by the state. The
punishments consisted of stringing up by the
thumbs, "sweating" and "watering." The first ex-
plains itself; sweating was shutting up in a close
box-cell without ventilation or light; and the last
named was no less than the celebrated torture prac-
ticed during the Spanish Inquisition under the
name of the "ordeal by water." Accounts of it
given by historians are almost identical with the
method then in vogue at Chattahoochee. The pris-

oner was strapped down, a funnel forced into his mouth and water poured in. The effect was to enormously distend the stomach, producing not only great agony but a sense of impending death, due to pressure on the heart, that unnerved the stoutest. When deaths occurred, as they did quite frequently, the remains were wrapped in a blanket and buried in a shallow trench that barely covered the remains from the air. Some horrible stories, too revolting to repeat in detail, are told of graves desecrated by domestic animals, and there was no record kept of the dead or those who escaped. In brief, the state turned over its charges body and soul, and thenceforth washed its hands of them. And this was not in the middle ages or Siberia, but in these United States, about a decade and a half ago.

During this administration escapes were frequent, and there are some tragic stories connected with them. The guards were often negro convicts, and the old maxim of slavery days, that a black overseer was the cruelest to his race, was proven time and again. One day a prisoner, a white man, made his escape and succeeded in penetrating the wilds of La Fayette County, some seventy miles to the south. In that section of Florida there are not only dense and trackless forests, but they are intersected by wide lagoons and palmetto flats, in which the tropical monotony of the scene is such that a man may wander for days and not be positive that he has made any actual progress. None dare venture into these wastes save trained backwoodsmen, and even they are often lost in the forest labyrinths.

In this natural man-trap the convict found himself. It was impossible to track him through such a jungle, infested as it was by wild beasts, alligators and horrible reptile life from the swamps, and there he was left to his fate. Months afterward a party of adventurous hunters discovered a sodden bundle of rags in a very lonely spot in the woods. They disturbed the unsightly rubbish and lay bare the bones of a man. The tatters of clothing bore the tell-tale prison stripes, and by a peculiarity of the shoes, one of them being a convict's brogan and the other a gaiter, the remains were identified as those of the fugitive who had disappeared in the forest. It was a dreadful death, alone in that awful solitude, and could the story of what he suffered be told in its entirety it would doubtless put romance to shame.

The story of this *regime* is one of almost unrelieved barbarity, and the absence of records make it almost impossible to give an idea of the state of affairs, except by isolated instances. For example: the guards were armed with muskets and bayonets. The latter were carried fixed, and when the squads returned at night they were called into frequent requisition to keep laggards in line. Often a man would drop of fatigue, and he would be instantly and mercilessly prodded with the cruel steel.

The legs and backs of nearly all of the convicts were covered with the scars of bayonet-wounds. The squads were run in, in this manner, to make it possible to work them up to the latest moment.

On one occasion there was a prisoner who gave considerable trouble by reason of his frequent attempts to escape. His name has been lost, but his number was forty-seven. At last he formed a plot to levant through one of the windows, and a fellow-prisoner who was in his confidence betrayed him to the officers. This furnished a good opportunity to get rid of him, and guards were stationed before the windows all night, to kill him as he came out. However, he suspected something wrong, and did not come. Next morning he was placed in the blacksmith shop and purposely left alone near an open window. The temptation was too great and he made his way through, to be shot dead by a guard who lay ambushed for him outside. I have these statements from the then deputy warden of the prison, who is now a resident of Jacksonville, and there is no doubt of their accuracy.

At last, shortly before the close of Governor Stern's administration, a great scandal, growing out of these atrocities, became so imminent, that a sort of compromise between the prison and the lease systems was effected. The convicts were divided; about half were sent to build a railroad between St. John and Lake Eustace, and the balance were left under Martin. It was hardly an improvement.

The line of the proposed railroad was through a virgin wilderness; there seems to have been no attention whatever paid to proper equipments, and the story of that terrible journey stands unparalleled in criminal annals. Dozens of those who went into the tropical marshes and palmetto jungles of Lake Eustace went to certain death. There was no provision made for either shelter or supplies. Rude huts were built of whatever material came to hand, and in the periods of heavy rain it was no unusual thing for the convicts to awake in the morning half submerged in mud and slime. The commissary department dwindled into nothing. I do not mean that there was some food or a little food, but that there was no food at all. In this extremity, the convicts were driven to live as the wild beasts, except that they were only allowed the briefest intervals from labor to scour the woods for food. They dug up roots and cut the tops from "cabbage" palmetto trees. Noble Hawkins, a ten-year Nassau convict, lived for fourteen days on nothing but palmetto tops and a little salt, and his case was but one of many.

Of course there is a limit to human endurance. It was not long before the camp was ravaged by every disease induced by starvation and exposure. The pestilential swamps were full of fever, and skin maladies; scurvy and pneumonia ran riot. Dysentery was most common, and reduced the men to a point of emaciation difficult to describe or to credit. Every stopping-place was a shambles, and the line of survey is punctuated by grave-yards.

The camp was at different times in charge of various captains, and under some of them the punishments were excessive. Hanging up by the thumbs was usually resorted to, and this led, one night, to a grisly tragedy. A negro convict was strung up for some infraction of the rules. Whip-cords were fastened around his thumbs, the loose ends flung over a convenient limb and made taut until his toes swung clear of the ground. The scared convicts huddled about the camp-fire and watched their comrade as he writhed, and yelled expecting every moment that the cords would be unfastened and his agony ended. But the captain had determined to make a salutary example, and he let the negro hang. Meantime the poor wretch's anguish was a hideous thing to see. They say his muscles knotted into cramps under the strain, his eyes started from his head, and sweat ran from his body in streams. An hour passed—then two. His shrieks had ceased and his struggles grown feeble, so they let him down and he fell to the ground like a log—dead.

It was then that the captain realized what a monstrous thing he had done, and he deserted his post, slunk away in the night, and was never heard of again. Here was a study for an artist. Night in the palmetto woods, the flaming camp-fire outlining the circle of frightened convicts and the miserable barracks where they slept, the distorted corpse upon the ground, and the panic-stricken officer creeping away among the trees.

Soon after the Drew administration assumed the state government, the horrible condition of affairs which I have outlined forced a change of some character. The building at Chattahoochee was entirely unsuited for prison purposes, and the lease system was turned to, as a last resort, very much as was the case when Georgia was saddled with that institution. Advertisement was made for bids and the Lake Eustace gang hired to Major H. A. Wise, a general merchant of Live Oak. The balance were sub-leased to Green Cheers, a farmer who lived in Leon County. My brother, W. F. Powell, and myself were employed by Major Wise to take charge of his camp, and thus began the system which has been more or less under my eye ever since.

The ragged battalion who disembarked at Live Oak were the survivors of those who had penetrated the wild morasses of Lake Eustace. The major part of them were negroes, but it was impossible to tell, as they stood, who were white and who were black, so incrusted were they all with the accumulated filth of months. The sight staggered me, but I saw at once that the first business on hand was to get them clean, and I ordered them to strip. It was not a difficult task, as scarcely a man of them possessed a whole garment, and I burned the vermin-swarming rags as fast as they were removed. Tubs of water were placed along the line; they bathed, and clean clothes were given them.

While this operation was in progress, my attention was attracted in particular to two white men, by reason of the singular appearance of their hands. They resembled the paws of certain apes, for their thumbs, which were enormously enlarged at the ends, were also quite as long as their index-fingers, and the tips of all were on a line. This deformity was occasioned by stringing up, and when one stops to consider the amount of pressure necessary to stretch out a man's thumb fully three inches, some idea can be formed of the severity of the punishment. The names of these two men were Robert and Eugene Weaver. They were natives of one of the northern states, and subsequently served out their sentence and were discharged by me.

Another member of the squad was a negro named Cy Williams, and as he had had a rather extraordinary history, I may as well tell it at this point. He was the first prisoner received by the State of Florida, and was entered in the books as No. 1. He did not know his age, but when he was a mere pickaninny, running about in the one garment that forms the costume of all negro youngsters in the South, he was arrested for stealing a horse. He was not large enough to mount the animal, and was caught in the act of leading it off by the halter, for which he was duly sentenced to twenty years impris-

onment. Warden Martin was somewhat puzzled to
know what to do with so small a convict, but he
finally invented a task that certainly reflects credit
upon his ingenuity. He placed two bricks at each
end of the prison yard, and giving the black baby
two more, ordered him to carry them to one of the
piles, lay them down, pick up the other two, which
in turn he carried to the further end, exchanged
again, and so on back and forth all day long, always
carrying two bricks. He was warned that he
would be whipped if he failed to pile the bricks
neatly or broke any of them. He grew up at the
task, and the constant abrasion of merely picking up
and laying down wore out four sets of bricks before he was put to other labor. Owing to the absence of all system, he received no commutation upon
the first ten years he served, but on the balance of
the sentence he received what is called in Florida
"gain time," making the entire sentence seventeen
years and some months.

Major Wise leased the prisoners with rather
vague speculative views, and the squad was sent
originally to the Santa Fe River, where they were
employed for some months in "ranging" timber.
Meantime he closed a contract with Dutton, Ruff
& Jones, dealers in turpentine, rosin and naval
stores, by which he engaged to deliver "gum" from
the vast tracts of pine woods owned by the firm
in the vicinity of Live Oak. The leading spirit of
the firm was Major Charles K. Dutton, of New York

City, who subsequently occupied about the same relation to the lease system in Florida as that of Senator Joseph Brown in Georgia.

It was evident that very few of these men were able to stand the exhausting labor of turpentine culture, and that it would be necessary to first get them into condition. However, we went into camp in the woods near a little station called Padlock. There we built a rude log-house, twenty by forty feet, for sleeping quarters. Like Solomon's temple, it was erected without the sound of hammer, and the roof was secured by a curious system of pegs and weights. There was not a nail in the structure, and it was altogether a fine specimen of wild wood-craft. On each side two sloping platforms ran from end to end, one built over the other, like berths in a steamboat. The prisoners slept on them, and midway between the two a long chain was stretched at night-time, on which they were strung by means of smaller chains fastened to their leg-irons. These latter were technically known as "waist-chains," and were attached in turn to the "stride-chain," which passed from shackle to shackle, with play enough to enable a man to walk by taking fairly short steps. As both stride and waist chains were riveted on, it would appear at first glance impossible for a man to remove his pants with his ankles thus fastened together, and in fact, when we first received the convicts, they wore them buttoned down the outside of the leg, like Mexican vanqueros.

But in time they learned to draw the garment down between the ankle and the iron, and then up and out; a simple but ingenious process, and slashed trousers were abandoned.

The front of this "cell-house," as it was termed, was not sealed solidly, but slatted, so as to permit a view of the interior at any time. At night it was lighted by pine knots burned on a sort of pyre in the middle of the floor, and a watchman sat with loaded rifle in front. The routine of locking up the men was about as follows: As they returned from work they filed in and took their places on the sleeping-platform. The building chain was then passed through a ring at the end of each man's waist-chain and made fast outside. A squad of guards were ready, torches in hand, and proceeded to rapidly scrutinize each link of the irons, a process familiarly known in camp as "chain search." This over, supper was served and eaten, and after a short interval a bell rang for every man to lie down. That was the last thing in order for the night, and if any convict desired to move or change his position thereafter it was required that he first call to the night guard and obtain his permission. I may say that the same system, with some immaterial modifications, is the one in vogue at the present day.

We named our camp "Padlock," after the station. Besides the cell-house, there were buildings of the same primitive character for the guards, but there

EXTERIOR OF PRISON.

Siberia, Page 19.

was no stockade, and the cooking was done hunter-fashion, on a bank of dirt under a lean-to shelter. The kettles and pots were suspended over it by bits of wire, and, in brief, all the other appointments were on the same scale. The food consisted of fat "white bacon," corn-bread and cow-peas—the latter a small red variety indigenous to the South. They were wretchedly prepared, of course, and in summertime I have often taken my penknife and scraped off a literal stratum of gnats from the top of the pea pan before sending it to the men.

We discarded the old methods of punishment from the start, and adopted the strap, which has been used ever since to enforce discipline, and has of late years been adopted by state law. It consists of a section of tough leather about a foot and a half long by three inches broad, and attached to a wooden handle. The castigation is applied below the loins, and the convict placed upon his knees with his palms on the ground. The clothing is then drawn back and the leather applied until, in the judgment of the captain, a sufficient punishment has been administered. There is no legal restriction, and never was, as to the number of blows, the frequency of punishment or by whom it shall be applied; but the rule has been that the warden, his assistant or the captain in direct charge of the camp, shall do the whipping. During the time that I was at the head of the lease system, I allowed no one else to administer punishment, as the matter was always un-

2

avoidably the source of more or less outside criticism, and I did not wish responsibility to be divided.

To return to the camp, the prisoners were worked in the woods in a radius of a few miles, and conveyed to and from the spot on what was known as a "squad-chain." In principle it was similar to a building-chain, but it was shorter and lighter, and the men were strung upon it by the rings of their waist-chains like ribs from a central vertebræ. Every man went on a trot. They kept this gait up all day long, from tree to tree, and as the labor is exhausting in the extreme, I have frequently seen men on their way back to camp drop of fatigue, and their comrades on the squad-chain drag them a dozen yards through the dirt before the pace could be checked so as to enable them to regain their feet. There would be a prodigious clatter of iron, a cloud of dust, a volley of imprecation, and the fallen man would stagger up, dash the dirt out of his eyes, and go reeling and running on.

But these scenes came later on, for the camp was for a long time virtually a hospital. I found the dysentery, with which most of the men were affected, almost impossible to check, and the mortality was terrible. The disease was of the same character as that which was so prevalent on both sides during the war, and many a corpse interred at Sing Sing was almost literally nothing but skin and bones. No records were kept of the number of deaths, and I am unable at this lapse of time to estimate them with accuracy, but it was a large proportion of our prisoners, and it was nearly a year before the balance were in what might be termed fairly good condition.

I shall frequently have occasion in this narrative to speak of trailing convict runaways with hounds, and I know that there is a prevalent impression that bloodhounds are employed for the purpose. This is an error, and I believe that the first and only experiment of that sort was made at the beginning of the Wise lease. Major Wise sent to New York and procured two imported blood-hounds of pure strain—one a male and the other a female. They were sent originally to the Santa Fe River, to the logging-camp, but afterward transferred to us at Padlock. The male died from the effects of the journey, but the other arrived in tolerably fair condition, and was certainly a formidable brute. She was as large as a calf, pied like a leopard, and looked less like a dog than some unknown wild beast. She spread consternation among the natives, and when they happened to encounter me with her they would abandon the road and take to the tall timber. I called the dog Flora.

The experiment was not a success. Beyond the intimidation of her appearance Flora had no especial value, and was vastly inferior to a deer-hound as a trailer. The hot climate proved too much for her, and she eventually succumbed to it and took the hydrophobia. I shut her up in a shed upon the first appearance of the symptoms, and the great brute, howling, foaming and dashing herself against the walls in her paroxysms, was a spectacle of such terror that none dare approach her. She crunched some heavy boxes that happened to lie inside absolutely into splinters, and in one of the fits she died.

The fact is that fox-hounds are used for man-hunting in nearly all the southern convict camps. They are probably a trifle less keen of scent than a deer-hound, but they have also a slower gait, which is an advantage, inasmuch as it enables the horsemen to keep up with them. But at any rate, their marvelous powers of following a trail hours after it has been made, holding it through turns and back-tracks and over traveled roads, almost surpasses belief. The fox-hound used for the purpose is slightly larger than a full-blooded pointer, and built a little heavier about the shoulders, but resembles it in general contour of the body. The head, however, is that of the typical hound—long-eared, sad-faced and deep-jowled. I can affirm that some of them are natural man-hunters, just as a colt is occasionally born with a natural trotting-gait. In training puppies at the camp it was my custom to order one of the "trusties" to run a few miles through the woods, and then put the dogs on his track. I have known them to trail the man over the most intricate routes, and eventually follow up his track into the cell-house and pick out the identical trusty where he lay, among a hundred other men, upon the sleeping-platform.

Another popular error in regard to chasing with hounds is that they attack the prisoner when they run up upon him. Such is by no means the case. The hounds are always closely followed by horsemen, and if they once get out of sight and sound the pursuit might as well be abandoned. In brief, they are simply guides, and when once the game is brought to bay, they are too wary to venture close enough to run the risk of a blow. I have known cases where dogs have been killed, but the convict invariably employed some strategy to entice them in range. On one or two occasions men have hidden behind trees, and the hounds, intent upon the trail, have been brained as they rushed past.

By what faculty they follow a track is a disputed question. They seem to have no difficulty in distinguishing the trail of one man from another, and it is certainly not in all cases by reason of an odor left upon the earth. I have one dog at the present writing that trails entirely by air; that is to say, he never touches his nose to the ground but invariably holds his head high, and in this attitude runs at full speed, immediately distinguishes cross-trails, and rarely makes a mistake.

There have at different times been some few men under me who, by a freak of nature or some inexplicable condition, left no trail and could not be followed by any hound. I do not attempt to explain it, but simply state it as a fact—one, by the bye, that has a bearing upon several cases I will detail further on. Whatever emanation lingers in the wake of the average human being and furnishes the mysterious clue to the dog was certainly lacking in their make-up.

CHAPTER II

In addition to the reasons that appeared upon the surface, there was another, and a potent one, for the employment of convict labor in the turpentine woods. The work is severe to a degree almost impossible to exaggerate, and it is very difficult to control a sufficient quantity of free labor to properly cultivate any great number of trees. The natives follow it more as a make-shift than a vocation, and are only too glad to abandon its hardships for any other character of work that comes to hand. The variety of pine from which the gum is obtained covers immense areas of Georgia and Northern Florida, and the process, which is curious and not generally understood, is as follows:

Early in the spring large oval cups, technically termed "boxes," are set into the trunks of the trees, close to the ground. They are several inches deep and hollowed out at the bottom to receive the sap. All this is done with a peculiarly shaped axe, having an extremely long blade, and it is needless to say the operation requires both strength and dexterity. When properly cut, the box has the appearance of having been made by a chisel, yet it is possible to hew one out with as few as nine blows of the axe. This of course requires a great expert, and few acquire that degree of skill. The average daily task of a convict is from sixty to ninety boxes.

Directly after the box is cut a triangular wedge is chopped out on each side immediately over the top. This is called "cornering," and is usually done by two men, one of whom strikes a right-handed and one a left-handed blow. The object is to expose a fresh surface of the trunk from which the sap may flow, running down into the concavity of the box. The sap is of a pearly color, thick and viscid, and the cornering usually fills the box for the first time. It is then dipped into buckets with a large lance-pointed tool known as a spoon," and almost a fac-simile, on a magnified scale, of a steel ink-eraser. The buckets are emptied into barrels which are collected by teamsters who range the woods with their wagons and deliver the products to the stills.

After the first flow is dipped a new incision is made by slicing out two slanting lines at the top of the cornering. A short tool called a hack, weighted at one end and armed with a crooked blade at the other, is used, and the operation is termed "chipping." The fresh flow refills the box, after which the chipping is repeated, alternating with dipping until the face of the box is so high from successive slicing that it cannot readily be reached. "Pulling" is then resorted to. This is identical with chipping, except that a very long-handled tool with a double blade at the end is used to cut the streaks, the workman reaching up and sometimes raising the face as high as twelve feet.

About the first of October the faces of the boxes are thickly coated with coagulated sap, and other work is suspended while this is removed, chopped off with implements something like gardeners' trowels. This occupies three or four months, and the routine is commenced over again. The entire product is distilled as gathered, heated in retorts and the vapor condensed through worms into the commercial spirits of turpentine. The residue left in the vats is rosin.

Chipping is the hardest work of all. It requires a man of immense stamina and in perfect physical condition, for he not only has to stoop continually, but drive the hack through the wood with one muscular exertion. The crooked blade curves the cut upward and inward, "shading," it is called, the purpose being to cast a shadow on the incision and prevent the sun from drying the fresh surface too rapidly. Each branch of the work is done by different squads, and they are worked as nearly as possible in lines—"drifting," it is called, and the word well expresses it—through the timber, some cutting, some chipping and some dipping. The guards follow at a little distance behind. Occasionally thick patches of undergrowth are encountered. Hills and dales are to be crossed and swamps skirted, and altogether, a cool head, good judgment and

steady nerve are needed to prevent continual escapes. But these qualifications were seldom ob-
tainable, for guarding was very poorly paid, and
this, as well as the other details I have entered into, have an important bearing upon numerous deliveries which subsequently took place.

We had not been long in camp at Padlock before
I discovered that we had an exceptionally dangerous and desperate class of men to deal with. Most
of them were "Cracker" outlaws and cut-throat negroes, sentenced, as a rule, for crimes of the most
atrocious character. The case of John Ponde will
suffice as an illustration and indicate the bloody
nature of certain of these wild woodsmen and their
contempt for law. Ponde was a white man, and had
settled in Bradford County, where he lived with
his wife in the style of the average squatter. He
was not on good terms with his father-in-law, but
nothing serious was thought of the matter until one
morning he saw the old man riding by on a horse,
and called his wife to the door.

"Do you see him?" he said.

"Yes."

"Well, take a good look at him; this is the last
time you will ever see him alive."

He was as good as his word. He followed the
old man to town, got on a spree, with him and the
two started back riding double, Ponde behind.
When they were nearly home Ponde wrapped his
arms around his victim and held him still while

he slowly and deliberately cut him to death with a
pocket-knife. For this crime he was sentenced to
prison for life.

It goes without saying that this type of men were
continually plotting for liberty, and many things
conspired to favor escapes—the wild nature of the
surrounding country, the necessity of working the
convicts out of doors, and most of all a deep-seated
and bitter prejudice among the citizens against
the lease system. Frightful stories of cruelty were
constantly bruited about; and while it was easy for
a fugitive to obtain a hiding place and assistance,
every possible obstacle was thrown in the way of
those engaged in pursuit.

The first serious trouble we had of the kind occurred in December. A guard named George Turner had charge of a squad working in the woods, and
in which was a white man named Freeman and
two negroes named McPherson and Perry, all desperadoes of the first order. Louis Fennison, a trusty,
accompanied the party, and had the privilege of
coming close to the guard to give him water, when
he desired it. At their first opportunity, Freeman,
McPherson and Perry took the trusty aside and
sought to enlist him in a plot to murder Turner
and set the quads at liberty. The plan was for
Fennison to seize him while he was drinking and
prevent him from using his rifle, while the others
rushed in and brained him with their axes.

The trusty pretended to agree—it would have

been suicide to refuse—and anxiously looked for an opportunity to warn the intended victim. He was watched so closely, however, by the plotters, that none occurred until at the very moment fixed for the deed. The squad was at the time on the skirts of the dense pine forest, and Turner, all unsuspicious, called for a drink of water. As he raised the dipper the murderous trio began to close in upon him, axes in hand.

"Look out, boss!" yelled Fennison; "they're goin' to kill you!"

The guard leaped back, leveled his rifle and called a halt, just in time to save his life. Word was sent into camp, each of the ringleaders whipped and ornamented with a fifty-pound ball and chain.

While in the woods next day, Perry, who had, by the way, only one year to serve, made some pretext to step aside, and picking up the huge ball attached to his leg, started off on a lope. The guard fired after him a few times, but the bullets flew aside, and finally a trusty set off in pursuit, yelling as he ran. Our commissary-man, Rodger Wah, hearing the uproar from the camp, leaped on a horse and galloped in that direction. He was not long in overtaking the fugitive, whose act was simply madness, for handicapped as he was by his irons, he stood not a ghost of a show of success. Wah shouted to him to stop, but he paid no attention to the order, and when the horse was close at his heels, began to run like a coursed fox, wheeling and doubling, until the commissary-man finally fired his revolver over his head to frighten him. But Perry was made of stuff not easily frightened, and he ignored the bullet as he had the order. Then Wah fired point-blank at him and sent an ounce of lead through his spine. The negro reeled, clutched at the air and fell, mortally wounded. A little while afterward he died.

This tragedy enormously intensified the popular feeling against the camp. The shooting was re-hearsed with the invariable embellishment of rumor, and generally denounced as murder. At the next session of the grand jury a true bill was returned against Wah, but before the case was called sen-timent had somewhat subsided, and the matter lan-guished in court and was finally dropped.

We were at Padlock camp for a year, and this was the most serious affair of the kind that occurred during that period. But there was no lack of other excitement, and it was during this sojourn that I had a most curious adventure. I was working a squad of fifteen negroes "dipping" turpentine gum in the woods. It had been a pleasant day, warm and genial, with no indication of storm, but just before quitting work I heard a dull, roaring sound and saw a singular figment of cloud bearing rapidly down upon us from the southwest. It was the dead-black color of soot and shaped like a vast balloon, the lower end sagging almost to the ground. I had never seen such a thing before, but I recognized it from descriptions as the famous funnel-shaped cloud that has figured in the history of so many terrible tornadoes, and I shouted to my men to lie down.

As the monstrous apparition approached us the noise increased to a roar and crash of sound that beggars all description. The earth vibrated under us, and I could see pine trees and innumerable debris turning over and over in the black swirl, like chaff in a puff of wind. I took it for granted that we were lost, but with one supreme shock the great cloud passed us and tore away with a strange bounding or hopping motion, and finally disappeared.

During the passage of the cyclone it was impossible to see or even think, but as it receded I found myself standing in the midst of my prostrate squad with at least half a dozen of the negroes clinging to my legs like scared children. They were frightened half out of their wits, as well they might have been, for we were right on the edge of the tornado, and the difference of a few yards would have swept us all into eternity. As soon as possible I started out to see what damage had been done, and made an amusing discovery. An old negro known as "Brit" was employed hauling gum barrels with a four-mule team, and was quite close to us at the time the storm-cloud appeared. He was in fact directly in the track, but in one of the jumps I have alluded to the monster passed over his head, tearing out a swath on each side and inclosing him in a tangled

circle of broken tree-trunks, like a barricade.
When we arrived on the spot the mules were lying
flat on the ground like frightened rabbits, and the
old man was on his knees, his eyes glued tight shut,
his very wool uncurled with terror, and his voice
lifted in that fervent prayer that only an African
can command:

"Oh, Hebbenly Fadder!" he moaned, "spar' yo'
sarbent! Take de mewls an' take de convicts;
dey all sinner-men, oh, Lawd! but I'se a berry use-
ful man in dis community, Hebbenly Fadder! Dey
carn't well spar' me! You'se done teached me a lesson, Lawd; you'se skeered me pow'ful, but don't
take me jist yet. Don't do nuffin' you might 'gret!"

We had hard work persuading him that the peril
was past, and harder work extricating his team
from the mass of rubbish that surrounded it. This
was the first and only storm of the kind that had
visited Florida in the memory of man. Its track
was well defined, from three to four miles long and
about 200 yards wide. It is swept clear of timber,
and this boulevard of nature's cutting can be easily
and perfectly traced to the present day.

I have frequently observed, during my entire
prison experience, that the period of the greatest
despondency and desperation in a convict's term
is immediately after he is received. The rude surroundings of the camp, the hard fare, the chains,
and the grinding toil combine to form an overwhelm-
ing conviction that he can never live to serve out

his sentence, and he is either seized with dull, despairing apathy or nerved to escape at any cost, according to what manner of man he is. Consequently I have made it my business to keep a close eye upon new men, and an incident which occurred about this time furnishes a good illustration of the matter.

We received a negro on a five-year sentence, and I put him to work in the woods. He was afflicted with an incurable malady, which, while it did not prevent his getting about, greatly preyed upon his mind, and a few days after he arrived, he called to me during one of my visits to the squad and asked me if I would do him a favor. I replied that I would if it lay in my power. Upon that he bared his breast. "Shoot me then," he said; "don't wound me, but shoot me through the heart. I can't do this work and there is no use trying. The sooner I am dead the better for me."

I told him that I could not shoot him down in cold blood, but if he was really anxious to court death, all he had to do was to run or make an attack on me and I would do my utmost to accommodate him. This view of the case did not strike him favorably, and I closed the interview by giving him a whipping and telling him to go back to work. In the course of the day he endeavored to get hold of a knife, for the avowed purpose of cutting his throat; but failing in that, he lapsed into a morose, brooding state, from which he rallied in a month or so,

THE DARKEY'S PRAYER.

Siberia, Page 37.

and eventually served out his sentence pretty cheer fully. His case was a sample of most others.

In the course of a year we had the woods well marked out in the immediate vicinity of Padlock, and built a new camp, called Sing Sing, four miles further on. In all of its appointments it was a considerable improvement on Padlock. We built two cell-houses, each a hundred feet long, and discarded the uncomfortable and inconvenient arrangement of double bunks. A single sleeping-platform was built on each side, and the building-chain run through eyelets in posts sunk at intervals in the ground. No stockade was considered necessary, and the yard was guarded by a man stationed at each of the four corners.

Everything was done by convict labor, and when the buildings were nearly completed and work in fact commenced in the adjacent woods, the first escape of the new camp took place. A negro, whose name I have now forgotten, but who was at any rate detailed for yard work, seized an opportunity one morning and dashed past the nearest guard. He was fired upon, and the sound of the shot reached my ears where I was working a squad at no great distance off in the woods. One of my most positive orders was that no weapon should be discharged on the premises, unless in case of escape; so I knew at once what had occurred, and surmising that the runaway would be apt to come in our direction, I called the squad instantly together, put them on

3

the squad-chain and ordered them to lie down. As soon as they were all well concealed, I rose up cautiously through the underbrush and looked toward the camp.

Sure enough, there was the man coming full-tilt toward us and heading a ludicrous procession. Every available man on the yard, including trusted prisoners, had joined in the pursuit. First came the cook, flourishing a huge butcher-knife with which he had been cutting meat at the time the alarm was given, and after him, in order, were several trusties and guards, all red-faced, panting and yelling frantically at every bound. I sallied out to head off the fugitive, but as soon as he saw me he made a sudden tack at right angles with his course. This was a cue to his pursuers, who also swerved to intercept him in the new direction, but the movement was observed and he tacked again, bringing him in line with me. Thus he was between two fires, but he repeated his maneuver so persistently, gaining a little every time, that I finally shot at him. At the sound he turned a somersault in the air and fell with a crash upon his face. I supposed, of course, that I had killed him, and the next instant the cook, who still led the procession, was astride of his back. When I reached the spot the negro had twisted his head around and was glaring up at the cook, who had his big butcher-knife poised in the air and swore he would kill him if he moved. It seemed that my bullet had barely grazed the fellow's head, but such an impact will easily knock a man over, and he was positive for the time being that most of his brains had been blown out. The cook was also a convict, and I shall frequently have occasion to refer to cases where one prisoner assisted in capturing another. Some of them were very remarkable instances of zeal, where zeal would naturally be least expected, but it was invariably at the cost of universal hatred among the balance of the men. The convict who so distinguished himself was marked for every affront that could be offered him, and in one case for death itself.

But I never gave too much credit to these self-appointed officers. It was not a sense of duty that prompted them, but axes of their own that they had to grind, and in many cases they would prevent an escape in order to inspire confidence and pave the way to getting away themselves. The trusty who figured in the instance I have just narrated was named Henry Stevens. Major Wise, the lessee, thought so well of the act that he naturally took him to Live Oak to drive one of his teams. This was the chance Stevens wanted, and he turned up missing one morning and has never since been heard of. Louis Fennison, the trusty who frustrated the plot to murder a guard in the woods, escaped not long afterward, and was next heard of in the city chain-gang at Albany, Georgia. We reclaimed him at the expiration of his sentence, and in later years, under a new lease, he escaped again with two oth-

ers, and is still at large. Thus instances might be
cited at a tiresome length, but these suffice to make
the point plain.

Very shortly after the camp was moved en masse
to Sing Sing we received two prisoners named
John Roberts and William Revel, farmers' boys
who were sent to prison for one year each. They
had relatives living all through that part of the
county, and Major Wise being well acquainted with
their families, ordered me, very much against my
judgment, to make them both trusties on the spot.
A few days passed and one morning they started
out to get wood. They did not return, and by night-
time it became evident that they had violated their
paroles and ran away.

Here was a ticklish situation. They belonged, as
I have said, to an immense system of intermarriage;
it was only too likely that the whole neighborhood
would be up and in arms to protect them, and such
was the sentiment against us, that there was not
a settler in a radius of fifty miles but would have
deemed it a pious act to give them shelter. In
brief, none of my guards would consent to join
in the chase, regarding it as an open invitation for
assassination.

Roberts' father lived no great distance away, and
thinking it probable that the fugitives had gone
there, I persuaded a backwoodsman named Buck
Harder to guide me to the spot. We reached it
at about eleven o'clock, by a long, tortuous route

through the forest. It was a one-story log cabin, standing in the midst of a little clearing and flanked by a few dilapidated out-buildings. A stick-and-dirt chimney rose above the ridge-pole of the dwelling and a few dried skins were extended against the walls. Beyond the outlying pines the moon swung high, and all was silent as the grave.

I ordered Harder to the rear and hammered on the front door. At last, after repeated knocking, a quavering voice called out:

"Who's there?"

"Strike a light," I answered, "and see."

"But what do you all want?" drawled the voice.

Strike a light and I'll tell you my business."

There was a long pause, and then came the slowest und of match-striking I ever heard in my life. It seemed an interminable time before light shone through the chinks, and then, determined to face the music at once, I burst open the door and rushed in.

The cabin contained only one room; a few withe-bottomed chairs stood on the floor, the bare cross-logs formed the ceiling, and a long, old-fashioned rifle, that had no doubt killed many a deer, hung with its accouterments against the chimney-piece. A fire was smoldering on the hearth, and some one lying before it covered with a quilt. An old, wrinkled-faced man, bent and grizzled, but tough as a knot, his white hair and beard disheveled and his whole aspect that of one just aroused from slumber, stood holding a light. His sly little eyes blinked against the flame as he regarded me, and rightly surmising that he was Roberts' father, I told him, pretty briefly, what my errand was.

"Sakes alive!" he exclaimed with every signal of dismay; "I can't believe it! Ye don't mean to say that thar fool boy's done cleaned up an' runned away?"

"That's it exactly," I replied; "and, furthermore, I want to find out what you know about it."

"Me!" he said in a grieved tone; "why, I don't know nothin' 'tall 'bout it. Ain't seed hide nur hair of the boy."

I looked around, and noticing a spare bed in one corner with the cover disturbed, asked who slept there.

"My darter," he drawled; "but she got cold and kim down 'fore the hearth."

This struck me as suspicious, and at any rate I made up my mind to know who was under that quilt. So I seized the corner and pulled it back, and instantly a pretty face, a pair of eyes, cute and black as a weasel's, peered up at me. It was a young girl *en dishabille*, and I dropped the quilt and retired in some confusion.

I did not leave altogether, but hid in the woods, after a search of the out-buildings, and watched the house. It was one of those bitterly cold nights that are occasionally experienced in sub-tropical climates, and by morning I was thoroughly benumbed and forced to go without making any discoveries.

But in after times I heard a curious story from this same girl who slept under the quilt. Her brother had gone straight from the prison to the house and told of his escape. During the day he remained in hiding, while a plan was carefully laid for his journey out of the country. Meanwhile he changed his clothes, hiding the convict stripes under the shucks in the corn-crib, and at dark a ruse was prepared to deceive me in case I should put in an appearance. To that end the spare bed was purposely rumpled to lead me to believe that he was concealed somewhere about the premises, and detain me there as long as possible—which afterward turned out as arranged. In point of fact, he left the house a short time before I arrived and made straight off. Not only this, but the lonely road between the clearing and the camp was patrolled by sympathetic neighbors, armed with their long-barreled rifles and prepared for a rescue at any cost in case I captured my man. Had I known this as I rode through those midnight aisles, I confess my feelings would have been peculiar.

Roberts was never heard of again, but Revel made his way to Georgia, where, strange to say, he sought and procured a position as guard at Jones' convict camp, near Waycross. We learned of his presence there and prepared to go after him, but he got wind of it and fled, and is probably still under cover in some of the abundant fastnesses of the neighboring states.

CHAPTER III

Meantime, what of the thirty and odd convicts turned over to farmer Green Cheers of Leon County, something over a year before? Mr. Cheers understood his business, but unfortunately his business was not the handling of convicts. He was a farmer simply, with very indistinct notions as to either the difficulties or responsibilities of the charge he had undertaken. There was a large, old-fashioned house on his place, and he used the upper story for his family, and the lower for the convicts, who were at that time known by numbers instead of their names—a plan since discarded. After the prisoners were once turned over to him, there was practically no inquiry made as to their welfare, certainly none by the state, which followed the good old custom in this regard; and they might as well have been in Africa, for all that was known of them until in the second year of the lease, when suddenly, by some means or other, the ugly secrets of the farm and manor-house came to light; and startling they were indeed.

It was learned that these miserable people had suffered constantly for food and clothing and the common necessaries of life. No attention was paid to cleanliness, or the conditions necessary to common de-

cency. The sick suffered and died without attention,
and the well were worked with less consideration
than is accorded to cattle. These are simply facts.
There were three or four women in the squad, and
what they endured cannot be easily or decorously
described in words. There was no system, no
records, and little or no management. I believe
Mr. Cheers lost considerable money by the enterprise.

Among other things, the very unwise course of
arming prisoners and using them as guards was
pursued, and this led to one of the most remarkable
deliveries on record. One of the squads was composed of twenty workmen and six guards—all convicts. Among the guards was a man named Joseph
Alston, who had been at one time quite rich and
what is familiarly termed a "high-roller."

Before the war he belonged to the close corpora-
tion of aristocrats who controlled all the large
Floridian plantations, but labor reverses gradually
absorbed his property acre by acre, and he sunk
lower in the social and financial scale, until at last
he committed a larceny of some sort and was sent to
the penitentiary for a term of five years. When he
was trusted with a gun he immediately began to plot
for liberty, and as he was a superior man mentally
to the balance, he soon had the other five guards
in his way of thinking.

When everything was ripe for action, these six
men, who had the full liberty of the place and

access to the stores, slipped one night into a room that was used as a sort of arsenal, and purloined all the spare weapons they could lay their hands on. They took guns and revolvers, old-fashioned army pistols, and plenty of cartridges, powder and shot and percussion-caps, nearly enough in all to arm the entire squad. These were concealed some little distance away, where they could readily be found, and when they took their squad out next morning they halted at the spot.

"Boys," said Alston, "who's tired of prison?"

"Here! Here!" cried everybody except one man.

"Have you nerve enough to stand at my back," continued the leader, "in case of a skirmish?"

"Yes! yes!"

Still one man was silent.

'All right. They are sure to come after us, and I guess we will have to fight our way out. We have weapons here for nearly all of you. Let every true man step out and get a gun."

With that the arms were distributed. The man who had not joined in the demonstration was sharply questioned, and for a while he had to talk for his life. He pleaded fear of failure, and it was finally decided to compel him to go along as a precautionary measure. Thus the fugitives started, headed by the six guards and making for a thickly wooded and swampy cleft not far from the Cheers place. As they penetrated it, the unwilling runaway managed to give the balance the slip in the underbrush,

and ran back. The others halted, intrenched themselves and awaited developments.

It was not long before the convict reached the
farm. He was breathless and wild with excitement,
and when he told his story Mr. Cheers immediately
gathered together a posse of neighbors and started
in pursuit. In a short time they reached the spot
where the fugitives were massed, and were greeted
by a volley that poured into them from behind
palmetto trees, back of logs and every available
lodgment in the thicket. They returned the fire,
and a pitched battle ensued that raged for hours.
The combatants on both sides were trained backwoodsmen as a rule, and versed in the tactics of
Indian warfare. They sought shelter and every
moment drew a galling fire. Gradually the posse
began to gain. They pushed by sallies into the
swamp, and hand-to-hand fights took place in the
thick of the morass, until at length the convicts
were routed. A number were captured, others shot
down, and the rest took advantage of the confusion
to push deep into the swamp and thus made good
their escape.

The facts of this strange fight were hushed up as
soon as possible, but it is reasonably certain that
there were several killed on each side and quite a
number wounded. Among the captured was Alston.
He eventually came under my management. I found
him a tall, slender, black-bearded man, with a cold,
determined face and quiet manners. He served out

a few years of his sentence, and through the influence of powerful friends at the capital obtained a pardon upon the condition that he would not drink "intoxicating liquors" in the future. Whether he fulfilled this unique condition I cannot say. He passed out of sight.

All these things resulted in the convicts being taken away from Mr. Cheers in the second year of his sub-lease. They reached us in about the same condition as those received from Lake Eustace, and some of them were clad in the filthy remnants of the very clothing they had worn at the time they received their original sentence in court. I had about the same experience in getting them into condition for the turpentine work, and will not dwell upon its details.

There were a good many odd stories connected with the convicts we had, that came to light from time to time, and I recall a singular accession to our ranks at about this period. During the old penitentiary *regime* at Chattahoochee, one of the negro sects at Live Oak desired to build a church. The congregation, with infinite pains, collected all the necessary material except the nails. This was a matter of great tribulation to them until one of the deacons, a big, tall, and very bow-legged African, produced a keg of the necessary article. He maintained strict silence as to where the nails came from, and the rest of the flock were divided in opinion between a miracle and a special interposition of providence. However, by a singular coincidence, Major Wise, who had a general store at the place, missed a keg of nails from his warehouse, and he proceeded to have the law on the good deacon. The jury refused to accept the miracle theory, and gave him two years in the penitentiary.

After doing a little of his time the prisoner escaped and was not heard from again until, years after, Major Wise happened to be at Eufala, Alabama, and noticed an extremely bow-legged black man hanging about the depot. It was the deacon. The Major recognized him at once, had him arrested, in spite of his pious protestations, and he was brought to our camp on a requisition. He served out the balance of his time without further trouble.

I have had occasion to mention the state of public feeling against the camp and, indeed, it has an important bearing in much that is told in this narrative. An incident occurring at this time is directly in point. Not only were the people exceedingly bitter on the subject of the lease, but stories of dreadful cruelties were freely circulated and generally believed. Among them was one in which it was said that I had killed a negro convict, stamped his brains out with my boots, and hid the body under an old church until I had an opportunity to bury it at night. This tale was told with every circumstance of truth, and eventually reached the ears of the Governor. Consequently I was very much surprised one day to receive a visit from a legislative investigating committee. I at once had the men drawn up in line and the roll called, which showed that none were missing, and, of course, settled the question, but I was anxious to learn who had started the story.

At last I traced it to a young man named Fry, but I could never find him. He had always "just gone," every place I inquired. One day, however, while working a squad near what was called the Macedonia Church, I learned that he was at a neighboring house and sent a trusty after him. A man named Hurst was lounging near the church door.

"Tell Fry to bring his shot-gun with him when he comes," he called after the trusty.

"What have you to do with this affair?" I asked him.

He replied, pretty stoutly, that Fry had told no lie about me and that he was prepared to vouch for him or for anything he said. Some further words passed in which I think I said that I could whip him and Fry together, if necessary.

"You can't whip me alone, yet," retorted Hurst; and, seeing myself in for it, I handed my gun to a guard and set to, not exactly according to prize-ring rules, but actively enough to soon leave me in possession of the field and put a stop forever to the murder story. Fry remained discreetly in-doors during the combat. Hurst afterward hired to me as a guard and made a good one. He was involved, later on, in an exciting shooting affray, which I will narrate at the proper place.

One great need at the camp at that time was a pack of reliable fox-hounds for trailing escapes. We kept a look-out for such animals, and one morning an old woman went past with three puppies bunched together in her arms. My brother called to her and offered ten dollars for the litter, which she accepted with alacrity, and thus we obtained a start. To any one interested in dog-breeding, the subsequent career of this little pack would be at least a novel story, and the history of the progeny that sprung from it is closely interwoven with the history of the camp. They were pure-blooded hounds, and also natural man-trailers, a thing that does not always follow, by any means. When they were still quite small I had a chance to test their power in a man-ner that would seem quite incredible to those not familiar with the traits of these animals.

Early one warm, pleasant morning, when the air was wonderfully still, but a dense fog hung over the lowlands, I was preparing to ride to the squads on my daily trip of inspection, when I heard the report of a rifle. This being the signal of danger, I listened to determine the direction. Such was the wonderful tranquillity of the atmosphere, that the sound seemed to pass me like something palpable and and go echoing for miles beyond. I knew about where the squads were; hastily gathering the three puppies in my arms, I leaped on my horse and put off at a gallop, when I was again arrested by two more shots from a different quarter. I faced about and made for the direction of the last reports, and reached a squad drawn close together in the woods.

The guard informed me briefly that a convict from some other gang had run past them, and that he had fired upon him, but that the fog was so dense that he could see nothing but a shadowy form through it and was unable to aim accurately.

This indicated only one escape, and getting the direction, I rode over to where the fugitive had passed and put the puppies down upon the trail. They were so small that I was doubtful of the result, but to my surprise, they took scent immediately and started off. I followed and was obliged to constantly check my horse into a walk to keep from stepping on them. It was a slow and probably a comical procession, but the little fellows stuck to it like veterans, toddling along on their short legs, until we had traversed a mile or so, when I saw our man looming through the fog right ahead. He had tired of running, and at the time was pursuing his way at a leisurely walk, imagining himself perfectly safe and little crediting the ability of my baby dogs to hunt him down. I shall never forget the look of disgust that came over his face when I shouted to him to halt and he saw who his pursuers were.

Convicts naturally enough hate the animals that have nipped so many hopes in the bud, and not long after this all three dogs were taken violently sick

BRINGING IN A PRISONER.

Siberia, Page 56.

with every symptom of poisoning, and two died. I ferreted the matter out and discovered that one Cyrus Cooks, then known as "number thirty-four," had given them powdered glass—a favorite prison poison. The survivor of the pack flourished to become the sire of a race of dogs famous in southern prison annals.

While we carried on the work steadily in the woods, Major Wise started a brick-yard on a small scale at Live Oak, and by the way, manufactured the first brick used in that place, which is now a flourishing little city. We sent over a squad of eight men in charge of a guard named Hurst (no relation to the man with whom I had a fight at Macedonia Church) to operate the brick machines. Hurst was a native, and apparently more richly endowed with good nature than good sense. The sun was very hot one day, and thinking to give his squad a treat, he sent to a neighboring house and purchased a quantity of buttermilk. The milk was passed around, and finally he and a convict named Sol Love stood drinking the balance. Love had once before escaped and was not only a desperate fellow but a conniver of the first water. He plied Hurst with smooth talk, and while the guard had his head in the buttermilk-can, imbibing the grateful fluid, all the rest of the squad took to their heels. Hurst, in his consternation, started after them, firing as he ran, and as soon as the coast was clear Love departed in the opposite direction.

4

This completed the guard's bewilderment, and he ran first one way and then the other, until all were out of sight.

The case was quickly reported, and Major Wise, a guard named McIntyre, and I started in pursuit. We held the trail up to the vicinity of the town of Sanderson, near which it became obscure, and we concluded that several, if not all, of the convicts were in hiding thereabouts. Not far from the town there is a railroad bridge, and as night was coming on and it was likely that some of the party would attempt to cross under cover of darkness, we concealed ourselves close by and watched. After it became quite dark, Major Wise and I went to town to get some supper, leaving McIntyre on guard. It subsequently transpired that he also got tired and left; but at any rate, as we came back, groping our way along, we ran directly into three men coming down the road. The surprise was mutual, but as they attempted to run we each seized one, and saw then that they were in prison garb. The third was rapidly making off in the darkness, and both the Major and myself drew our pistols and fired at him. The black figure seemed to reel for an instant, but at the next the night had swallowed him up.

The men we caught were two of the brick-yard fugitives, named Peter Reddick and George Gomez, and the other was the redoubtable Sol Love. We were satisfied with what we had bagged that night, and it was altogether too dark to search further for Love; but next morning we looked over the ground and found indisputable evidence that he had been wounded. We discovered a place where he had stretched himself by a log and bled freely, but the trail took us to a dense swamp in which it was lost.

About two weeks later a rumor came that a strange man had died under mysterious circumstances in a house on the outskirts of the town of St. Mary's. Investigation proved that it was Love. Our bullets had pierced his chest, but as he was a man of herculean strength, he had dragged himself from the swamp to the dwelling where he died, which was occupied by a friend of his. He was so far spent with suffering and fatigue when he arrived that it was impossible for him to rally, and thus ended a desperate man.

Reddick was shortly after the principal in another attempt to escape, that terminated rather grotesquely. He seized a favorable opportunity to make a rush from the yard, and was tearing along at a furious rate when a guard saw him, called on him to halt, and then fired. The bullet went right through his hat, stunning and scaring him so badly that he dropped on all fours and ran like a monkey to a corn-crib which was sitting on piles above the surface of the ground. He scrambled underneath and stretched himself carefully at length, for dead. He was dragged out as stiff as a poker and revived with the strap. Reddick is still in prison, now on his fifth sentence, and has made innumerable attempts to escape, but has always been unsuccessful. Between terms at the Florida prison, he did one at Albany, New York, and is at present under twenty years sentence for thirteen burglaries. He is an expert at what is known as "second-story work."

It might reasonably be supposed that among so many men willing to risk life for liberty there would be others nerved by desperation to a further step, and that suicides would be frequent. But this was not the case. During my fourteen years experience there has been no instance of the kind, and in this particular our prison records are unique. However, there have been attempts—three during our stay at Sing Sing, and they were sufficiently harrowing. We had a negro preacher named Watson, sent from Madison County for stealing cotton. One day his guard threatened him with a whipping for laziness, and the dread of it preyed greatly on his mind. At last he determined to kill himself. He was in the woods at the time, cutting boxes, and seizing his box-axe by the helve, he sawed the keen edge back and forth a dozen times into his throat, completely severing the windpipe and inflicting a horrible wound through which his tongue dropped. The pain unnerved him and he let the axe fall and tried to call for the guard, but only a ghastly, whistling sound came from his mutilated throat.

Thus he stood for several minutes, a picture for a nightmare, staggering, beckoning with his bloody fingers and pointing to the open gash. The guard recoiled in horror, refused to go near him, and sent for me. I sewed up the wound as best I could, and as the jugular vein had escaped by the merest chance, the man eventually got well; but suicide was ever after a subject in which he took no interest.

The next case was that of Thomas Jump, a Hernando County backwoodsman, who was sent to prison for murdering his brother-in-law. He had lived the usual life of a shiftless "Cracker," hunting and fishing, and hard work did not agree with him. He was put to "chipping," and presently stopped in disgust. The guard told him to go to work or he would have him whipped. At the word "whipped," the wild backwoodsman, who had never in all his life suffered a blow in anger, started as if a bullet had struck him. His eyes flashed fire.

"Do what?" he cried.

"Have you whipped," replied the guard coolly.

Jump pondered awhile in silent rage.

"Then it will be the first time," he said, "since my mammy used to do it."

The bare possibility of such a thing stuck in his mind and in a few moments he called wildly to the guard to shoot him, and then attempted to knock his own brains out with the weight attached to his hack. He struck himself hard enough to fell an ox, but his skull was too thick and he survived the hammering. He was afterward pardoned out and lived to be glad of his failure.

The third would-be suicide was Simon Moody, a Bradford negro, who, under circumstances of peculiar atrocity, murdered a white man who had raised him. For this he was sentenced to prison for life; and when the camp-agent called for him at jail, he made some excuse to borrow the jailer's knife, with which he cut his throat from ear to ear. He was stitched up and lived, but, like the preacher Watson, he ever after abhorred the very name of suicide.

While, as has been seen, there were few who were willing to deliberately end their career, there were many who were willing to resort to desperate expedients to avert labor. The most curious case was that of a man named Clow, a druggist and a very well-informed man, who was under seven years sentence for school-record forgery. He was incorrigibly lazy, and having but one eye he determined to totally blind himself to escape work. He procured a needle and tried to hire a fellow-prisoner to hold it while he drove it into the pupil of his remaining eye. He was afraid to undertake the job alone, for fear of mutilating himself without accomplishing his ends. I learned of the matter and punished Clow severely, promising him a good many repetitions if he tried the experiment. This stopped him, but he moped and pined away until he finally died in prison.

James Peterson, a professional thief sent from Gainesville, was a man of the same stamp. He made up his mind not to work, and when sent into the woods to cut boxes, drove his axe through his foot. It was a very severe gash, but was healing and he was able to hobble about, when I sent him into the yard one day to split wood. He grumbled a good deal, and when he reached the woodpile placed his foot on a block and deliberately cut it again across the old wound. The blood spouted out in a perfect torrent and he was carried into the hospital department. For this act he paid a dear penalty. The wound, reopened as it was, refused to heal; both foot and leg swelled to enormous size and finally gangrene set in. After lingering in great agony, he died.

Feigned insanity and pretended sickness were also common dodges. We had a giant of a convict in camp named Jim Johnson, and one morning while in the woods he stuck his axe under his arm and began to gibber idiotically at a tree-top. He could not be moved or silenced, and finally the guard chained him to a pine, clearing the ground round about of sticks and stones, and went on with his squad, first sending a trusty after me. When I arrived he was still talking gibberish to the boughs, and as insanity does not usually set in that way, I concluded the gentleman was shamming. I laid my whip on him pretty vigorously, and presently he came to his senses and begged to be allowed to go

to work   I told him to go ahead, but in a few minutes he resumed his tactics and began wildly cutting down a tree instead of cutting a box in it,
making strange noises at the same time. On this
occasion I prolonged the punishment until he
admitted the ruse and promised to drop it in the
future. He had no more attacks after that, and
made it a point to take new prisoners aside and
warn them in a fatherly way against the insanity
dodge.

A female prisoner also tried it on in a somewhat similar manner. She simulated epileptic
fits and did it to perfection, writhing, shrieking,
and finally lying so still and inert that her breathing could not be detected. On one occasion,
while she was in this condition, I put my finger on
her pulse and found the tell-tale artery beating as
steadily as ever, proving conclusively that there was
no collapse. She was punished, and that ended the
fits.

CHAPTER IV

Of the native outlaws who were in our camp during our stay at Sing Sing, no three more conspicuous examples could be found than Columbus See, John G. Lippford and John Williams. See was a twenty-year man, and Lippford and Williams for five years each. Of the three, Lippford was the most intelligent; he had been convicted of some complicated land fraud; but they were all fearless, determined, inured to hardships from childhood—in short, typical specimens of the wild, southern backwoodsman. It was this trio who plotted and carried out a very original and remarkable prison delivery.

By good conduct and an oily tongue, See managed to inspire sufficient confidence to obtain the position of cook, and as such he had the run of the yard. Shortly afterward the guards began to miss rifle cartridges, but as these are always in considerable demand for hunting, they jokingly laid the loss at one another's door, and nothing much was thought of it. I had at the time a small squad composed exclusively of white men, and Williams and Lippford were members of it. They usually worked in the woods, but one day I left all but one of them on the yard to build a shed. Including some

negroes, there were, in all, fourteen or fifteen convicts about the premises, and they were guarded by
W. J. Hillman, since captain of a convict camp.
Hillman had in some way managed to incur the
enmity of nearly all the white convicts, and they
hated him very cordially. There was only one
other guard on the place—the night watchman, who
was asleep in his room in the guard-house. The
commissary-man had gone bird-hunting that day.

This, then, was the situation when See came
through the yard, apparently on some errand connected with the kitchen. He passed close to Hillman and the instant he was behind him wheeled and
grabbed him around the waist, pinioning his arms
to his side. The next moment they were fighting
like tigers for possession of the guard's gun.

Hillman, who realized fully the feeling of the
men toward him, and the small chance he would
stand when once disarmed, struggled with the
strength of desperation, and would probably have
worsted his assailant had not two other men
dropped apparently from the clouds and taken a
hand in the fray. They were Lippford and Williams,
who had deliberately leaped from the top of the
high shelter where they were working, and escaping
injury by a miracle, joined with See and soon had
the gun.

Lippford instantly cocked it, and pointing it at
Hillman's head, ordered him to lie still. It is
needless to say he obeyed. See then ran into the

guard's quarters, secured the nigh-twatchman's rifle, and going to the rear of the cell-house, dug up a lapful of cartridges, which he had been burying, one by one, for weeks.

By this time they were joined by five others, and the camp was in their hands. After See dug up his ammunition he made a bee-line for the kitchen, with the full intention of then and there killing a negro named Henry Duncan, who was assistant cook, and whose life he had often sworn to take on account of some fancied affront. Duncan saw him coming, and realizing his extreme peril, rushed out and ran like a deer, taking the direction in which the commissary-man was hunting. Common prudence now dictated that the men leave at once, but the temptation to "get even" with Hillman was too strong; the long-restrained hatred broke forth, and they cursed him in every vernacular they could lay their tongue to.

His life, for the moment, was not worth a copper, and See covered him with his rifle where he lay on the ground, and attempted repeatedly to shoot him, but Lippford snatched the muzzle away.

"I can't live satisfied until that man dies," cried the convict, seeking to bring the rifle-sights on a line with the guard's head.

"For God's sake, See!" urged Lippford, "don't put our necks in a halter for a grudge."

At length this counsel prevailed, and the eight men took their departure in a sort of triumphal procession, singing at the tops of their voices. Before going they broke into the dog-kennel and took with them two hounds used for trailing. Seven or eight negroes refused to go, and remained.

I had a house near by and my wife witnessed the whole scene from the front door. When she saw Hillman disarmed, she ran to a bureau and taking out a revolver of mine waved it to him. A few moments later one of the escapes, a negro, dashed past.

"Jim," she called, "go back to camp!"

"Can't do it, Miss Lizzie," answered the darky grinning; "dis yere too good a chance!"

Finally Hillman came for the pistol and started on horseback for Live Oak after help. As he rode off the yard Duncan and the commissary-man came rushing over a wooded slope. The harrowing experience had so changed Hillman and he had turned so black in the face from suffusion of blood that Duncan thought he was a negro in the act of escaping, and shouted to the other to shoot him down. The guard yelled out his name just in the nick of time, and galloped away.

As soon as possible after we received the news, we formed a posse and started in pursuit. We traced the convicts to the Suwanee River, which they crossed, and there the trail was broken; so we were obliged, reluctantly, to abandon the chase. None of the eight men were recaptured, although we occasionally heard from them as they pushed south.

The fact was that, while repeatedly seen, they were such notorious and acknowledged desperadoes that no citizens dared to halt them. I should explain that when I speak of citizens, both here and in other places in this narrative, I use the word in the sense applied in my calling. Just as in Utah all who are not Mormons are known as Gentiles, so in prison vernacular all who are not convicts are alluded to as citizens. The party of fugitives would enter the lonely and isolated cabins of the section they traversed, and force the settlers to give them such food and shelter as they required. At one place they traded one of our guns for a load of provisions.

Of the two dogs they took with them, one, a female, returned and afterward had a litter of puppies that were destined at a later day to participate in some exciting scenes themselves. The other, the sire of the litter, which they carried along or made away with, was the last of the three purchased, as I have related, by my brother to start a pack. He was a magnificent trailer, and I regretted to lose him.

It may be interesting to trace the subsequent career of the three ringleaders. Lippford went to Marion County, and in time the officers learned of his whereabouts and a posse went to capture him. He had cleared a little place in the woods, built himself a cabin and was living the life of the ordinary settler. He was in the house at the time the posse appeared, and when they reached the edge of the

clearing he made a sudden dash from the door and
rushed toward a dense and trackless swamp that
bordered on the place. When the officers saw that
he was about to escape in its impenetrable recesses,
they fired on him, and a bundle he was carrying on
his back fell to the ground. Lippford staggered
on and disappeared in the morass. That was the
last ever seen of him, but as two buckshot holes
were found passing clear through the bundle, it is
safe to say that his bones lie somewhere in the dark
morass that swallowed him up.

Williams met his fate at Brookville, Florida.
He was hiding in the vicinity, but in the course of
time he grew bold and would occasionally come into
town for a spree. His identity was at the time unsuspected, but on one of these carousals he went too
far, and in a spirit of pure drunken deviltry he shot
down an inoffensive negro upon the street. He
took flight, sobered by the enormity of the act, and
was instantly pursued by a throng of citizens and
officers. A running fight ensued, and a deputy sheriff
named John Steele shot him dead. His body was
subsequently identified.

I have reason to believe that See is still alive,
and shall have occasion to again allude to him. He
went into an unsettled portion of Taylor County,
where he lived the life of a wild man, terrorizing
the few who met him and holding his domain by
force of his sinister reputation. Occasionally the
citizens of the county would appeal to the officers

to remove so undesirable a resident, but, as far as I know, no one ever had the hardihood to attempt it.

Time and again during these days, the turbulent and desperate nature of the prisoners broke forth. Some weeks after the capture of the camp which I have detailed, I sent a squad of eight men into the woods in charge of a new guard named W. B. Phillips, a tall, raw-boned, wild-looking native— rather harum-scarum, but a nervy fellow and a dead shot. They had not been out very long before three of the squad—John Jacobs, James Goings and Will iam Alexander—dropped their tools and ran.

Phillips was instantly all excitement and began whooping like a Comanche, but he retained enough presence of mind to open fire. He first drew down on Goings, and at the shot the man fell to the ground, pierced through both legs. It was the shock, however, more than the wound that upset him, and he staggered to his feet again and disappeared in the underbrush. Phillips' next shot was at Alexander, and he also showed signs of being hit, but kept on nevertheless. We afterward learned that the bullet had struck him in the side, inflicting a painful but not a serious wound. By this time Jacobs was nearly 300 yards away, lumbering along and greatly hampered by his chains, which were so short as to prevent him from taking a running gait. It was one chance in a hundred, but the guard took a farewell shot at him, and by a curious accident the bullet struck the stride-chain, cutting it in two. Thus unexpectedly relieved of his impediment, the fugitive bounded like a deer and soon vanished. We did not hear anything more of him for years, and my subsequent experience with him, which was to say the least peculiar, I will relate further on. Alexander also made good his escape and was last seen in Mobile, Alabama, but Goings was less fortunate.

The night following the delivery, I was sitting in my house when a little girl from a neighboring settler's rushed in, as pale as a ghost.

"Oh, Captain Powell!" she exclaimed, "there's a wounded prisoner just passed our house!"

"How did he look?" I asked, hardly able to believe that any of the runaways were still in the vicinity.

"He has both legs broken," she said, "and is pulling himself along with sticks."

Still incredulous, but willing to investigate, I went back with her, and, sure enough, found the track of a man in the dew that lay heavy on the grass. He had been half-crawling and half-dragging himself, by thrusting two sticks in the ground, and the marks were very plain to be seen. By that time it was too dark to do anything that night, but early next morning we took the trail. It was easily traced by the crushed herbage and occasional spots of blood, and much to my surprise, for I knew the man must be very weak and badly wounded, it led

A CLEVER RUSE.

us clear to Live Oak. There it was lost on the hard roads, and we made diligent search for some hours, but were unable to get trace of our man.

We were about to leave when we learned that the night before some one had broken into the house of Colonel White, afterward Judge White, a prominent citizen of the place. There was something peculiar about the burglary. The thief, whoever he was, had made no effort to take any valuables, but had stolen nothing but food and was apparently in a great hurry to get away. All things considered, I concluded to search the premises. They included a large vineyard, in the rear of which was what is called a "sink-hole." These are common in the lime stratum that underlies much of Northern Florida, and are simply deep caverns open at the top and often having a spring of living water at the bottom. This one was densely masked by trees growing in crevices and luxuriant vegetation, and we clambered down to explore it. Crouched upon the slippery rocks at the bottom, and utterly exhausted by pain and fatigue, was our missing prisoner.

We carried him back to camp and he eventually recovered, but how he made so long a journey in his condition is a mystery only to be explained by indomitable nerve.

It so happened that other shooting affrays followed in close order. The convicts knew full well that when they ran they took their lives in their

5

hands, but there was no lack of men prepared for such a risk. The guards, in emergencies of the kind, could not leave their squads, and the only messenger they could send was a bullet. It was hard, I admit, but if blame attached to it, it was the system that should receive it.

Two cases of the sort occurred in one day. In one of them a guard named Hurst, whom I have already mentioned, figured. He had in his squad a veteran sailor named Williams, and the men were chipping pines. This operation necessitates stooping, and finally Williams stuck his hack into a tree and faced about.

"Look here!" he said to the guard, "do you fellows expect a man to work standing on his head?"

"I don't care what you stand on," replied Hurst, "just so you chip those pines."

With that the sailor dashed off through the woods. Hurst fired and the bullet struck him in the hip, knocking him head over heels. In time the wound healed, but Williams persisted that the leg was entirely paralyzed, and went hobbling about on crutches, doing no work at all for the balance of his time—some two years. I frequently accused him of shamming, but the prison physician thought otherwise. On the day of his discharge my judgment was vindicated. He made perfectly sure that he was free, and then broke both crutches across his knees, roaring with laughter.

"Ha! ha! ha!" he shouted; "a man that can't beat his way in prison ought to be fried in oil!"

On the day that he was wounded, a negro named Frank Johnson also attempted to run, but was shot down by his guard, Louis Richard. It was a coincidence that he also was wounded about the thigh, and it turned out to be a serious matter for him, for the joint stiffened permanently. He suffered greatly, and was discharged at the expiration of his sentence, lamed for life.

It may be well to note, in connection, that this narrative is the only existing record of escapes. Strange to say, no official register was kept or authorized by the lessee, and when the convicts were turned over by Major Wise to his successor he was unable to furnish anything but a list of the men he then had. In consequence it is an undeniable fact that there are at this day dozens of escaped convicts living throughout Florida, who could not be successfully reclaimed by process of court, through inability to trace their cases or prove that they ever did escape.

It goes almost without saying, that in the rude back districts there was many an atrocity perpetrated in the name of the law, and instances of a monstrous nature frequently came under my observation. Such a case was that of a negro named Tony Tucker, who to my certain knowledge died from the effects of an almost incredible piece of barbarity. We received him from Sumpter County at about this period in events, and when he arrived at camp he presented a singular and horrible appearance. He seemed to be suffering from an enormous goitre, if a goitre can be imagined consisting of a circle of separate swellings that puffed his neck out of all semblance to anything human, and extended up upon his head. It was caused in this wise: When arrested he was some distance from the jail, and the officers bound his hands and fastened one end of a long chain around his neck. They attached the other end to their buggy and started off at a brisk trot. By a desperate effort the negro kept up for a while, and then he fell repeatedly and was dragged through the dirt for yards before the horse could be slowed down to enable him to regain his feet. He reached the jail more dead than alive, and in a little while he was in the condition I have described.

Each separate link had ground into his flesh and produced an abscess, and the pressure threatened every moment to strangle him, besides producing intolerable pain. I lanced the neck in perhaps twenty places and gave him some relief, but he was mortally hurt and really dying by inches when received. He lingered for a long time, being a man of powerful physique, but eventually expired in the greatest agony. This is no overdrawn or highly colored picture, but simply a statement of facts. I never learned the names of the officers who so cruelly misused him.

It may be remembered that our cell house at
Sing Sing was a double structure—two buildings
side by side. The doors were not customarily locked
at night; the fact that the prisoners were linked
on the building-chain, and an armed guard patrol-
ling the front wing being deemed sufficient protec-
tion. One night a convict, whose name has been
lost, cut his chain in two and crept off his bunk
toward the door. The guard was slowly pacing
from one house to the other, and when his back
was turned the prisoner made a sudden dash for
liberty. He flung the door wide open, thus inter-
posing it between himself and the guard, and
whipped around the corner of the house. Before
the night watchman could fire a shot he had disappeared in the darkness.

We had the dogs on his track directly; but he
was the fleetest footed man I ever followed, and he
beat us in a fair race—the first and last case of the
kind on record. Not only did he outrun the swift
hounds through the pitchy darkness, but he did it
so easily that as he passed through watermelon
patches he would sit down and refresh himself
with a melon or two before resuming his flight.
We concluded it was no use chasing such a cham-
pion sprinter, and gave him up.

It was about this time, or near it, that a curious
affair, hushed up as speedily as possible, came under
my notice.

One day six prisoners were received in camp from

Brevard County on a five-year sentence each, for cattle-stealing. They were middle aged, substantial looking, and while they had the rough-and-ready exterior of frontiersmen, they were of an altogether different type from the class that usually finds its way into prisons. Two days later a message came in hot haste to send the men to Live Oak, as they had been granted a new trial. Accordingly they were sent away, and that was the last I ever saw of them. The explanation was afterward made that there had been some irregularity about their first trial, but I subseqently learned that the "irregularity" in question consisted of an extraordinary conspiracy, made possible by the peculiar condition of affairs in the section where they lived. In order to understand it, it must be known that Brevard and several adjoining counties were largely given over at that time to the cattle business. The market was Cuba, and vast herds ranged through the cane brakes and grazed on the rich uplands. Those who engaged in the business on a large scale grew rich, and it was no unusual thing for rude backwoodsmen, almost reared in the saddle and often not able to write their own names, to have from twenty-five to fifty thousand dollars in Spanish gold in their rough log cabins. The retainers of these cattle barons formed small armies; they were entirely isolated from the world, and they ordained things to suit themselves. Of courts, law-officers, or any restraining influence whatever except

force, there was none. Occasionally feuds would
spring up, usually arising from some quarrel over
the ownership of cattle, and were settled Indian
fashion, by a merciless bushwhacking warfare in the
woods. Many a skeleton lies moldering among the
palmettos to-day, the fruit of such encounters, and
many a smoke-stack stands as a monument of the
cabins burned and pillaged in these fierce internal
strifes.

It was in this country and amidst these conditions that the six men who were so briefly my prisoners lived. They were all stock-raisers on a small
scale, and in that capacity incurred the enmity of
some of the cattle barons I have alluded to. As
they were desperate and determined fellows, it was
deemed inadvisable to attempt to frighten them out
of the country, and a plot was finally formed to get
rid of them by sending them to prison. I have said
that there were no courts. They proceeded to organize a bogus one in a cabin belonging to one of
the rich stockmen. Judge, jury, court officers and
lawyers were impersonated by his cowboys, and a
pretended sheriff was sent out to arrest the victims.

Of course such a ruse would not have deceived a
man of experience for a moment, but not one of the
six had ever been in a court before in his life, and
while they held the principles of law in contempt,
they had a superstitious awe, common to natives,
of its outward forms. Consequently they came in,
hats in hand, and gravely faced the spurious judge

and villainous-looking cowboy jury. Lawyers were furnished them, and they were arraigned on the charge of cattle-stealing. The solemn farce of trial was proceeded with, and it is needless to say that they were promptly found guilty and the judge sentenced them to five years apiece in prison. Had the least suspicion of the truth entered the minds of the prisoners, there would surely have been bloodshed then and there, but they saw nothing wrong and were overwhelmed with grief at their conviction. No time was lost, but one of the conspirators, personating a deputy, started at once for prison with the party. I cannot say exactly how they came to be received without the fraud being detected, but it was probably due to carelessness in handling the commitment papers. At any rate, when the matter leaked out, the state officials were horrified at the boldness of the act, and lost no time ordering the release of the prisoners and in as far as possible suppressing the facts of the affair. It is possible that a damage suit was feared, but if so, the state was mistaken, for once they learned how they had been duped, the half a dozen quondam convicts were intent on nothing except to get back and take personal revenge.

It was said that there were lively times in Brevard County when they returned, and that it needed a good deal of hot lead as salve for their wounded feelings; but the stories came up from the wild country by word of mouth and varied considerably in detail. I am only sure of the fate of one of the six. His name was Jonnaker, and very shortly after his release he was riding at break-neck speed on an Indian pony when they fell headlong into a sink-hole, and both man and beast were instantly killed.

CHAPTER V

Of all our prisoners at camp Sing Sing, the one whose case attracted the widest attention and who was, in many respects, the most remarkable character, was Richard or "Dick" Evans, ex-sheriff and ex-city marshal of Pensacola, who received a five-year sentence for as cruel and barbarous a murder as was ever committed in Florida, which is saying a good deal. He was the singular creation of very singular circumstances. Coming originally from the North, very poor and altogether obscure, he grew to be a political power of the first magnitude in his city. He arrived at just the right time for an unscrupulous adventurer to make money. Florida was under radical rule; wholesale looting of the public funds was going on everywhere, and Pensacola was a hot-bed of political corruption and general immorality of every description. The city never saw wilder days, even when the Spanish buccaneers used its harbor for an anchorage and built their fortifications on its hills. The land-sharks, outlaws, blackmailing officials, and desperadoes from every state that thronged the approaches of the harbor were as rapacious, infamous and unrestrained as the pirates of other times ever dared to be.

It was while affairs were in this condition that
Dick Evans put in an appearance, and soon opened
a saloon and dance hall on Polifax street, a thoroughfare given over bodily to vice. His establishment was in the midst of similar dives, bagnios,
groceries and every sort of dead-fall in which the
drunken sailors, who formed the main patrons,
might be lured and robbed. Evans himself was a
man of desperate courage and considerable intelligence, and his place soon became the headquarters
of the political rowdies, wire-pullers and ward-
heelers of the town. There was a cluster of rooms
in the rear where gambling was carried on, and he
naturally gravitated into the position of "boss" of
the politics of his section.

As he prospered he was not content with one
place, and opened another establishment for negroes,
which was speedily the rendezvous of all the black
ruffians in Pensacola. It was known as "The Tin
Roof," and a sort of variety performance with colored performers was given every night. It was an
infamous den, and run ostensibly by a negress with
whom Evans lived openly as man and wife.

It seems incredible that such a character could be
elected to any position of trust, but he was nevertheless made at different times both sheriff and city
marshal. One night while he held the latter office,
a political meeting was held in the city and broke
up in something like a riot. The street was full
of men fighting, when Evans rushed into the thick

of the fray, whipped out his revolver and shot five men. Such, however, was his political influence that he was never prosecuted, and the crime for which he was sent to prison was the murder of a young man named Calvin Griffin, in his own saloon. Griffin was intoxicated at the time, and reeling up to the bar, seized a pitcher and said in drunken folly:

"I am going to break this pitcher and pay for it." Thereupon Evans sprang on him like a tiger and beat his brains out with a chair. It was undoubtedly due to his powerful political friends that he escaped the gallows and secured his comparatively light sentence.

I found him a sturdy, athletic man, on the right side of middle-age, with a set, hard face, black hair and mustache, and a very restless eye. He was sullen and embittered over his sentence, and I have no doubt determined from the first to escape; but he had sense enough to adopt some strategy, and conducted himself so well that he was eventually made hospital steward. The hospital department was merely a division of the cell-house, and the whole building was guarded at night by one man who sat with his rifle before the slatted door and thus could see at all times what was going on inside.

One night the guard heard a suspicious grating sound, and located it as proceeding from where Evans lay stretched on the sleeping-platform, covered with his blanket. In a few moments he was convinced

that the convict was sawing his chain in two, and
he naturally supposed that the next thing would be
a dash for the door. Here he used very bad judgment, for, instead of immediately giving an alarm,
he sat perfectly quiet, his finger on the trigger,
ready to shoot down the man on the first demonstration.

I have never approved of leading convicts on to
proceed with any infraction of the rules after I have
once discovered it, but the guard gave Evans every
opportunity to make the dash he supposed he con-
templated, desiring to catch him red-handed. The
sawing continued for some time and then stopped,
and the prisoner, after tossing about a little, finally
lay quite still. Satisfied that the door was about
to be besieged, the guard feigned sleep at intervals, and then would walk a little distance away and
back again, but every time he looked through the
slats he could see the rigid outline under the blankets.

Several hours passed thus, and the watchman grew
puzzled. He was morally certain that Evans had
cut his chain, but why he did not make the dash
was something he could not understand. At last
he sent for me and explained the situation. Much
annoyed that he had not summoned me before, I
rushed immediately into the cell-house to investigate, and the instant I laid eyes on the bunk something about the profile of the blankets struck
me as peculiar. I went to them and found they

were hung across a bunk plank, which had been raised out of its place and set up edgewise, a gap where it had been leading beneath the platform. The bird had flown.

There was a trail through the sand under the bunk, showing where he had crawled, and I followed it, expecting every instant to encounter the fugitive, until it led me to the rear of the cell-house. There a hole had been cut through the logs and masked by a board set up before it. Evans had crawled out and vanished, dropping in his hurry a pair of pants, most ingeniously fashioned out of an old blanket. These we picked up in front of the aperture.

I called the hounds, and as soon as possible rode off in pursuit. They took the trail well, although the night was extremely dark, as happened upon many another chase. In fact, fortune seems to favor fugitives in that particular. Our direction was toward the Suwanee river, and from the actions of the hounds there was no doubt but that we were close in Evans' wake. It afterward turned out that the baying had just reached his ears, and here a thing occurred that shows the desperate courage and illimitable nerve of the man. The moment he heard that fatal sound, a bold and perilous ruse flashed into his brain. I can best explain it by telling what he did. He never hesitated an instant, but whirled about in his tracks and came running back to meet us. As I have said, it was partly

dark, and when he judged by the sound that we
were almost face to face, he gathered himself together and leaped far to one side of the road. He
barely struck the earth when we swept past, the dogs
keeping the old track, as he had anticipated they
would, and leaving him there.

The fugitive did not wait, but rushing into the
road again, pursued his course toward the camp
over the same track that he had originally taken
in his flight. Meantime the dogs ran steadily,
until they reached the point where he had heard us
and turned, and, without slackening their speed,
they also turned and followed the scent back.

Evans was almost midway to the camp when the
baying sounded in his ears again. This was exactly
what he had calculated upon, for it was his plan,
as it subsequently proved, to double the hounds
back, expecting that they would continue on the
first track clear to the cell-house, thus giving him
an opportunity to retrace his route to the Suwanee
River. Once there, he knew he was comparatively
safe, for water effectually breaks a trail.

Again we pressed him close, and again he faced
about and ran back. For the second time he
cleared the road with a wide bound, and we passed
him. But human cunning is no match for the marvelous instinct or perhaps marvelous intelligence
of a hound trained to the hunting of men; and
instead of following the first track back to the
camp, the dogs merely ran to the point where he

had doubled upon himself, and doubled also. All this was done without the slightest hesitation, and proves conclusively that a good dog has no difficulty in distinguishing between two trails made a few hours apart by the same man, even when one overlaps the other.

It was bewildering, this weaving back and forth in the darkness, but I had conceived some notion of Evans' plan and trusted implicitly to my guides. In perhaps half an hour we pressed the fugitive close again. This time the melancholy baying meant to him failure of his subterfuge, so ingeniously planned and daringly carried out; but his indomitable nerve never left him. Hunted down and exhausted as he was, he turned and came up the road. A less determined man would have surrendered then and there, but he coolly determined to try the same tactics over. He leaped aside and we passed, but only for a moment. The dogs, weary of this game of hide-and-seek, and after running for a few yards, they stopped; seemed puzzled, sniffed the air, and then made for a tree that stood dimly outlined by the roadside. They circled round it, loudly giving tongue, and I knew I had my man at last.

It was too dark to see, but I was convinced that he was behind the tree-trunk and called on him to come out. There was no reply.

"I see you, Evans," I called again, "and if you don't come I will certainly shoot you."

A JAIL DELIVERY.

Still silence, save for the barking of the hounds and blowing of my winded horse in the road.

To approach in that profound gloom would have been simply an invitation for him to brain me with the first knot he could lay his hands on, and at last, at a venture, I fired my revolver in the direction of the tree. The explosion filled the midnight woods with echoes, and Evans, while he made no move to come out, stirred sufficiently to expose the white outline of his shoulder. I dropped my revolver sights as nearly as I could upon this mark.

"Come out!" I shouted, "or I will kill you!" and fired again.

This time there was an immediate response.

"Stop! Captain," came a voice from the gloom; "that last bullet knocked the bark in my face. I'll give up."

Upon that he stepped to the edge of the road. Just then Mr. Mills, of the camp, rode up, and leaving my horse with him, I walked over and searched the runaway. I was afraid to remount, for once in the saddle I could not see him, and, linking arms with him, we made our way back to camp in that fashion, arriving just before day-break.

During the balance of our stay under that management, Evans made no more overt attempts, but his bull-dog determination never left him, and, as it afterward proved, he was only waiting for a favorable opportunity.

6

About this time I had a guard named Bill New-land, who was the hero of two surprising adventures, one of which resulted in a long, arduous and thrill-ing chase. We had been using double-barreled shot-guns in guarding and had just then substituted Win-chester magazine rifles. Newland had never handled a repeating gun before, and it was an entertaining novelty to him. Armed with the weapon, of which he was as proud as a boy with a red sled, he took a squad of eight men and a trusty into the woods and immediately sat down on a log to examine the mechanism of the magazine. Presently he tried to see how rapidly he could operate it, and in jerk-ing the lever up and down a shell was discharged on the "carrier" before it reached the barrel, and as it set off several others in the magazine, the explo-sion was something tremendous.

The gun was blown to pieces; a fragment of the wreck struck Newland a smart blow on the chest, his face was filled with burnt powder, and fully be-lieving he was killed, he fell backward over the log and lay there. A general escape would undoubtedly have taken place but for the extraordinary fidelity and presence of mind of his trusty, a man named William Filer. Before the eight convicts, several of them desperate men, recovered from their sur-prise and realized the situation, he had them strung on the squad-chain, the end locked, and was stand-ing guard over them with a bludgeon. In this order he got them back to camp, the guard bringing up the rear and looking like the sole survivor of a big railroad wreck.

Newland was not much the worse except for his burns, and thinking he had learned a good lesson in caution, I put him to guarding a squad that worked near a marshy place called Gum Slough. One of his men was a villainous negro named Griffin, who in addition to being a desperado was a cunning schemer, always plotting mischief, and I was surprised to find that Newland had apparently taken a great liking to the fellow. I warned him that the man was a sly rascal who probably had some deviltry in his mind at that moment, but Newland scouted at the idea.

"Why, Griffin is one of my very best men," he said; "there's no more harm in him than in a little four-year-old child."

"There's no more harm in him than in a little four-year-old wolf," I replied; "and you had best keep him under the gun."

I failed to convince him, and in brief he made a sort of pet of the man. This he had occasion to bitterly regret.

One afternoon Newland was sitting down in the woods reading a letter, his gun leaning against his shoulder, when Griffin offered him some "chink-a-pin" nuts he had just picked.

"Come and give them to me," said the guard— thus violating the rule that a convict shall never be allowed to approach within a certain distance.

He held out his hand abstractedly, still reading the letter, and Griffin with a quick movement dropped the nuts into his outstretched palm and seized the gun. He leaped back, cocked it, and presented it at his head.

Newland was thunderstruck, but Griffin paid no attention to his plaints, and as he was immediately joined by a couple of the other convicts, the three forced the balance of the squad to accompany them, and all moved off. Newland followed, begging and pleading for his gun and recalling his numerous favors, until Griffin finally turned on him.

"Yes, you white ——— !" he said menacingly; "you were very kind to me, and if you will just follow me down into this swamp I will show you how kind I can be to you."

At this the victim of misplaced confidence concluded that discretion was the better part of valor, and not only dropped the chase but left the country, and I have never laid eyes on him since.

After proceeding a short distance, the five men who had unwillingly accompanied Griffin and his party found an opportunity to give them the slip, and hurried back to camp. They arrived at about nightfall, and when they told their story I instantly gathered my dogs together, and with Major Wise and T. J. Leverett, a guard, started in pursuit. The hounds took the scent beautifully, and we followed them through the dense forests, the tortuous lagoons and tangled brakes of Gum Slough, heading toward the town of Houston. We kept the pace all night long, guided by the yelping of the dogs, and day broke on the chase. At last, tired out and discouraged, Leverett left us, and Wise and I pressed on toward Live Oak, the trail still hot. Meantime, however, the dogs began to show signs of fatigue. The long and closely sustained effort was too much for them and they gave out. But I felt that I had gone too far to give up and I resolved to see it through, if I had to go alone.

Now that we were without the dogs, we were forced to follow the trail by such scraps of information as we could pick up on the road. Fortunately we were so close behind the fugitives that we encountered numerous people who recollected seeing them pass, and in this connection a curious incident occurred. We encountered a party of negroes driving in an ox-team, and Major Wise checked his horse to make some inquiries of the driver, a weazened and cunning looking old darky. I was impatient, and called out at a venture:

"Don't talk to that old rascal! He is the very man that knocked their shackles off."

This random shot struck home, and the effect upon the old fellow was electric. His eyes bulged out, and he attempted to stammer a denial, but the words died on his lips, and he too evidently regarded me as a conjurer of a very high class; for only a short time before, he had actually knocked the leg-irons off the runaways, and was subsequently arrested for it, and the very dints of the hammering found on his wagon tire. But, of course, we knew nothing of this at the time, and rode on.

At Lake City, Major Wise was so overcome with fatigue that he stopped and took the train back to his home at Live Oak; but I pressed on, and by dint of careful inquiry, I got track of my men on an old public road running to Gainesville. This was a valuable clue, for I remembered that I had heard one of the fugitives, a man named Thomas Nettles, often speak of one Prince, his brother-in-law, who followed the trade of shingle-maker at Gainesville. I felt sure that they were on the way to his house, after help and clothes, and without taking the trouble to make many more inquiries, I hurried on in the direction of the town. Night fell, black as ink, when I was near the Santa Fe River. I did not know the country, the water was high, and the question was how to cross. A settler whom I encountered directed me to where he said the stream was spanned by a natural bridge, and I soon located the place by his landmarks, but could see no crossing. I had no idea what the natural bridge looked like, and time was too pressing and the darkness too extreme to make a prolonged search; so, taking chances that the water was shoal, I urged my horse in. The next moment he was carried off his feet and swimming wildly for the other side.

It was a situation to make one's hair stand on end. A few belated stars shone in the sky, but their faint light did not penetrate the murky darkness that hung above the waters. I felt the flood swirl and lap about my legs, and my ignorance of the locality and of the extent of the inundation forced the realization home, that good luck alone could extricate me. Could the runaways have seen me whirling down that inky current, they would no doubt have considered their chances very much better than mine.

The truth was that the river was so swollen by freshets that it could no longer pass under the natural bridge, and had overflowed it, spreading over the adjoining woods and palmetto flats, and converting them into an enormous swamp. Although I did not dream it at the time, the top of the bridge was almost beneath us as my horse struggled along, and at length I found myself among a growth of partially submerged trees on the other side. My horse floundered up to a little palmetto "tussock," lifting above the rock, and I let him stand and blow a while. I peered about, through the gloom, and gradually I discerned near me what appeared to be the stranded remains of an emigrant's outfit. A wagon was caught between two trees and hung with one side canted up, half in water and half out, while boxes, bedding, and household utensils floated about in melancholy confusion.

As I surveyed this flotsam, I noticed a light glimmering in the distance and made for it. It proved to be a camp-fire at which two bedraggled men and a woman were drying their clothes. They told a harrowing story. They were the owners of the stranded outfit and were pushing across the country, looking for a place on which to settle. That night in attempting to make the ford, just as I had done, they were caught in the current and forced to abandon the wagon. They put the woman in a box, and the men swam out, pulling her along between them. Everything they had in the world was left in the swamp, and they sat by the little fire, homeless, helpless, and despairing.

I had only time enough to hear this story and then pressed on to Gainesville, which I reached after a continuous ride of seventy-two miles. I tried to find some local officer to assist me at this point, but by bad luck everybody was either away or busy, and I was again left upon my own resources. I learned that the house of Prince, the shingle-maker, was on the outskirts of the town, near a dense canebrake. I located the place, and as night came on, hid myself in the vicinity to watch. The probabilities were that the three fugitives were by this time all armed, and the outlook was somewhat exciting.

This night was also very dark, but at length I saw two figures coming across lots to the house. The door was opened to them, and as they stood momentarily outlined against its square of light, I recognized Griffin and Nettles, the former carrying a rifle. They had not even removed their prison stripes.

Without waiting a moment, I slipped up to the door and knocked.

"Who's dat?" called out Prince instantly, and I could hear his voice tremble.

"A man that wants to buy some shingles," I replied, in a feigned tone.

"Hit's mighty late at night t' talk erbout shingles," said the negro, evidently open for a bargain, but still suspicious. We parleyed for a while, and although he seemed ready enough to talk, he would not open the door.

"Look here, my man," I said at length; "I never saw you in my life, and if you don't come out, how the deuce am I to know that you are the right one, when you come to my house for pay for your shingles?"

This argument convinced him, and he cautiously unfastened the lock and stared out. As he did so, I caught a glimpse, over his shoulder, of my two convicts retreating by the rear door. I dashed around and fired two shots almost point-blank, but it was too dark, and the negroes reached the cane-patch ahead of me. It was perfectly useless to pursue them into its recesses, and after all my pains, I was forced to go away empty-handed.

When the sheriff, who was away at the time, returned, I put him on the track, and both negroes were caught a few miles from town, working in a cotton-patch. They claimed that the third man left them at Welburn, and at any rate he was never captured. The old negro ox-driver whom I have mentioned as meeting on the road was subsequently arrested upon the confession of the runaways, who stated that they had met him in their flight and that he had hammered off their shackles. This was, of course, aiding and abetting, and the case was a perfectly plain one, but the negro escaped punishment by a means that shows very clearly the extreme carelessness in keeping up the records at headquarters. After all the evidence for the state was in, and it was most conclusively proven that the prisoner had removed the irons as charged, his attorney simply asked that Major Wise be compelled to prove that the runaways were legally state convicts. This could be done by the commitment papers which accompany each man to prison, but, alas for the Major, he had neglected to file them and they were lost. The consequence was that he was unable to show that he had a particle of legal right to pursue the men, and the cunning old darky was discharged.

It is due to a noble animal to say that I could never have made my long ride—the longest of the kind in Florida prison annals—had it not been for the nerve and stamina of the horse I had. His name was George, and he was a splendid bay, full of fire and intelligence I raised my dogs with him, and they were the best friends imaginable. It was a pleasant sight to see them bounding around him, licking his face, and if by chance one of them hes-

itated before him on the road, he would walk carefully around to avoid tramping on him.   He would
follow me all through the turpentine woods and in
the chase, dogs and horse worked like one machine.
George is fifteen years old now and is a good horse
yet.

CHAPTER VI

Some time in 1878 a very savage and unmanageable dog spread general terror in the city of Savannah. He was a cross between a blood-hound and a bull-dog, but was a sort of brute monstrosity, with a strange-looking, round head and an enormously muscular body, pied like a leopard. This singular beast was perfectly unmanageable from a puppy. He acted at all times like a mad dog, and had no other instinct than a ravening desire to bite, rend and tear anything that came within his reach. I suppose that he was kept as a curiosity on account of his remarkable malformation; but in the course of time he became so dangerous to the community that the city council ordered the police authorities to kill him or have him removed out of the limits.

Major Wise happened to be in Savannah at the time, and offered to take the brute. The police were only too glad to get rid of it, and gave it to him on condition that he would never bring it into Savannah again. Major Wise at first attempted to keep this formidable monster about his premises, but he soon saw that he did so at the peril of his life, and sent it to the convict camp. I was a little puzzled to know what use to put the creature to. It is well enough to have a watch-dog that is savage to others so long as he is tractable with one's self, but this one was as willing and anxious to bite me as anybody else. It was out of the question to turn him loose in the yard, and finally I struck the happy idea of tying him at night to the door of the cell-house. His presence there made it absolutely impossible for any one to come in or out. Guards, trusties and convicts were all one to him, and he flew impartially at anybody who approached. In this capacity he was a great success, but the difficulty in handling him made him a constant nuisance. I worked with him for a year, trying to teach him to know me and obey my voice, and at the end of that time was as far off from such a result as at the beginning. When I tied him up for the night I would be obliged to lead him along with a club in one hand, and I usually had to knock him down half a dozen times before we reached the post where he was fastened. If he happened to get loose during the day, he would rush at anything he saw, regardless of obstacles. On one occasion he was chasing a trusty who ran for his life toward the cell-house, and finally got behind a post, which the dog ran into full tilt and nearly knocked his brains out. The career of this monster, for he was nothing less, ended shortly after. I was leading him along one day when he suddenly turned on me and seized me by the hip, and I had a desperate fight to beat him off.

I concluded that he had lived about long enough, and had him dispatched with an axe.

These recollections, which go well into the second year of our stay at Camp Sing Sing, bring me to a gloomy and memorable tragedy, which has passed into prison tradition, and is told with many embellishments, around the convict camp-fires to this very day. It came about in this wise: Among our trusties was a one-armed man named Jesse Simpkins, who had been sent to prison from Madison County, and customarily accompanied the squad of a guard named Gilchrist. In spite of his mutilation, Simpkins was a powerful man, and aside from being an inveterate yarn-spinner, he was to be depended upon in most emergencies. He was extremely unpopular among the prisoners, who regarded him as a spy.

One day, while in the woods, two of Gilchrist's squad edged gradually off among the trees and then suddenly dropped all pretense and ran. The guard fired on them several times, but failed to bring either down and as they were rapidly disappearing through the timber and underbrush, he shouted to the trusty to catch them. Without hesitating a moment, Simpkins bounded off, and as he was a remarkably swift runner, it was not long before he overtook the pair. They had carried with them their heavy dip-irons, which are very formidable weapons, and brandished them menacingly when they saw the trusty appear.

"What do you want?" asked one of them.

"You," replied Simpkins laconically.

"Well, you get out, mighty quick, or we'll crack your head open!"

"You'll have me to catch first."

The two fugitives made a dash at him, but Simpkins was fleet of foot and had no difficulty keeping them at a distance. When they stopped he stopped also, and when they advanced he retreated, always holding them in sight. In a few moments they saw that they had no time to waste at such a game and plunged into the woods, the trusty dogging their steps like a hound. Whenever they looked back he could be seen slipping among the trees, alert, determined, implacable.

It can readily be understood that to men escaping, in the midst of hopes and fears and all the manifold and multiplied anxieties of flight, such a situation would soon become intolerable. At first they were merely enraged, but finally the man's steadfastness struck them into a kind of panic. It was like being followed by a ghost. Time and again they rushed at him, but he easily eluded them and slid away like a shadow through the bushes. They tried strategy.

"Simpkins," called one of them, "we're tired of this. Come, let's talk the thing over, and go back together."

"You start back and I'll keep after you," replied the trusty.

"My God!" exclaimed the baffled runaway, "how long are you going to keep this up?"

"Jest as long as you do."

"We'll kill you, sure."

"Start in any time you want to."

The two men stared blankly at one another and resumed their flight. It was a question of who lasted the longest. The route lay through twelve miles of virgin wilderness, and several times they thought they lost him in the forest depths, but, to their bitter disappointment, the next clearing would reveal their pursuer, still holding the trail. They sought to ambuscade him, they tried to double on their track, they attempted to outrun him, all in vain—he was too swift and wary for them. It had long since become a matter of life and death, and had they encountered, Simpkins' bones would certainly have been left to bleach in the fastness of the woods.

Some of the ruses they employed to trap him had the ingenuity of desperation about them. Once, one hid in the underbrush and the other rushed on ahead. Simpkins, following the convict in advance, was thus lured almost into the arms of the one in ambush, but as he prepared to spring out, the breaking of twigs betrayed him, and the trusty had just time to dart aside. Both turned and endeavored to close in upon him from different directions, but he was too wary for them and escaped their clutches. After that the woods were unfavorable to a repeti-

SIMPKINS ON THE TRAIL.

Siberia, Page 109.

tion of the strategy, and the pursuer was able to keep both men in view between the tree-trunks.

At last they reached the Suwanee River, the trusty right behind. The place is a lonely waste of woods, the river running darkly between stretches of desolate morass—a spot that seemed designed by nature for a tragedy. Night was coming on, and there they paused and agreed that one should swim first, while the other held their pursuer at bay. One plunged in, gained the other bank, drew himself out, dripping and exhausted, and called on his companion to follow. Simpkins was hovering close to the other as he leaped, and when he rose from the plunge, seized a huge stone and hurled it at his head. The aim was true; he cracked the man's skull like paper, and spattered his blood and brains into the water.

The corpse turned over and over and floated down the stream, while the other runaway, horrified at the sight, darted like a madman into the woods. Simpkins coolly watched the effects of his blow, turned on his heel and retraced his long journey through the forest. It was late at night when he arrived at camp, and we had come to the conclusion that he had joined the others in their flight. When he told his story and insisted that he had killed one of the men, nobody believed him. His reputation as a fabricator was remembered, and it was generally supposed that he had made up the tale to cover his lack of success in the chase. But about a week

7

later he received sudden and unexpected confirmation. Governor Drew, who had a mill some distance down the river, notified Major Wise that the
body of one of his convicts had been taken out of
the water at his dam, and that the skull bore marks
of fracture. The corpse was identified as that of
Simpkins' victim, and thereafter his reputation for
truth became rehabilitated. The other man was
never heard of.

At this time and in this connection, I have another case to mention that was probably a tragedy,
and certainly a mystery. To begin at the begin
ning, I received notification to go to Monticello
after a life-time prisoner, a negro named Dave
Walker. He had made something of a history for
himself before I received him. It seems that he
was a desperate fellow and determined to escape.
In some way he obtained possession of an iron bar,
and one day when Mr. Hurst, the jailer, opened the
cell door, he struck him a terrific blow with it.
Before the stroke could be repeated, Hurst shot
him in the head. The bullet struck in front of one
ear, and circling under the skin, emerged behind
it, inflicting a mere flesh-wound, but sufficient to
knock the man over. He was thereupon placed in
a dungeon, where I found him when I arrived. He
was called upon to come out, but muttered some in-
articulate words and refused to obey. Finally I
went in after him, and groping around in the dark,
laid hold of the fellow's foot and dragged him out.

He pretended that the wound had rendered him stone-blind, and I had to lead him to the depot and put him on the cars. On the way to the camp I thought I would try the effect of a little scare.

"Walker," I said, "I think I can cure that blindness of yours."

"How's dat, Captain?" he asked.

"Well, I have a piece of leather fastened in a wooden handle that I will apply to your back a few dozen times. It's a great cure for bad eyes."

He turned this over in his mind, and at length he called to me.

"Captain," he said, "now's I come to try I b'lieve I can see a little."

"All right," I replied cheerfully; "the strap will cure you entirely."

"I guess I can see 'bout as well as I ever could," he said, and dropped the little ruse then and there.

We had a side-camp called Custer, near the railroad track, which I had placed in charge of Mr. T. J. Leverett, whom I have mentioned once or twice before in this narrative, and whom I will have occasion to allude to again, in a somewhat tragic connection. I left Walker there, warning Mr. Leverett that he was a desperate and tricky fellow and likely to embrace the first opportunity to escape. My prediction came true. A short time after, while working near the edge of an inclosure, he jumped the fence and ran. He got out of gun-shot safely, and Leverett immediately took his trail with a couple of my dogs that happened to be at the side-camp.

It was in the morning, and in making my daily rounds I arrived on the spot an hour or two later. I had three dogs with me, and after I heard the particulars I rode off to reinforce Leverett. I met him coming back.

"Where is your man?" I asked.

"I have lost him," he replied. "He ran into a little lagoon, and the last I saw of him he was in the middle of it."

"Why didn't you go on the other side," I continued, "and take his track again at the place where he came out?"

"That's just the point. He didn't come out. I was all around the lagoon, and I couldn't find his trail anywhere."

This struck me as rather peculiar, and I asked him why he had not shot when he saw the man.

"Oh, I shot," he replied; "but when the smoke cleared away I couldn't see him any more. You might as well go back," he added; "it's perfectly useless to look for the man."

It was as Leverett stated. The lagoon was a very small one, and there was absolutely no trail coming out of it. The approaches were thoroughly beaten and it would have been simply impossible for him to have emerged undiscovered, so I believe I may state positively that whatever became of him, he did not come out. I cannot say what happened to him in that little area of swamp, but he was never heard of again, and the mystery of his disappearance excited no little discussion in the camp.

My lines have been cast so largely among the hard realities of life that it might be reasonably inferred that I do not believe in ghosts, yet I have at this point a ghost story to tell. It was what might be called a family affair, and has no connection with my experience as captain of the camp; but as it occurred at about this period and made a deep and lasting impression upon me, I will narrate it at the risk of general disbelief. It was the ghost of a little child that came to me, and it happened thus:

My brother and myself both had houses near the camp. My wife had been for some time wishing to visit her family in South Georgia, and finally made the trip, taking with her the children, including our youngest boy, a baby five months old, to whom I was much attached. All through the arrangements I was oppressed with a vague and indefinable presentiment of calamity, but as I could give no reason for it, I could not well oppose the visit. They had been gone three days, and at night, after counting the men and going through the usual routine at the camp, I went home and retired. But I could not sleep. The shadowy forebodings that had weighed upon me grew into a keen sense of danger —I knew not what—and thrilled me with apprehension. Finally I fell into a troubled doze, from which I was suddenly awakened at about eleven o'clock by hearing my baby cry, plainly and distinctly, seemingly right in the room.

I knew the child's voice in a thousand, and thinking my wife had returned, I sprang out of bed. I was alone.

Completely nonplussed, I walked to the door and listened. Meantime the crying had ceased, and at length I persuaded myself that my senses had tricked me, and went back to bed. The next moment the cry sounded again, loudly, piteously—my child's own voice, and somewhere in that room.

I was wide awake, and when I found positively that no one was there I put on my clothes, and greatly agitated, went to my brother's house, where I told him and his wife the story, adding that I was positive that something had happened to my baby.

Of course they laughed at me, insisted that I was dreaming, and finding the matter altogether too incredible for belief, I returned home, where I tossed on the bed until morning, listening in vain for a repetition of the cry.

I could not shake off the memory of the visitation, or the conviction that it conveyed a warning, and during the morning I told my brother repeatedly that I was sure some accident had happened the baby. Before noon a boy came galloping up on horseback with a telegram in his hand.

"There is the bad news," I said; and so it was. The message was from my wife, calling me to

Georgia and telling me that our little child had been burned to death.

My distress, as I instantly started, may be imagined, but surely not described, for the certitude was impressed upon me that the dead child's last cry for help had been to me. It was raining hard, but I did not notice it. Yet this storm followed me like a Nemesis, delayed me twice by washouts, and when I arrived the baby was buried.

The rest is soon told. My wife had taken the child to bed, had missed it in the night, and it was found dead in the open hearth where it had crawled and fallen. It was the night I heard the cry, and happened, as nearly as could be judged, at about eleven o'clock.

I will close this chapter with an event which at one time threatened to have considerable influence upon my fortunes. The universal bitterness against the camp and all officials connected with it, culminated at about this period in the indictment of myself, my brother, and my brother-in-law, Mr. R. A. Mills, who was a guard, for cruelty to prisoners. The true bill was returned at Live Oak, and the trial created a great sensation in the county. The prosecution had secured a number of volunteer witnesses among the neighbors, while I had eight of my guards summoned. The prisoners themselves were disqualified under the law from taking oath, and consequently could not testify.

Feeling ran high, and the community took sides

so generally against us that nothing but a clear conscience and the knowledge that I had in no case gone
beyond the strict letter of my duty, held me firm.
No man knew better than myself the defects and
hardships and miseries of the lease system, but I
did not feel that I could be justly saddled with
these. I was employed to perform certain duties
under certain conditions, and I performed them.
That was the long and short of it, and I faced the
music.

When the witnesses for the state were placed
upon the stand, they rehearsed the same vague
stories and general rumors that had been circula-
ting for over a year, but were unable to cite a single
fact. The truth is, there were no facts to tell.
The life of a convict was hard, and the punishments often severe, but they were not inhuman, and
were invariably necessary, not only for our safety but
for the safety of the peaceably disposed prisoners.
In the lapse of fourteen years, I can conscientiously
say that I never whipped a convict in my life, whom
subesquent circumstances showed to be undeserving
of it.

The principal witness was a woman, the wife of
a settler, and she swore that she had seen me knock
a prisoner down, stamp on him, and then whip him
with a big stick. She was asked, upon cross-exam-
ination, whether she knew Captain Powell by sight,
and replied that she did. My lawyer then indica
ted where I sat with my brother-in-law and brother,

and asked her to say which of the three she referred to. She promptly pointed to Mills, a mere boy, who did not resemble me in the least, and when the state closed their case, the judge dismissed it without calling a witness for the defense.

This ended the matter as far as I was concerned, but my brother was pursued with a persistency that smacked strongly of personal spite. He was reindicted, and foreseeing that he would eventually be bankrupted by attorney's fees, he left the business and engaged in farming in South Florida. I stuck to my post, but words cannot describe the petty and continued annoyances to which I was subjected; but I had a dogged determination to live down defamation, and I am happy to say that I succeeded, and lived to see a reversal of public sentiment.

In my recollections of this time or about this time, I have not the exact date, there is one of an odd escape that is not only interesting of itself but has something to do with events transpiring later on. We had two convicts named Alexander Lege and Nathan Shell. The former was a big, burly fellow and the latter a slip of a boy, a mulatto or an octoroon, at any rate very light-skinned and possessed of unlimited nerve. These two plotted to escape and one day dashed into the woods. The guard sent a few vain bullets after them, and they disappeared.

The news was carried to camp, and I put the dogs upon their track. It appeared that after traveling

together for a short distance, they quarreled, as
men in peril are frequently foolish enough to do,
and separated. It was the means, however, of Shell's
delivery, for the trail we took was that of his companion, and in the course of the day we ran upon
him. He was a curious spectacle when he hove in
sight. In his intense anxiety to get rid of his suit
of stripes, he had stripped it off altogether and went
on his way stark-naked, trusting to luck to find an
opportunity to steal an outfit from some settler's
clothes-line. None appeared, and when captured
he was so scarred with brambles and covered with
dirt and perspiration that he resembled some wild
man of the woods. We did not hear of Shell for
years afterward. He had struck directly through
the woods, was more fortunate than Lege in dis-
carding his prison suit, and eventually reached a
point in Central Florida where he was for the time
being, safe.

CHAPTER VII

I will beg the reader's indulgence at this point to call attention to a parallel that the great majority of people probably believe could not exist in this country without attracting general notice and exciting universal comment. In Mr. George Kennan's celebrated papers upon the Russian exile system, he fully describes the "Kameras," or cell-houses, in use in Siberia, and his articles are accompanied by numerous illustrations. I will venture the assertion that if any Floridian convict was shown these pictures without the accompanying text he would be prepared to swear that they were ruins of the camp in this state. It is not merely a slight resemblance, or even a marked resemblance, but the two are absolutely identical in every essential detail. The main difference is that there is no building-chain used in the Siberian cell-houses, the prisoners being given the liberty of the room after they are locked in. The sleeping platforms, called "nares" in Russia, and those in use here are exactly alike; such scanty arrangements as exist for personal cleanliess are similar, and the general arrangement and construction of the building and the stockade are the same. The lowest order of Russian prisoners are fastened with stride and waist chains exactly like those used in Florida, and there is a coincidence of little details that is perfectly amazing to one familiar with both systems.

Mr. Kennan states that when he visited one of the Kameras he was horrified to observe that the whitewashed walls were stained a dusky red for some distance above the sleeping platforms, and was told that the stain was made by the prisoners who crushed there the innumerable vermin that infested their beds. Mr. Kennan need not have gone so far away from home. In summer time these insect pests were almost impossible to exterminate, and it took only a few weeks for the convicts at the camps to paint a dado on the walls exactly similar to that which Mr. Kennan observed. These are unpleasant tales, but most of the minutiæ of life in the state chain-gang is extremely unpleasant, and without allusion to it the hardships cannot be understood. Barring the climate, it is certainly the Siberia of America. I have had occasion to speak of the loose adminis-tration of the law in those days, and the phrase only partially describes the situation. Alachua County in particular seemed to regard the prison as a sort of clearing-house for its pauper incumbran-ces, and while we were in Sing-Sing we received from there a blind prisoner and an idiotic one. The blind man was accused of stealing a gun, an article that such an unfortunate would be scarcely supposed to covet. We put him at work at a pump and he proved to be a rather remarkable fellow. He learned to find his way to his post without difficulty, and after he served out his sentence he made a good living in the neighborhood by cutting timber. He struck as true a blow with the ax as a man with sight, and by some instinct or other managed to get out of the way of falling trees. The idiot gave us a good deal of trouble. He was sent into the woods and tempted by the luscious appearance of the turpentine gum, essayed to eat some. He came back with the stuff solidified all over his face—a spectacle for gods and men—and did little or no more work for the balance of his term.

While I am on the subject of queer fish, I should by no means omit reference to a certain trusty known as John Key West, so called from the place of his conviction. The woods adjacent to the camp were full of a variety of large ground-tortoise, known throughout the south as "gophers" and esteemed as great delicacies by the colored population. John Key West had an inordinate appetite for gophers. Boiled, fried, stewed, or fricasseed, it was all one to him, and the unfortunate gopher that he encountered in the forest might as well give himself up for lost.

One day he went with his squad into the woods, and after his work was done, took a dip-iron and started for the crest of a neighboring hill, announcing that he intended to dig a gopher. These creatures burrow deep into the sandy soil, and nothing further was thought of the incident until the guard, collecting his squad together in the evening, noticed that John Key West had not returned. He sent a negro trusty up the hill to investigate, and presently he came bounding back yelling at every jump. He said that upon reaching the summit he looked about and saw a captive gopher and John Key West's hat, but nothing else. The sand near by appeared to be disturbed, and scraping there he unearthed a human foot, attached apparently to a body farther down. He did not stop to make further discoveries, and the whole party proceeded hurriedly to the spot.

There, sure enough, was a monstrous foot sticking stiff and stark above the sand, and as it was recognized by the brogan as belonging to John Key West, several laid hold of it and pulled and tugged, but in vain. The guard sent to the house of a Baptist minister close by, to borrow a shovel, but the good man replied that they could not kill convicts and stick them in gopher holes and then expect to dig them out with his tools. So the men went to work with their dip-irons, and at length unearthed all that was mortal of John Key West. He had evidently captured a gopher, tracked another to its lair and then dug deep into the hole after it. With sportsman-like enthusiasm he had crawled head-first after his prey when the sand caved in and buried him alive. But the ruling passion was strong in death, and when they pulled out the corpse, the other gopher was found clutched

in its stiffened hands. I think that had John Key
West been asked how he would like to die, he
would probably have chosen this way.

Dick Evans was not the only ex-officer we had at
Sing Sing. There was another in the principal of
a very noted case, of which the facts were as follows: Gus Pottsdamer, a prominent young Jew,
was city marshal of Lake City, and some bitterness
arose between himself and the sheriff, a man named
Henry. They met, and a hand-to-hand fight ensued,
in which both drew weapons, and Pottsdamer shot
his opponent dead. The evidence showed that
Henry was beating him over the head with his pis-
tol-butt at the time the shot was fired, but the marshal was nevertheless found guilty of murder and
sentenced to life imprisonment.

I received notice from Major Wise to come in
person to Live Oak for a prisoner, and not knowing
who it was I rode in, carrying an old shot-gun that
I desired to have repaired. The case had created
a sensation all over the state, and there were good
grounds to fear that the prisoner would either be
lynched by one faction or rescued by another. When
the train from Lake City pulled in, a large crowd
had assembled about the depot, and five men with
shot-guns first disembarked. Then came the prisoner, a frail, pallid young man, so loaded down
with chains, handcuffs, shackles, and manacles of
every description that he could hardly walk, and
another guard of five men brought up the rear.

Almost all of the prominent Hebrews of the state came pouring out of the cars after this procession.

The guards closed in and Pottsdamer hobbled to Major Wise's office, where the formalities of turning over a convict were complied with. These concluded, some one asked where the posse was to convey him to the penitentiary, and Major Wise stepped to the door and called me in. A roar of protest immediately went up, and both the sheriff and Colonel Taylor, the state's attorney, who was present, insisted that a rescue would certainly take place. When they learned that my shot-gun was empty and destined for the locksmith's, their fears redoubled, but I said that I would risk it, and told them to take off the irons. At first the sheriff refused point-blank, but I told him emphatically that I would not walk a man four miles in that condition, and at length he handed over the keys. I removed all the chains and manacles, returned the mass of hardware, and we started off down the road alone. Of course I had no trouble and we arrived at camp all right, but the episode was not unnoted by the Hebrews who witnessed it. Without knowing it, I made some stanch friends, and had occasion in after years to know that this race never forgets a kindness in adversity.

Pottsdamer spent thirty days in prison and was then released on bail, pending a hearing by the Supreme Court. He remained at liberty a little longer period, when the decision of the lower court

HADLEY AND HIS SWEETHEART.

Siberia, Page 128.

was affirmed and he was ordered back to prison for life. He was brought in with less ceremony than on the former occasion, and for a month his friends worked like beavers in his behalf. At the end of that time they secured a pardon for him. Pottsdamer subsequently moved to Live Oak where he became a leading business man, and was elected sheriff a few years ago. He is inclined to take his convict experience good-naturedly, and is fond of speaking of me as his "old boss."

I had then and have still a good many men in prison, who not only followed stealing for a livelihood while they were free, but were so unregenerate that they kept up the practice after they donned the stripes. One of them was a trusty named William Hadley, known as Number "54." Part of his duty was to carry dinner at noon to the men who worked in the woods, and complaints began to come in that the rations were short. The cook took a solemn oath that he sent the requisite number of portions, but when they reached the men, they had always contracted in some mysterious manner. Hadley protested that he knew nothing about it and seemed grieved that his integrity should be questioned.

I concluded to play the detective in the matter, and one day I first counted the bread and meat, and then when "54" started I put off quietly in his wake. I had followed him some little distance when he swerved from his route and made for the

8

cabin of a well-known young negress, who if not fair, certainly had the reputation of being frail. He went into the house, and after remaining a moment pursued his way to the squad. Satisfied that it was in this cabin that the mysterious shrinkage took place, I lingered in the neighborhood and presently Hadley came jauntily tripping back from delivering dinner, carrying the empty pan in his hand.

The few negroes of the vicinity greatly prized "corn pone," while fat pork was regarded as a delicacy that might well tempt one to desperate deeds; so I immediately and correctly surmised that the missing portions had been left with Hadley's inamorata, and that he would pause for a tete-a-tete, before returning to camp. So it developed. The dusky belle came out to meet him and together they repaired to their trysting place, which proved to be a nest amidst the thick branches of a great prostrate pine tree. I gave them time to bill and coo a while, and then suddenly appeared on the scene. No ghost ever created greater horror and consternation. They were unable to speak, and simply stared at me with big milky eyes, while they obeyed my order to come out.

I told Hadley to get down for punishment, and handing my strap to the negress, requested her pretty shortly to lay it on to the best of her ability.

She looked at me appealingly, and hit her lover a few gingerly strokes. He glared around with a world of reproach in his face.

"Lay it on!" I shouted, for what I wanted was to get Hadley mad.

Bang! bang! bang! went the strap.

"Keep it up!" I ordered.

Bang! bang! bang! this time with a will.

Hadley ground his teeth. At this stage, the negress fully believed that her life depended upon her vigor, and she beat a devil's tattoo upon the prostrate trusty. At last I judged him to be in a properly wrathful condition, and putting on a finishing touch or two myself, I told him to get up. He rose sullenly to his feet, and the negress, who was breathless with her exertions, began to move off.

"Hold on," I said; "I have a little business with you first. Get down where Hadley was."

"Why, cap'n—" she began, but I cut her short.

"Get down!" I thundered, and she mechanically obeyed. I handed the strap to Hadley. "Now put it on," I said.

An instantaneous change came over the darky. His sullen look disappeared like magic, and he snatched the leather as drowning men snatch straws.

Revenge is sweet. He whirled the strap and brought it down with a resounding whack.

"Oh, Lord! Oh, Mr. Hadley!" yelled the negress.

"Give it to her, Number 54," I said; "remember how she tanned your hide."

He settled down to business at the word, and the scene of their late loves reëchoed to the thuds of the strap and the screams, pleas, and protests of his

quondam sweetheart—to all of which he turned a
deaf ear.

"Oh, Mr. Hadley!" she roared, "you tole me to
come! You knows you did!"

"You lie, you hussy!" he heartlessly replied, and
bent his exclusive attention to the flogging, which
I must confess was artistically performed. When
I thought that she had obtained a good lesson and
Hadley's revenge was sufficiently glutted, I bade
her get up and be a good girl in future. The meat
was never short after that.

With all his faults Hadley was a good fellow, and in
matters of importance could be depended upon.
Ater serving out his sentence he went to work in
the extensive saw-mills of Drew & Buckley at Ellaville. One day a convict ran away, and for some mysterious reason the dogs refused to track him. He
was evidently one of those peculiarly constituted
individuals, that I have mentioned elsewhere, who
leave no trail. At any event, the hounds hung back,
would not take the scent, and we gave the man up
for lost. That night at about twelve o'clock there
was a thunderous knocking at the stockade gate, and
Hadley strode in, hauling along the runaway by
the scruff of the neck. It appeared that he had
taken the direction of Ellaville and accidentally
encountered the ex-trusty, who at once recognized
him. The fugitive claimed that he had been sent
to look for a convict, who had run away, but Hadley was too old a prison-bird to be caught with

such chaff, and he promptly took him in. I paid him ten dollars for his trouble, and he went on his way rejoicing, declaring that all convicts who wished to get away had best give Ellaville a wide berth.

Sometime afterward there was a wreck on a log train, which hauled enormous loads of timber from the woods, over a private railroad belonging to Drew & Buckley. A gigantic pine log had slipped cross-wise on its car and, striking against a tree near the track, derailed the whole train, smashed the engine, and killed several workmen. Hadley was on the train and went down with the wreck. He was taken out with both legs broken, but he was one of the kind of men who are hard to kill; and when convalescent, he came hobbling out on crutches to pay the camp a visit. One of the guards commented upon the dangers of his new vocation, and he assented emphatically.

"If Governor Drew wants to keep dat train ob his," he said, "he better not run ober me. Sakes alive man! I jes' tored dat ingine all ter pieces!"

I last heard of old "54" in Jackson County, where he got into trouble. He had a quarrel with a notorious woman, who drew a dirk and tried to stab him, but he whipped out a revolver and put a bullet through her heart before she could strike the blow. He was tried for murder but acquitted, and has since drifted out of sight.

The turbulent history of Major Wise's lease sustained itself to the bitter end, and terminated in fact with a highly sensational episode—one that gave us an insight to the character of a man subsequently destined to make much trouble. At the close of the third year at Sing Sing, and the last year of his lease, bids were again advertised for and the convicts were let in a body to the South Florida Railroad Company. This contract was concluded a few months before the close of the year, although it did not go into effect until January 1. Of course in the interim the Wise lease was in force, but by some means or other several of the convicts conceived the idea that they were then the property of the railroad company, and that no one else had a right to work them. The chief promulgator of this theory was a man named Walter Shavers, a desperado who feared nothing, and who took an impish delight in inciting others to mischief.

He talked fourteen of his comrades into his way of thinking, and when I came to call the men out in the morning, these conspirators took their stand by the door armed with clubs, and refused to move. They had nerved themselves to desperation, and, like the mutterings of a storm, I heard the word passed back and forth, to stand firm. I was very much surprised at such a demonstration, and inquired the cause of the strike. Shavers stepped boldly to the front, bludgeon in hand.

"We don't intend to work for Wise," he said. "The railroad company has leased us, and we won't come out for anybody except their men."

The balance of the convicts, some seventy-five in all, were huddled in the rear of the cell, thoroughly intimidated. It was my desire to save them all trouble over what was so palpably an error, and I attempted to reason and explain, but Shavers cut me short.

"I have told you the reason," he said; "we don't intend to come, and now you can make the most of it."

Then I realized that it was time for heroic treat-ment, and flinging open the gate, I called on those in the rear, who were evidently not parties to the revolt, to come out. They obeyed with a rush, and the impetus carried Shavers and his fellow-plotters with them.

Once outside, all weakened and went upon the squad-chain but the ringleader and two others, who declared that they would die then and there before they surrendered. I looked around and saw a huge trusty who went by the sobriquet of "Jack o' Diamonds"—I forget what his real name was. He was a herculean fellow, his eyes were snapping at the prospect of a fight, and he was evidently itching to take a hand in it.

"Jack," I said, pointing to Shavers, "throw that man into the cell."

At the word he pounced upon him like a cat, and a wrestling match ensued that would have put pro-fessionals to shame. Both were very strong, both in deadly earnest, and their very sinews cracked as they swayed back and forth, grappled, and rose and fell. The whole camp looked on in breathless excitement. It was nobody's fight for a while, but at last, Jack o' Diamonds obtained a back lock on his man, lifted him off the ground with a supreme effort and hurled him through the open cell-door.

I slipped the latch and called assistance to put the other two in. This was accomplished without much difficulty, and, accompanied by two men, I stepped inside to discipline the trio. One submitted gracefully, but Shavers had to be held down while he was whipped, and the other I tied hog-fashion. When the three promised submission, I turned them out and put them on the squad-chain; but no sooner was the key turned in the padlock at the end, than Shavers shouted to the others to stand by him, and they all attempted to break off.

"Are you all curs?" he yelled. "Give me a hand and we'll snap this chain like a string!"

We had them at a disadvantage however, and I began at one end of the chain and went down the squad, whipping them all. This quieted things temporarily, and I took advantage of the lull to send them down the road toward their work, and dispatch the others in different directions.

Although he had been twice punished with sufficient severity to subdue any ordinary man, Shavers was still unconquered, and after nis squad had gone a little distance, he seated himself and declared positively that he would not work. The guards sent for me, and I found Shavers sitting at the side of the road, sullen and defiant.

"Haven't you dropped this yet?" I asked.

He replied by a furious look.

"Will you get up and go to work?"

"No!" he exclaimed. "Whip me—kill me if you want to, but by — I will not give in!"

"That rests with you," I answered. The other convicts were beginning to move uneasily, mutter and look at one another, and I felt that affairs were critical. Such an example could have but one result, and that a general revolt, in which blood would surely be spilled. So when I applied the whip to him again I did not spare him, and at last he yielded and gave up the struggle. That was the end of the strike. We subsequently kept a close watch upon Shavers, and he served out his sentence of five years without any other serious trouble. But he was a curse to the camp, incessantly watching for an opening, desperate, embittered, and revengeful, and having withal the dangerous influence among his fellow-prisoners that a man utterly careless of life is sure to possess.

CHAPTER VIII

I was employed by the East Florida Railroad Company to continue with the prison. Their lease was for two years, and the breaking up of the old camp and removal of the convicts to their new quarters was a formidable undertaking. The last of the year found us in the midst of bustle and preparation. We decided to take the cars from Custer, our side camp, which stood quite near the track, and was four miles distant from our headquarters in the woods. The start was made at four o'clock in the morning, just at that black margin between night and day, when the moon had set, and not a single star relieved the deep gloom of the skies. Each man carried a torch, and the long procession filed slowly out of the cell-house, and wound its way through the inky depths of the forest, looking like some unearthly troop of hobgoblins, that would melt into thin air at cock-crow. To add to the grotesque impressiveness of the scene, the negroes struck up one of those strange, wailing, unintelligible chants, that are born in the mouth of every genuine African, and the echoes caught the weird melody and moaned it back and forth for miles.

Many of the men were sick or maimed, and every few moments a torch would go down and show where someone had fallen. The others staggered under enormous bundles, and bristled with frying pans, stew-pots, skillets, and almost every imaginable utensil of camp-cookery, for we not only carried all of the camp equipments, but every man brought along that little hoard of private possessions that a prisoner is morally certain to accumulate, if he stops long in one spot. At the latter end of the journey we were obliged to place the weaker ones on horse-back. I dismounted myself and lifted a sick convict in my saddle, and in this order we reached Custer. Such a moving-day was never before seen in Florida.

The railroad company sent four freight cars to the camp, and we divided the convicts among them, well guarded and on squad-chains. An engine was furnished, and between the schedules of other trains we ran to a point near Jacksonville, where we disembarked, and had a further journey of six miles on foot to the camp, which had already been prepared by free labor. It was on what was known as Trout Creek, and the route lay over the partially finished grading of the then new Jacksonville & Waycross Short Line. When we left the cars, we found the adjacent fields literally packed with spectators, most of them negroes, and so eagerly did they press forward, that the cordon of guards we hastily threw out could scarcely keep them back.

Our procession left the gaping crowd behind, and toiled, hampered as we were by the sick, over the rough roadway, through cuts and across log-spanned creeks, until, thoroughly tired out and at about dark, we reached the camp.

The appointments were vastly better than those of Sing Sing, a substantial double cell one hundred feet long had been constructed, together with suitable guards' quarters, kitchen and other buildings, and the yard inclosed by a solid stockade. Many little details, however, were lacking, and as there was no building-chain, we literally surrounded the house with guards, on the first night. For many days we were occupied in supplying those little details that experience alone can suggest. The convicts were then put to work constructing the line of the Jacksonville & Waycross Railroad.

I did not originally accompany the party as captain, but as first assistant; and the reasons for this management may be gathered in part from what I have already told. It was the earnest desire of the Plant Investment Company, which was the owner of the railroad and the real lessee, to free the system, as far as possible, of the odium that then attached to it, and as I had been captain under Major Wise's regime, and had received, of course, a share of the smirching, it was deemed expedient for some one else to figure as the head. A man named Henderson, who had been a guard at the Georgia prison, was sent or and placed in command. I felt that I had always done my duty and that this was only a concession to popular opinion, so I spared nothing to render things as amicable as possible. But I must confess that Mr. Henderson and I did not live very happily together. He went upon the assumption that the prisoners had been barbarously abused during the Wise lease, and never missed an opportunity to draw them out upon the subject.

> "A rogue ne'er felt the halter draw,
> With good opinion of the law."

says the proverb, and it will be readily understood that many of the convicts, and particularly ignorant negro convicts, were delighted at this opportunity to make things unpleasant for their old captain. They certainly told some monstrous stories.

It was only human nature, but I felt keenly the false position it placed me in, and I several times sent in an application for dismissal, but the railroad company insisted that I remain.

I stood these trials with what patience I could command, and applied myself to my work, which was the management of the construction train. Among other things the company gave me strict orders to allow no unauthorized person to pass on the grading where the convicts were at work, or to approach nearer than certain limits, and this rule led to two ludicrous incidents. We had pushed the grading about a mile beyond the end of the track when, one day, Mr. H. S. Haines, the general superintendent of the S. F. & W. Railroad, came out upon a special engine to pay us a visit. The East

Florida Railroad Company was part of the S. F. & W. system, and Mr. Haines' position made him chief of us all.

He dismounted from the engine and walked a mile or so up the road, to where the picket line of guards was extended. A long, big-jointed native named Press Ambrose, who was, by the way, a thoroughly good fellow, but as obstinate as a mule, presented his rifle and halted him.

"My name is Haines," shouted the superintendent; "I have a right to pass here."

"No right that I know of," replied Ambrose, coolly.

"But, man, I'm superintendent of the road."

"That may be," said the guard, "but I don't know you."

Mr. Haines was beginning to get annoyed. The long walk had tired him and he was anxious to inspect the grading.

"Look here," he called, "I have no time for any fooling. My name is Haines, H. S. Haines, and I'm general superintendent of the S. F. & W. Railroad. Now let me pass."

"If you have no time for foolin'," replied Ambrose slowly, "you'd better be moving off, for you're foolin' away your time powerful talking to me."

Mr. Haines scratched his head. Finally he lost all patience.

"Oh, confound it!" he exclaimed; "I can't stand here all day. I'm going across anyhow."

Ambrose instantly covered him with his rifle.

"Mister," he said earnestly, "I don't know who you are, but if you move one step toward me, you do it at the risk of your life."

The superintendent looked into the muzzle of the rifle and looked into the face of the guard. He saw death in both. He paused, pondered a moment, and then turned on his heel and walked back to the engine. He had the engineer blow the whistle for me, and subsequently passed through the lines, under my escort. Before he left he said: "Who is that guard at the end of the line?"

"Press Ambrose," I replied.

"Keep him under all circumstances," he returned; "he knows his business."

Labor, on the line of the road, was being carried over a wide and dangerous quagmire known as Fox Swamp. An embankment was thrown across it, and one squad was at work at one end and another in about the middle. Late one afternoon, a negro tramp came along, and, desiring to cross the swamp, made a detour around the first squad and crawled up the embankment some little distance beyond. Just then the men at work in the middle started in, and their guards, catching sight of the negro, ordered him to go back out of the way. He retreated a little distance, which brought him near the lines of the other squad, and immediately several rifles were leveled at him and he was warned away. He was between two fires, and with his teeth chattering and eyes protruding, he ran first in one direction and then the other, until the two squads came so close together, that he was brought to a standstill.

"Get out of the road!" shouted one set of guards.
"Keep back!" warned the other.

At last he gave a yell of terror and jumped off the embankment into the quagmire. He sank up to his neck in the slimy ooze, and the bog would have undoubtedly claimed him for its own had not the squads stopped and quickly let down men to pull him out. He was escorted to the further side and when last seen was footing it up the right-of-way like a scared deer.

In the course of three months we moved to Camp Hillyard, thirty-two miles from Jacksonville, on the line of the road. This camp was substantially like the other, although in general appointments it was again its superior, and, indeed, from the beginning of the railroad lease, it was apparent that better times had set in. The Plant Company managed their charge generously, the food was good and abundant, and no expense was spared to keep the standard of the camp at a first-class point. Nevertheless, one of my earliest experiences was unpleasant in the extreme. Measles in a virulent form were in the neighborhood, and the disease broke out upon me, while on a car with my gang. I went in and on the way picked up a sub-foreman named Jason Moore, who was also just taken ill. William Rich, one of the guards, was attacked at the

BATHING THE PRISONERS.

Siberia, Page 145.

same time, and I left them at the camp and went to my home at Live Oak, where I remained until convalescent. Not long after my return, Moore, who was a capital fellow, died of the disease, and Rich followed him a little later. One in three was rather a close call, but this was as nothing to what followed, for the camp was destined to shortly become the scene of a frightful and devastating epidemic— a prison horror, in fact, of the first magnitude. I will explain, as best I can, the circumstances that attended it and leave the reader to draw his own conclusions.

The weather in the fore part of the year was cold and inclement, but Captain Henderson abandoned the old plan of bathing inside the cell-house in tubs, and on Sunday would marshal the convicts in the yard, stark naked, and turn the hose upon them. The water was icy, a keen wind was often blowing, and the effect of such a bath was to chill the men to an almost paralyzing degree. I have seen burly fellows turn literally blue under the stream, and stagger like drunken men from the shock. They would go shivering into the cell-house, don their clothes in dead silence, and then sit apparently half stupefied around the fire.

Not a great while afterward, one of the convicts, who came in laughing and singing, to all appearances never in better health and never in better spirits, was seized with a sudden and violent pain in the back. In a little while he screamed out that

9

his whole spine was like a bar of red-hot iron. Then he went into convulsions, so uncontrollable that it was impossible to hold him, and his head bent until it touched between his shoulder-blades. Alternately he writhed and yelled and stiffened with reactions that left him rigid. This torture continued for a few hours, when he died.

Next night, while this mysterious and terrible taking off was still the subject of general conversation and conjecture, two other men were seized with symptoms identical with the first case. Both lingered in agony for a while and both died. For many a man this was the beginning of the end. The strange malady that came so swiftly and killed so surely was one of those quick and deadly types of spinal meningitis, that make it, when it once obtains a foothold, the most terrifying scourge known to humanity.

After that the camp became a human shambles. Man after man was stricken down, and while many recovered, the deaths predominated, and their appalling suddenness and the uselessness of any precautions invested the visitation with a superstitious horror impossible to describe. Every man felt that death walked beside him, and no one who laid down at night could say with any certainty that he would be alive by morning. The disease seized its victims with absolutely no warning, and indeed most of those who were attacked seemed to be in unusually buoyant health just before they felt the first pang. Men fell back in paroxysms while they were eating, while they were cooking, while they were talking, with the words half-uttered on their lips. Little groups would be seated on the edge of the sleeping platform, waiting for the bell that was a signal to retire, when one of their number would turn livid, stare blankly for an instant at his fellows, and then fall back, writhing in mortal anguish. Sometimes two or three would be attacked out of one party, and their comrades, pale with the knowledge that death had brushed their very elbows, would creep under their blankets and lie trembling until morning.

Our hospital acccommodations were limited and they were almost immediately overtaxed. In a week or two the cell-house itself was half full, and the spectacle of the stricken, the dead, and the dying half-crazed the balance with fear. New victims were almost invariably seized at night-time, and as evening advanced, terror could be seen to visibly lay hold of the squads. They worked mechanically, spoke almost in whispers, and seldom talked to one another. As they entered the cell-house, they flinched and hesitated at the door and cast haggard looks inside, as if they expected to see the plague· standing in some material form, ready to strike them down. The scenes that constantly repeated themselves can only be partially described in words. Here is an example: One morning at break of day, when the men began to stir, a yell of dismay came from the sleeping platform.

"Oh, my God!" came a voice from among the newly awakened convicts; "there's a dead man here next to me!"

"Here's another, stiff and cold!" said a cooler prisoner, who had just made a similar discovery in another quarter of the building.

There was silence for a moment, broken by the awe-struck tones of a third convict.

"There must be three then," he said, "for the man beside me is dead, too!"

The cries of these three, as they lay in mortal travail, had been drowned by those of the stricken all around them, and had not awakened their companions, worn out as they were by nights of sleepless anxiety. The corpses, distorted by the pangs of death, and stiffened to the posture in which life had left them, were hastily carried out and buried in a potters'-field, that was already rivaling the roster-roll of the camp. So the days wore on.

The only treatment we could employ was that of counter-irritants. The backs of the sufferers were blistered heavily with cantharides. Tubs of boiling water were kept in the cell, blankets were dipped in them and then wrapped around the body. Often the skin would come off in patches, but this seemed to be all that would give relief or hold out any hopes of a cure. Those who recovered convalesced slowly and felt the effects for months.

The panic was by no means confined to the prisoners. One day, ten of the guards stepped into the headquarters in a body and asked for their discharge.

"We like the place," said their spokesman, "but life is sweet."

This left us very short-handed, but we needed nurses more than we needed guards, so it did not materially interfere with the work. Those in charge could not leave, and we simply had to summon such courage as we could and see it out. It must be remembered that we had none of the facilities of a city, none of its ready and abundant aid, but were alone in a rude convict-camp with this pestilence for a guest. It raged until it might fairly be said to have exhausted itself for lack of material. Twenty-seven died in one week, and while I am unable to state, from lack of hospital records, exactly what the total mortality was, it is no exaggeration to say, that it fairly decimated the camp, and it was a long time before affairs dropped into their accustomed channel and we recovered from the shock of the visitation. I was myself attacked, but it was a comparatively light case and I was soon able to be up and about again.

My recollection of the early days of the railroad lease is not altogether one of gloom, but is enlivened by several incidents of a different character. One of our guards was a raw native who had been raised in the piny forests, and who was as complete a specimen of the backwoodsman as I ever laid eyes upon. This guard invited me to a country entertainment known among the natives as a "frolic," and we started after dark for the scene of the festivities. A frolic is about the only relaxation these people have, and bears the same relation to them that a fashionable ball does to the denizens of cities. I may add that the affair is generally all that the name implies.

We plunged into the wilderness and made our way through miles of dense woods, underbrush, and palmetto thickets until at last the merry strains of a fiddle broke upon our ears, and we emerged in sight of a log-house, overflowing with people. An uproarious welcome awaited us, and we were soon in the thick of the fun. It was a curious sight to unfamiliar eyes. The walls of the house were lined with guests, who crowded back to clear a space for the dancers, and blazing torches of "fat" pine cast a grotesque and flickering light upon the assemblage. No waltz, schottische, or polka found place among the dances. Such things were as unknown to the simple dwellers of the forest as Greek to a South Sea Islander. The partners merely faced each other and executed a sort of double shuffle, more or less garnished with pigeon-wings and such fantastic figures as the inspiration of the moment suggested.

The fiddlers were home artists. It had "come to them natural," as the backwoodsmen say, and they sawed away at such good old southern country tunes as "Miss Cindy," "Run, Nigger, Run," and "Liza Gincy." There were plenty of pretty "cracker" girls, blushing and giggling in the corners, and big, raw-boned, young woodsmen, looking a little sheepish and embarrassed before so many people, but bound to have a good time, all the same. By and by things warmed up, the rustic belles conquered their diffidence, their beaux came gallantly to the front, and merriment went on apace.

I found that my guard was a very popular character, and the fact that I was a captain at the camp secured me more attention than I knew what to do with. The party grew more and more hilarious as the night wore on, the dancers capered their level best, the fiddlers sawed away for dear life, the pine knots flared and flickered, and now and then somebody would emit a whoop, and the echo would be taken up by the deer-hounds outside until they filled the forest with reverberations. At intervals one of the men would inform his friends, in a husky whisper, that he had "a quart hid out in the woods." This meant moonshine whisky, pure from the secret stills of the wilderness, and an immediate adjournment would be made to sample it. At midnight the festivities were at their height, and I managed to escape, against the hospitable protests of all the frolickers. But before I was allowed to depart I was obliged to accept at least a dozen invitations to attend similar entertainments that were being planned in the neighborhood, and as I afterward concluded that one frolic was enough for a year or so, I have no doubt that I missed a good deal of fun.

CHAPTER IX

Part of my duty, under the new prison administration, was to act as forwarding agent to bring in new recruits, and in this capacity I had a number of novel experiences. The first of any moment was a trip I made after Jack Powell.

Powell and his step-father, a man named W. A. Durden, were settlers living in a thinly populated district near the town of Ochesa, on the Appalachicola River. They were convicted of the murder of a neighbor, and the jury in their verdict returned Durden guilty in the first degree and Powell in the second. The jury was composed of backwoodsmen, unfamiliar with legal terms, and by first and second degree they intended to merely enumerate the prisoners, Durden first and Powell second. They wanted both hung. Consequently when Powell was sentenced to life imprisonment, their indignation knew no bounds. They considered that justice had been cheated, and determined to take the law into their own hands.

Powell was in custody at Appalachicola, and for security placed in the upper story of a store-house, where he was guarded by a heavily armed sheriff's posse. This was the situation when I arrived, and the sheriff scowled at the idea of my getting him away, alone. He turned him over to me with great reluctance and the squad of guards accompanied us in a body to the boat which I took, up the river, for Chattahoochee. I saw no signs of any lynching party at Appalachicola, and concluding that it was a false alarm, I rested easy until we neared Ochesa, when my prisoner reminded me that it was his home, and expressed some apprehension that a vigilant committee might be in waiting.

His fears proved well-grounded, for when we came in sight of the landing, a party of determined looking men appeared around the corner of a solitary warehouse that stood near the river bank. We stopped to discharge freight and passengers, and looking around the deck of our little craft, I noticed a number of flour sacks piled aft. I pointed them out to my prisoner and told him to go and secrete himself behind them. He immediately suited the action to the word, and I stationed myself at the gang-plank, drew a heavy Colt revolver, and awaited developments.

I did not want to make any blunders, but I felt reasonably sure that the men ashore were lynchers. They had an indescribable, half-uneasy, and half-resolute air, and all carried rifles. A negro was the first person on the gang-plank, and as he passed me he whispered: "Look out, boss! Dose men gwine ter take Powell way from you, suah!" This laid all doubts at rest and I made up my mind immediately to allow no one else to come aboard.

Meantime the group by the warehouse consulted together and finally moved toward the boat, one of them in advance and evidently the leader. As he put his foot on the plank, I ordered him to halt.

"I know your purpose," I said, "and you cannot come on board this boat."

"It's none of your business that I can see," he returned, stopping however, "whether I come on board or not."

"I'll make it my business to the extent of putting a hole through you if you attempt to cross that plank."

We parleyed for a moment, and then the party threw off all concealment and openly declared that they intended to take Powell.

"He deserves death," said the spokesman, "and seeing that the law didn't hang him, we will. We are here to get him, and if necessary we will commit another murder in doing it."

"Men," I replied, "if this man deserved hanging you should have hung him before he was sentenced to the state prison. He has been turned over to me, and it is my duty to protect him, which I will surely do. As far as another murder is concerned, I think I can get as many of you as you can of me, and you can rest assured that I will blow the first man off that gang-plank that puts his foot on it."

The lynchers hesitated and looked at one another. They were reckless backwoodsmen, all of them, insensible to fear; but it is a pretty well-established fact in the history of mobs that where certain death awaits the one who takes the initiative, there is never anything done. Had they been able to make a rush, I could never have saved the situation, but none of them cared to adventure on the narrow path down the gang-plank. The captain of the boat, who was very much alarmed, approached me at this juncture and begged me to give up the prisoner and save trouble, but I covered him and ordered him to stand back and keep out of the fracas. Eventually we got away from the landing in safety, but several of the lynchers ran down the bank and shouted that they would have their man before morning.

At this it dawned upon me that I was probably just at the beginning of my trouble, for owing to the imperfect facilities for travel at the time it would be necessary for me to stop at Chattahoochee Junction over night, before I could get a train east. Now Chattahoochee Junction was about the worst place in the world to stop, under the circumstances. There was nothing there except a warehouse and a small hotel, and at the latter there was no prospect of obtaining accommodations, as the landlord had an inveterate aversion to entertaining an officer with prisoners. I had good reason to know of this rule of his, for on one occasion he had refused me even a meal, when I was taking a convict to prison. The town of Chattahoochee was two miles up the river, but it was a town in name alone, containing nothing but a few shanties and a general store or two. So there was every prospect that I would be obliged to remain with my charge out of doors all night at the Junction.

I conjectured that all these facts were well known to the lynchers and, as Ochesa and Chattahoochee were no great distance apart, they would head me off at the latter place and atttempt to seize my man sometime during the night. This it turned out was exactly what they intended to do, and the land route being much shorter than that by water, they were at the Junction in full force ahead of me.

On the way up the river, I racked my brain for some plan to escape them, and finally hit upon one.

The boat's trip did not end at Chattahoochee, but it kept on up the river to Bainbridge, Georgia, where it was due to make connection with a train for Waycross. My scheme was to get off when the boat made a landing, as if I intended to stop, but jump on again at the last minute and keep on to Bain-bridge.

In pursuit of this ruse, I stepped off with my prisoner at the Chattahoochee Junction wharf and walked with my prisoner up the bank, directly through the crowd of lynchers, who eyed us menacingly. They fully believed that they had us in a trap, that we would be obliged to spend the night in the open air; and I afterward learned that elaborate plans were laid for an attack under cover of darkness. They never dreamed of my taking Powell through Geor-

gia, for the impression prevailed that it was unlaw-
ful to carry the prisoner of one state through another.

I looked around, as if in search of some place in
which to spend the night, listening meantime with
keen anxiety for the boat's whistle. At last it blew,
and telling my prisoner to run for his life, we made
for the wharf at full speed and gained the deck just
as the cable was cast off. The lynchers saw through
the trick a moment too late and came crowding
down to the landing, cursing and waving their guns,
but we were already in mid-stream, and I waved
them adieu from the deck.

After this narrow escape, all went well. We
made connections with the train at Waycross, went
from thence to Dupont, Georgia, and then to Live
Oak, from which place we reached Jacksonville and
the convict camp earlier than we could have done
had I stopped over night at Chattahoochee.

The people of Ochesa were so exasperated at the
escape of Powell from their clutches, that it was
necessary to remove Durden to Tallahassee, for safe
keeping. His sentence was eventually commuted
to life imprisonment, mainly on account of his venerable appearance, and he was certainly a singular
spectacle when he arrived at the camp. His beard
reached to his waist, and his hair fell far below his
shoulders. Both were as white as snow, and he
could tie his enormous mustache back of his head;
great, shaggy brows overhung his eyes, his nose

was like the beak of a hawk and he was as wild and alert as a catamount. A visitor at the Florida State Prison to-day might see an old man, much bent and quite decrepit, who hobbles around the yard with a stick. He is too feeble to do any regular work but potters occasionally at some little odd job, and dozes between times in the sun. His face is almost expressionless, listless, vacant, except for his eyes, which have a sinister look and now and then flash with the fire of other days. His hands tremble a good deal, and he tells in a thin, quavering voice, how he used to be able to kill a deer every time with a rifle, but thinks he would have to use a shotgun now. When he gets out, he says he intends to hunt considerably and get back his health, and if this prompts a question as to his hopes of liberty, he broods a while and then mutters piteously that he guesses the governor will pardon him pretty soon. He has guessed so now for thirteen years. This is what time and prison experience have made of the wild old woodsman. His step-son, Powell, died in the stripes, and I shall have occasion to mention him again, further on.

Shortly after the trip I have described, Henderson's career as captain ended. He had received an order from headquarters to do a certain piece of work, and taking it upon himself to disregard it, was relieved, and the camp was turned over to a sub-foreman named Jack Forrester, to hold temporarily until I returned from one of my trips. Henderson went back to Cedartown, Georgia, where both he and Forrester originally came from, and the last I heard of him, he was a guard at a convict camp there. When the position of captain was tendered to me, I declined it, preferring the lesser responsibility of the other situation; but events soon culminated in throwing me into the old harness again.

During Forrester's administration, which was brief, Walter Shavers, who will be remembered as the desperado who led the convict revolt at Camp Sing Sing, committed a robbery at Jacksonville, and as he was a professional criminal and thoroughly incorrigible, Judge W. J. Baker, of the District Court, sentenced him to ten years' imprisonment. When this sentence was passed, Shavers sprang to his feet.

"Curse you!" he exclaimed, dramatically; "you can sentence me for ten hundred years if you want to, but mark my words, you white-headed scoundrel, I will escape and come back and kill you inside of a week!"

Several officers laid hold of him and pulled him down, and he was hurried out of the court-room; but as he reached the door he turned and shouted back:

"Look for me in a week, and consider yourself dead!"

Judge Baker turned pale and pondered silently. He knew the desperate character of the man, and the threat so preyed upon his mind that when I came to Jacksonville after the prisoners of that term, he sent me word to keep Shavers well guarded and not give him the slightest opportunity to get away. I repeated this warning to Captain Forrester, who laughed and remarked that Shavers would be an old man before he got away from him. However, he reckoned without his host.

A few days after Shavers arrived, he was put to work with a squad in a deep railroad cut, then in course of excavation. At dinner-hour the guards sent to a neighboring house and procured a huge pot of boiled "greens," which they grouped themselves around, at one end of the cut, and proceeded to devour. The convicts were in the middle, and this left one end clear. In a few moments seven of them made a dash for liberty. As they ran out, the balance of the squad, who did not attempt to escape, rose in confusion and were thus interposed between the guards and the fugitives. This may have been part of a cunning plot, and may have been merely an accidental circumstance, but at any rate it prevented immediate firing, and, before the guards could obtain a clear shot, the runaways were practically out of range. They reached a belt of adjacent timber in safety, immediately disappeared, and, in brief, all made good their escape. Among the number was Walter Shavers.

Captain Forrester was present at the time of the delivery and at once sent word to Jacksonville.

SHE SAT THERE AS RIGID AS DEAD.

Siberia, Page 163.

Judge Baker heard the news with consternation. It was in direct confirmation of the first part of Shavers' threat, and having no doubt that he would carry out the balance if he got an opportunity, he lost no time in surrounding himself with detectives. I arrived in the city the next day with some prisoners in charge, and the request of Mr. Drain, the agent of the railroad company, I remained over to assist in searching for Shavers and guarding the judge.

We had reason to believe that our man had made his way straight to Jacksonville, where he would have little difficulty in hiding away, as he was a gambler and thief by profession, and hand in glove with all the very large criminal' negro population of the place. This made it unlikely that he would be found upon the streets, and for two weeks I searched the rookeries unremittingly, day and night, and made it my business to penetrate every den where I thought it at all probable he might be. Jacksonville's poorer quarters have a dense and teeming aspect that is out of proportion to the size of the city and resemble those of a metropolis. This is particularly true of the tracts on which the lower element of negroes have settled. These are packed with tenements, threaded with crooked alleys and blind passages, and full of squalid little courtyards, that were, in those days, roosts for human birds of prey of every description. Vile bagnios, dance-halls, tumble-down groggeries, and indescrib-

10

able dead-falls abounded, while in the many gambling dens of the locality the famous negro dice game of "craps" or "oontz" was in full blast every night.

This was exactly the sort of neighborhood that Shavers would naturally gravitate into, and I haunted it persistently night after night, hoping to encounter him. Early one morning, while darkness was still intense, I was on one of its narrow streets and saw a bright light shining through the chinks of a door and heard the hum of voices inside. It was a house that I had sometime before "spotted" as suspicious, but I had found no means of entering it, for the place was carefully guarded, and the door opened to none save those known to be habitues. To use force was out of the question, for besides the odds that I would be apt to encounter, such a step would scare away the game, if there. I made sure that a pass-word was used, and while I was cudgeling my brains for some scheme to get hold of it, a man came along and knocked in a peculiar manner at the door.

I immediately stepped behind him and, when the door was opened, walked in, before the sentry could stop me, at the same time drawing my pistol. I found myself in a robber's roost of the ugliest type. Several gambling tables were in the room, and a crowd of sinister-looking negroes around them, engaged at play. Others looked over their shoulders, and still more were carousing with a dozen or so of abandoned women, who mingled in the throng. The scene was illumined by big, smoky lamps, bracketed against the wall, and several drunkards snored, all oblivious, amidst a litter of torn cards upon the floor.

The sudden apparition of a stranger, revolver in hand, seemed to turn everybody into stone. The gamblers sat as if transfixed, open-mouthed and staring; those who were coquetting with the women stopped in the middle of a caress and a dead silence fell as I rapidly surveyed the place. I realized that I must make the most of the surprise I had occasioned, and, without speaking, I quickly made a round of the room, scrutinizing everybody briefly, but narrowly. One young mulatto woman was seated against the wall and wore a large, old-fashioned sun-bonnet. She sat there as rigid as the dead, but her eyes snapped as they momentarily met mine. I recognized no one and was gone the next minute, all, without a word being spoken. I gained a dark corner of the street, keeping the house still in sight, and from there I witnessed the result of my visit.

Instantly I disappeared, the spell was broken, and the place in an uproar. Frightened negroes poured out in every direction like a swarm of bees, and the uppermost thought on the minds of all seemed to be to find a spot where they might hide. The silent quarters awoke to the slamming of doors and echoing of footsteps along passage-ways, and before the excitement calmed down, I quietly slipped away.

When two weeks had passed away without a sign of Shavers, or an attempt upon Judge Baker's life, that gentleman's apprehensions abated somewhat, and I returned to the camp, leaving the case in the hands of the local authorities. It chanced in after times, that I had under me as convicts some of the very men who were in the room at Jacksonville on the night of my somewhat ghostly appearance among them. They told me, and the story has been amply corroborated, that I looked Walter Shavers in the face on that occasion. It seemed that when he arrived at Jacksonville, he went immediately to the house of a woman he knew, and was dressed in a full outfit of female attire. His somewhat feminine cast of countenance lent itself to the disguise, and he was the young mulatto girl who sat against the wall in the gambling den. He remained in Jacksonville for months, and time and again passed the very men who were searching for him. This bold and clever villain is still at large, and as he was entirely too well-known to elude the recognition of some one who would be morally certain to betray him within this lapse of time, he has prob_ably gone north, or is in some other penitentiary under an assumed name.

CHAPTER X

About the middle of March, 1881, my duties as prison agent took me to Key West, the famous city of cigars, where we were notified that seven prisoners awaited transportation. As it lies on an island, off the west coast, I took passage from Cedar Keys on the "Lizzie Henderson," a steamer plying between that point and Havana, touching Tampa Bay and Key West on the down-trip. This lengthened the journey considerably, but it was the best I could do at the time. The Lizzie Henderson was a stanch little craft, and well for me, as it afterward turned out, that such was the case.

According to schedule, we were to stop but a short time at Key West, and I arranged to put in an appearance with my charges immediately before the boat cast off, and thus avoid crowds. The captain promised to blow the whistle as a signal, and then wait for me, and I proceeded to the jail.

Some of the prisoners were Cubans, and knowing the excitable nature of the large Cuban population of Key West, I had kept my coming as quiet as possible; but the news spread in some way, and I presently saw through the jail window, that the stree was black with people. They were apparently actuated simply by curiosity, but I knew that escapes would be almost certain if we ventured among so many, and took steps to circumvent them. I ordered an omnibus brought quickly into an alley in the rear of the jail, that seemed to have been unnoticed by the throng, and proceeded to hand-cuff the prisoners.

When I had the irons on six men, I looked around for the seventh convict, and was amazed when the sheriff pointed to a very pretty and handsomely dressed young woman seated by the door.

"There is your seventh prisoner," he said.

I had noticed the girl when I entered, and sup-posed her to be his daughter or perhaps a member of some charitable, visiting committee, for she had every appearance of intelligence and refinement, and rather shocked I stepped to where my valise stood, to put away the extra pair of cuffs. She under-stood my purpose, and supposing that they were about to be placed upon her wrists, she lost the composure that she had maintained up to that moment and burst into wild sobs. I looked at her with a sinking at heart. She was a tall, pale girl, with not one of the unmistakable marks of vice, and if, as I began to surmise, she had been well reared and was there through some error of justice, I dreaded to think of the fate that awaited her— the only white woman among a horde of depraved negresses and desperate and abandoned men in an isolated convict camp with nothing, absolutely nothing, to sustain or fortify her for the ordeal. I thought then and still think that no matter how guilty, a better end would have been gained in releasing her there, while she was impressed with the menace of prison, but unhardened by its experience. Her story was a singular one, and I shall have more to say of it presently.

We succeeded in partially quieting her, when the boat's whistle sounded and the party were hurried to the omnibus. The sheriff jumped up in front and put the lash to the horses, but although we went at a gallop, the crowd immediately discovered the ruse, and we were soon in the thick of it. Most of the people were Cubans and tumbled over each other to get near to the omnibus. "Adieu, amego," they shrieked, "adieu! adieu!" It was pandemonium.

It must be remembered that it was no ordinary situation to the actors. From their point of view, I was taking their friends across the water to prison exile in a strange land, of which they had heard vague rumors and always horrifying ones. The entire wharf and for blocks around was a dense, clamoring mass of people, and it was with the utmost difficulty that we got near the boat. By dint of fairly driving over all obstacles, we managed to describe a turn and back the vehicle up to the end of the gang-plank. Two sailors stood ready to cast off the cable.

"Now run for it!" I shouted, and my little party

went aboard with a rush. I jerked the gang-plank in after them.

At that moment a strange and pathetic incident occurred. A grizzled old Spaniard, his wrinkled face all running with tears, leaped from the wharf to the deck, and one of my prisoners, a young native named Marcellus Fernandez, sprang forward with despairing gesture. They meant no harm; they were father and son, devoted to one another with all the passionate affection of the Spanish race, and the old man could not bear to see his boy taken into captivity without one more farewell. The boat's propeller was beginning to revolve; there was no time for sentiment or explanations; so I caught up the poor old fellow in my arms, he was as light and thin as a child, and literally threw him back. He alighted all right; but the haggard face of his child, looking across the now rapidly widening interval of water was too much for him, and he threw up both arms and went crashing down in a swoon. The last I saw of him, the crowd was carrying him away.

The vessel had covered but a short distance from the wharf, when the captain rushed excitedly to the bell and signaled the engineer to stop. He had just made the curious discovery that we had a dozen or so of the Cuban spectators on board. It appeared that they had slipped over the gang-plank before we arrived at the dock, hoping to thereby obtain a good view of the scene, and afterward were so absorbed in contemplating my prisoners that they did not notice that we had pulled out. When they observed this circumstance, the uproar they raised was like the jabbering of a hundred parrots, all at once. They screamed, gesticulated, and swore by all the saints on the Spanish calendar, that they were ruined unless the boat put about at once. The captain replied that if he touched the wharf again, he was satisfied that the crowd would board him, until they sunk the ship, and at last he compromised by sending them back in a row-boat. We stood to until it returned, and then steamed on, the crowd watching us to the very last.

The vessel's next stopping-point was Havana, and we steamed away southward toward the turbulent, Spanish-ridden, little island that lies only ninety miles across the gulf. I turned all my prisoners loose once we were at sea, believing that they would rather take their chances with me than with the leopard-sharks that thronged those waters, and they roamed over the deck at their will. That night we cast anchor in the beautiful harbor of Havana, under the lee of the ancient fortress of El Moro. There was scarcely enough light to appreciate the picturesque surroundings of this port, which is one of the loveliest in the world, and the soft night air was our most certain indication that we were in the tropics. We did not make a landing, but discharged cargo by another boat, and as soon as possible started on the return trip.

I had retired to my berth and was sleeping soundly, when I was suddenly pitched head-foremost across the cabin, and before I could recover myself, I was hurled in the other direction. The vessel was pitching like mad, and there was a deafening tumult, in which I could distinguish the crashing blows of the waves, like so many quick cannonshots, and between them the sharp snapping of cordage, the pounding of feet overhead, and the deadly missile-like humming of a swift and concentrated wind.

The uproar and the shock bewildered me, but I managed to reach the dead-light window and throw it open. It was black as ink outside, and instantly a shower of spray washed in and left me drenched. I made my way outside with difficulty and found that we were in the midst of a gulf tornado.

Such visitations are the terror of sailors in these waters, and they say that they are like the typhoons of the Chinese Sea. I am willing to take their word for it. This one swooped down upon us without a particle of warning, or at least the signs of its coming had been so slight that the first any one knew of its presence, we were in the midst of it. Any description of mine would convey but a slight idea of its incomparable fury. It did not bear to one fixed point, but fell upon the water like a flash, tearing it in all directions. The vessel seemed to pitch in every way at once, and in fact was so battered to and fro by the waves, and so constantly overwhelmed by them and stood almost literally upon her beam-ends, that it was very doubtful whether she would survive. At one time, when every soul was clinging for dear life to whatever substantial thing happened to be at hand, and the tempest had reached a volume that simply stunned one out of the power of thinking of anything, except that death was right at hand, the sailors ceased their exertions and gave up the ship for lost. It proved that this was the turning-point of the tornado, and its violence abated with a swiftness that was almost as bewildering as its fury. In what appeared to be an incredibly short time after this, it had passed us by.

We escaped by the merest luck. A hundred times during the storm, the chance of a point in any direction of the compass would have sent us to the bottom, and we realized it with a reaction of feeling that I shall never forget. The tornado left a dead calm in its wake, and as the vessel rocked on the flattening waves, like a tired child panting after a struggle, the officers investigated the extent of the damage. It was discovered that the strain had cracked the stout iron of the boiler from end to end and the propeller was, of course, useless. As soon as possible, all sails were set, but there was then hardly a cap full of wind stirring, and we lay for a long time becalmed, with intervals of snailing progress that was scarcely perceptible. I was anxious enough to get ashore again, and the delay seemed almost intolerable. It took us thirty-six hours to make the trip to Cedar Keys, and the balance of the journey back to camp was accomplished without any incident worthy of note.

To return to my young woman prisoner: She had heard tales of the convict camp and was prostrated with terror and grief. She wept bitterly during the whole trip, ate nothing, and arrived in a pitiable condition. Her sentence was for one year, and at this point I may as well tell her brief history with us, and her story prior to that time, which I learned from several sources and am satisfied is true.

Her real name was Maud Foster, and her father is in business in New York City. The family was well-to-do, eminently respectable, and she had been well-reared and carefully educated. But she was of a romantic disposition, had probably been reading trashy novels, and in a fit of pique or some freak of heaven only knows what, she ran away from home with another silly girl, and the two went to Cuba. It is needless to say that they did not find any of the noble dons or gallant hidalgos that their fancy had painted, but were simply very much of strangers in a very strange city. In a short time their senses partially returned to them, but as they were ashamed to go home and did not know, in fact, exactly what to do, they came to Key West. By that time their money was pretty nearly gone, although they had plenty of clothes and some jewelry, and it can be readily imagined that these two New York girls, now thoroughly disenchanted, were in a state of mind bordering on distraction. At this point one of those smooth young villains who lay in wait for unprotected women, scraped an acquaintance with Maud and stole a valuable ornament from her. She immediately complained to the police, and they prepared a complaint which she was requested to swear to, but upon reading it she found that it charged too much, and pointed out the errors. Thereupon another was drawn up and she subscribed to it.

The man was arrested, and at his hearing the girl was asked whether she had signed a certain complaint. She was greatly agitated, and in her confusion supposed that the first document was alluded to and replied that she had not. On the strength of this denial, the young thief, who was much exasperated and had influential friends, procured her arrest for perjury. I have endeavored to state the case as plainly as possible and am aware that it appears preposterous that such a charge could lie. But the man, as I said, could command influence; she was a stranger whose story sounded highly improbable, and she was rushed into trial, found guilty and sentenced, before she realized her danger. Then she gave herself up for lost, and shame prevented her from communicating with her parents and friends. The girl who ran away with her did what might reasonably be expected. She went to the bad, and in time returned to Cuba as a member of the demi-monde. Such is the true story of the fate of these two foolish runaways, and it certainly furnishes food for reflection.

When I reached the convict camp with the unfortunate girl she was in such a flutter of terror that she walked right behind me, clinging to my coat. I had inspired her with some confidence, and she was afraid that I might leave her alone among all those people. Henderson spoke to her roughly, and his words sent the blood rushing to her face, while her limbs fairly sank under her. It was altogether a sorrowful sight. I regret that I ever saw it. I felt sorry for the girl, and as time passed it hurt me to see how shame and desperation did their work. She donned the stripes in a paroxysm of wild grief, but before long she hardened herself to her degradation and abandoned herself to it. It made a bad woman out of her, and her beauty was practically all that remained of her former self. I attempted to remonstrate with her one day, but she stopped me with a passionate gesture.

"My God! Captain!" she answered bitterly. "You talk of my degrading myself! You must be jesting with me. How can I degrade myself more than I am? I am at the bottom ground now and I have quit caring what I become."

During her confinement in prison she wrote privately to her mother, but adopted a curious subterfuge to conceal her disgrace. She dated all her letters from Cuba, sent them to her girl friend, who mailed them so as to secure the proper post-office stamp, and forwarded the answers from Havana to the convict camp. In this way she kept up the deception for a whole year. While she was in the deepest despondency, she would sit down and write a cheerful, spirited letter describing imaginary scenes and travels. I had not the heart to interfere with what seemed to me a pardonable piece of duplicity, for at any rate she was determined to bear her burden alone. The answers she received were undoubtedly from a person of refinement.

The last I saw of this singular prisoner was on the day following her discharge. She had ordered her clothing, which was elegant and costly, to be sent to Jacksonville, and happening to be in that city, I noticed a finely attired lady drive past in an open carriage. She smiled at me rather wanly, and for a moment I failed to recognize in her the woman I had last seen in convict stripes. I believe she afterward went to Cuba.

I had no sooner delivered the Key West prisoners than I had orders to report to Pensacola for a noted desperado named Jim Ota, whose subsequent career furnished numerous incidents in prison history. He had been convicted of burglary, coupled with assault with intent to ravish, and sentenced to life imprisonment. The atrocious character of the offense, coupled with the fact that the complainant was the wife of one of the leading citizens of Pensacola, raised popular indignation to such a pitch that the jail was several times besieged by lynchers, and the prisoner was only saved from their clutches by the strength and determination of the sheriff's posse. Ota had both Indian and negro blood in his veins and was a cool, clean-cut fellow, with determination stamped visibly on his face.

I have alluded to the difficulties of travel in those days. They were extreme. To reach places that are now only a few hours' journey by the air-line railroads, we were obliged to make long detours, and the only route to Pensacola from Jacksonville was by way of Montgomery, Alabama, from thence to Mobile and then back, via Flomaton Junction.

A reference to the map will show that this is almost a loop. I arrived thorougly fatigued, and after only a few hours' stop took the train again with my ticklish charge, whom I well knew I must watch every moment. I was altogether three days and nights without sleep, and as the journey progressed I fell into a state of exhaustion not easily described.

My mind was bent to the imperative necessity of vigilance, but nature was meantime asserting herself, and I began to move and act automatically.

The result was a curious dual state. I was awake and yet asleep, and I wondered with keen apprehension whether Ota noticed anything peculiar about me, and whether I would be able to move in case anything happened.

At Waycross, two friends of mine came aboard the

ATTEMPTED ESCAPE OF JIM OTA.

Siberia, Page 182.

car and addressed some questions to me. My eyes were wide open; I saw my prisoner and knew perfectly what was going on, but I was so chained by fatigue that I was unable to speak and sat motionless, staring at them like one mesmerized. It was some time before I could break the spell.

"That man is a dangerous prisoner," I exclaimed at last, "and I am dead for sleep. For God's sake watch him awhile for me."

I barely heard them say "yes," and then fell back almost in a stupor. At the last station my friends aroused me, and Ota and I reached the camp all right. I mention this incident to show how severe the strain often was upon the officers in those days.

Tampa was another bad point to reach and the route was curiously indirect. I went there shortly after the experience I have just narrated. First I went by rail to Callahan and then took a new road completed to within a few miles of Ocala. At that point a stage was advertised to connect with the train and carry passengers to Tampa via Ocala. The stage proved to be a two-seated, primitive wagon, remarkable for its absence of springs and general discomfort, and as there were a couple of lady passengers with an abundance of trunks, we were terribly cramped and crowded. The distance was over a hundred miles; the road was indescribably bad in places, and we reached our destination half dead. I found but one prisoner, a six months man, and not relishing another wagon experience I concluded to take a steamer to Cedar Keys and thence proceed by rail to Jacksonville. I had to hire a sail boat to reach the vessel which lay across the bar, six or seven miles away, and was then obliged to use in all four different modes of travel, to bring in one man.

We passed through Bradford on our way to Jacksonville, and to save time I wired to the sheriff to have his prisoners at the train. Accordingly he was at the depot with three men, one of them a savage-looking negro, whom he informed me would escape if he saw the slightest chance. I ordered them on board, but this fellow, whose name was Smith Oliver, refused to budge.

I laid hold of him and after a sharp tussle managed to get him on the cars, just as the train pulled out.

I took a seat in the rear of the men, and for the next hour or two Oliver kept furtively looking around at me. I cautioned him against these tactics, and while I was speaking, he sprang to his feet and leaped for the open car window, head first, like a diver. He was half-way out before I could lay hold of him. I seized his legs and drew him in, struggling desperately, although he was manacled and the train was going at full speed. As soon as I got him into the seat again I drew my revolver, and presenting it at his head told him that the next time he moved or looked around I would blow his brains out. Under this powerful persuasion he remained quiet for the balance of the trip.

When I turned him over to Captain Forrester, I told him of the character of the man, and a few days later he fully sustained his reputation. He was with a squad on a construction train moving at full-speed, and while passing over a twelve foot embankment he seized an opportunity to leap off. He wore a "stride-chain" on his ankles at the time, riveted from shackle to shackle, but strange to say, he alighted unhurt and instantly darted off into the timber. Captain Forrester was on the train, saw the leap, and jerked the bell-cord. The engine was reversed, and when the speed of the train was slackened a little, he also jumped off. However, he was not as sure-footed as the negro, and rolled head-over-heels to the bottom of the embankment.

When he regained his feet, his eyes were so full of sand and he was so jolted up generally that he had no idea which direction the fugitive took. Thus he made good his escape.

CHAPTER XI

A bad example is just as dangerous in a convict camp as elsewhere, and the day following the escape of Smith Oliver, described in the last chapter, two other prisoners leaped from the train at nearly the same spot. They were both white men—Jack Powell, whom I saved with such difficulty from the lynchers, and Thomas Nix, a big, gaunt "cracker," who was under fifteen years' sentence for an infamous crime in which his daughter was complainant.

A few shots were fired, but they reached the woods in safety, and as I happened to be at the camp, I was detailed for the pursuit. I surmised that the men would separate as soon as they gained cover, for they were an ill-assorted pair, Powell being a loutish, chuckle-headed fellow, while Nix, with all his rough exterior, was sharp as a needle, and, moreover, an adept at woodcraft, perfectly at home in the wilderness, and as skillful at hiding away as an Indian. Such a man would not be likely to encumber his flight with a companion, and when the dogs took a trail that led straight to a densely overgrown swamp, I felt sure that this was Nix and not Powell I was following.

I rode through the rank fringes of the morass right behind the dogs, and presently the track began to

lead toward a wild region know as "Trail Ridge."
This is a chain of little eminences lying along the
St. Mary's River, in the midst of a country almost
unknown to the outside world, although it has been
penetrated and occupied, to some extent, by adventurous settlers, and outlaws hiding from arrest.
But what made the chase assume a very serious aspect when it entered this domain was that nearly
all of the settlers subsisted from the proceeds of
illicit whisky. Hidden in secret spots all through
the swamp and forest were their rude stills, and
although the profits were beggarly, these moonshiners, like all others of their class, believed that they
had a perfect right to manufacture all the whisky
they wanted, and were prepared to assert it to the
bitter end. Consequently they regarded all officers
in general and United States marshals in particular
as their natural enemies. They bitterly hated anybody and everybody connected with the law, and
would not hesitate for a moment to bring down
such game with their long-barreled rifles, and
I fully realized that I had entered hostile territory.

It was impossible for a stranger to penetrate the
bewildering maze of tropical wood and undergrowth
that masked the approaches to Trail Ridge, so I
was forced to hire a native as a guide. I did not
have unlimited confidence in him. He had a shifty,
evasive manner, common enough among the country people, but under the circumstances it seemed

to me highly suspicious, and I made up my mind that the chances were about even that he would lead me into a trap.

I kept my eyes on him, determined to put a hole through him at the very first sign of treachery, but he made no move to confirm my suspicions and led the way steadily toward the St. Mary's. The river is a deep but narrow stream, that has driven its channel through the midst of a pestilential swamp, abounding in quagmires and pretty nearly overgrown with lush, heavy vegetation. Its approaches are thick with palmetto trees, growing on little hummocks that rise above the stagnant water and are festooned with slender parasitical creepers, which keep up a constant, fantastic motion, no matter how still the day, and have an uncanny air of reaching out and grasping at the passer-by. The huge, fan-like palmetto leaves, interlacing overhead, darken the scene even at midday, and millions of southern water weeds tangle in inextricable confusion in the gloomy reaches underneath. Rotting tree-trunks barricade passage everywhere; fat, bloated water-moccasins, indescribably loathsome in appearance, wriggle through the ooze; the stench is fearful; poisonous little winged insects cloud about one's head like smoke; now and then the checkered snout of an alligator slides through the slime; big spiders, spotted red and black, and venomous as serpents, scramble up their airy ropes, and as night advances, the croaking of marsh frogs and hooting of owls combine in an infernal chorus that smites the ear like thunder.

We entered this foul morass, sometimes walking, but more often crawling and floundering. Occasionally we came upon a little tongue of land intersecting the quagmire, and found these bits of solid terra-firma almost invariably occupied by some squatters. There would be a small clearing, perhaps a little garden cultivated by the "wimmen folks," and the rudest imaginable cabin, surrounded by a "snake" rail fence. Here the possessors of the place lived in perfect security and almost perfect solitude. It was getting dark when I knocked at the door of the first house for the purpose of making some inquiries, and the greeting I received was characteristic.

"Who's thar?" called out somebody, without opening to me.

I briefly explained.

"We ain't seen no convict," replied the voice, "and we ain't lookin' fur none fur you."

"How far is it to the river?" I asked.

"Look-a-here," said the voice again, and this time it was menacing; "if you all have business anywhar's else, you'd better go right off an' 'tend to it!"

It would have been folly, suicide perhaps, to linger, and I followed the advice. Happily the people at the next house were better disposed, and gave some valuable information. They had seen a convict passing through the woods, with his stripes on, and a singular hat, made of tree moss, upon his head. There was no doubt, from the description, but that the man was Nix. He was evidently pushing toward a place called King's Ferry, which was the only point where he could cross the river.

Upon obtaining this information, my guide told me that he had a boat hidden not far away, and we pushed to the spot where he drew a rude bateau from among the reeds of the river's margin. We both scrambled in and paddled through the gathering darkness, to the ferry and beyond, making all the inquiries possible. But Nix was too clever for us. Several people had seen him, noticing particularly his curious cap, but he might have taken any one of a thousand different directions afterward, and night made his escape sure. The wilderness had swallowed him up, and it was years before I found the broken end of the trail, to pursue it hundreds of miles away amidst scenes of considerable greater peril. I will tell the story at the proper place, and leave him for the present as we left him then.

Powell had, it afterward turned out, gone but a short distance into the swamp, where he secreted himself for two or three days, until hunger drove him out. Then he went to the house of a settler and begged for food. Help was quietly sent for and he was captured and brought ignominiously back to camp.

It may be remembered that among the runaways from Sing Sing was a negro outlaw named John Jacobs. He had baffled pursuit and it was not until this period that we heard from him. The news came from a wild district in Marion County adjoining the Ocklawaha river, which he had penetrated, and occasionally did work for farmers in the neighborhood. Although remote from any town and practically hidden in the forest, his evil name followed him, and in time the sheriff, Pump Crutchfield, was notified that he was there. He forwarded the information to us, and I was sent after the fugitive.

I went to Ocala, the county seat, where I met Crutchfield, and we drove near where Jacobs was said to be. We had minute information. He had hired to a farmer and was then at work in a large cleared cabbage-field, plowing. But so wary was he that he never stirred without a weapon at hand, and we were warned to take him suddenly or there would either be bloodshed or another escape.

We found the cabbage-field easily, and there, sure enough, was my old prisoner, diligently turning a furrow, with a rifle hung to his plow-handle. The clearing was surrounded by thick woods, and the question was how to take him before he could break for them. It was done by a bit of strategy. I left Crutchfield hidden at one side, with instructions to rise at the proper time and attract his attention, while I executed a flank movement from the other. I then crept along the underbrush, and gaining the desired point, waited until Jacobs turned his plow and began to move away. Upon that I jumped noiselessly over the fence and tiptoed after him. He did not hear my footfalls on the soft ground, and presently I was close to his back. At this juncture, Crutchfield slowly rose up from behind the fence. The negro stopped and surveyed him dubiously. He did not know the sheriff, and it was obvious that he was debating in his mind whether to stand his ground or run. While his eyes were fastened upon him, I suddenly seized him by the collar. A more astonished darky never gasped. He jumped clear through the plow-handles and tried to snatch his gun, but I had my pistol against his head before he could reach it.

"Do you know me, John?" I asked.

He twisted his neck around and rolled his big, white eyes upon me.

"Good Lawd, yes! Cap'n," he ejaculated; "what on dis yearth you want wif me?"

"You owe the state of Florida a little work, John," I replied; "so you'll have to drop this job until you square up the debt."

I slipped the bracelets upon him and we filed out of the cabbage field. I intended to go back by river, so Crutchfield left us with the team, and I and my prisoner proceeded to a little landing on the Ocklawaha, where the Silver Springs boat, owned by Colonel Hart, stopped on the way up. The river

schedule was very uncertain, and although the boat
was due at dusk, hours passed without its putting in
an appearance, and the few passengers grew tired
of waiting and went home, leaving Jacobs and me
alone. There was no town at the landing nothing
but an old freight house and a dilapidated wharf,
built out over the water. This wharf was so low
that the river weeds had overgrown it from end to
end, and all that could be seen of it, in fact,
was a square of green, rising a little above the other
reeds and vegetation that grew in the shallows
near the bank. The surroundings were desolate in
the extreme. Night was upon us, and I began to
realize that I was in an ugly position, particularly
as it was possible that the boat would not arrive
before morning. There was no moon, and it was
soon difficult to see more than a foot or two
through the thick, tropical darkness, into which
my prisoner might at any moment dash and make
his escape.

As night fell, woods, swamp and river awakened
to a din of animal voices. Swarms of owls screeched
and hooted right over our heads, long-drawn cries
came from the forest, and the water around the
wharf seemed literally alive with alligators. These
monsters emit a hoarse bellow, something like that
of an angry bull, but louder, and that night they
fairly shook the earth. Between the roars I could
hear the vicious swish of their tails, and it seemed
highly probable that some of them would crawl up

among the weeds of the wharf and take a nip at our legs. Jacobs was breathing hard, and I felt instinct ively that he was half-frightened and half-meditat ing a dash.

"John," I said to him finally, "if an alligator would happen to grab you just now, you would stand a poor show with those irons on your wrists."

"'Deed I would, Cap'n," he replied fervently.

"Well," I continued, "I'll tell you what I am go ing to do. I won't see a man killed if I can help it, and I intend to take those cuffs off even if you run away from me."

He protested that such a thought had never en tered his mind, and I slipped one of the locks. While pretending to unfasten the other, I snapped the loose cuff on my own left wrist and then said cheerfully:

"Well, John, if a 'gator gets you now, we'll both die together, and by the way, if you make any at tempt to escape, I will be pretty sure to put a bul let into you."

He did not reply, but I could see the whites of his eyes as he glared at me indignantly through the darkness. We sat down on the wharf and waited. The owls and alligators kept up their dismal concert, and a night never passed slower or more wearily. Now and then Jacobs would say in a hoarse whisper, "Don't shoot me, boss!" "All right, keep quiet then," I would reply. At about one o'clock the boat's whistle sounded like sweet music in my ears, and shortly after I was on board, cramped, tired out and entirely grateful. We arrived at camp without further incident, and Jacobs made a good prisoner for the balance of his time.

While acting as prison agent, I had another experience with Sheriff Crutchfield that was, to say the least, lively. He notified us that an escaped prisoner named Beverly Lewis had been seen, hanging around Ocala, and I went after him. We learned that he was to be at a negro festival on the outskirts of town, and thither went Crutchfield and I, to surprise him, if possible. At the suggestion of the sheriff, who thought that the man might otherwise see me and take the alarm before he could be caught, I secreted myself in the vicinity and he went to the house. He saw Lewis in the crowd, and without waiting to call me, rushed in and placed him under arrest. But the game was not so easily bagged. Lewis instantly broke away, tore through the crowd and jumped right into the open fire-place. The chimney was a frail affair of mud and stick, occupying an aperture in the rear of the house, and the whole back of it gave way before the fugitive. The last Crutchfield saw of him he was disappearing through the ragged opening.

I saw the fiasco, and both Crutchfield and I started on a run for the opposite side of town, where a sister of Lewis lived, and where we supposed he would be likely to go at once for arms and assistance. It was quite dark, and as we neared the spot I saw a man running at the top of his speed in our direction. With no other thought than that he was Lewis, I gave chase, and coming up with him in a little street, I clapped a pistol to his head and ordered him to surrender. The man threw up his hands and stood there, chattering and gibbering, while I discovered that it was a case of mistaken identity, and left him no doubt under the impression that he had been attacked by a highwayman and had a narrow squeak of it for his life.

We saw no more of Lewis, but he was foolish enough to linger about the town and eventually meet his death at the hands of Crutchfield. One day, sometime after the little comedy of errors I have described, the sheriff caught sight of him slipping along a back street, and ordered him to halt. Lewis looked around, instantly recognized his whilom captor at the festival and began to run like a deer. Crutchfield rushed after him, but as it became plain that the negro had the best of the race he drew a heavy revolver and fired. The bullet passed clear through the fugitive; he leaped in the air and fell on his face, dead.

These adventures were continually alternated by my journeys after newly convicted prisoners. Notification came that there were recruits in Marianna and in Washington County, and my trip after them resulted in another odd experience with the moonshiners. In order to reach the localities named, I was obliged, as usual, to take a circuitous route. I went in over our own line of railroad to Bainbridge, Georgia, where I hired a buggy and driver and struck across the Florida boundary, southward. The drive was pleasant as far as Marianna, but soon after that we entered the wilds. The country there is practically a virgin wilderness, and the main industry of the scattered settlers is the distillation of illicit whisky. This district is the terror of United States marshals, and those who have gone into it have usually stayed here. At least they have not come out yet. I did not take prisoners at Marianna, intending to stop on my way back, and drove as directly as possible toward Vernon, the county seat of Washington County.

As we made our way through the primal woods, our solitude was broken by a woman who rode up to the buggy on a mule. She was sallow-skinned and sharp-featured, and her flimsy calico gown hung limply on the many angles of her form. Her head was half buried in a huge sun-bonnet, and altogether she appeared to be a simple, unsophisticated native. I took in these points over the edge of a newspaper I was reading, and when she came quite close she opened a conversation with my driver. In a short time I discovered that she was plying her tongue with considerable shrewdness, and was evidently bent upon finding out who we were and all about us. Putting one thing with another, I made up my mind that she was a spy of the moonshiners, and took occasion to let her know what my business was, for I had no relish for being shot by mistake.

"Don't you all have nothin' to do with the courts?" she asked innocently.

"Only to get men after they are sentenced," I explained.

"Oh!" and she fell into a brown study. Presently she said, in an off-hand way: "If you folks wants to know whar anybody lives hereabouts, I reckon I kin tell you. I know nigh about everybody in these here woods."

I hastened to decline this bait.

"I don't want anybody but my prisoners, and I don't know or care who lives here. Much obliged to you but I know the way to the jail and that's enough."

This satisfied her to some extent, but she still plied her questions. Finally I turned the tables and asked a few myself.

"How far are you going, madam?" I inquired.

"Oh, just down the road a bit," she replied.

The "bit" proved to be twelve miles, during which distance she followed us like a shadow, prattling on all the way, and then, evidently convinced that I had no United States warrants to serve, she turned suddenly into a side trail and disappeared. I subsequently learned that I had taken her correct measure. She was a well-known native female detective, who guarded the avenues of approach for the moonshiners, and it was a cunning stranger who penetrated the country without her knowledge. For

A FEMALE DETECTIVE.

all I know to the contrary, she still patrols the road on her old mule.

At Vernon I found nothing but a few dilapidated dwellings, a court-house that looked like a corn-crib, and a jail "down by the creek." The sheriff was a veritable Poo-Bah, being also, I think, clerk of court, postmaster, road-supervisor, and probably mayor, marshal and coroner. At all events, he was vastly the most important personage in the village, and kept the only house of entertainment there. He informed me that he would have a fine supper prepared for me, and a little while later I sat down before a dish of boiled potatoes and one of boiled eggs. That was the supper for which I was charged three dollars, and I instantly recognized the landlord as the original type of the Florida summer hotel pro-prietor. In the morning I handed my papers to the sheriff. They called for two prisoners. He exam-ined the documents and drawled out:

"I'm all-fired sorry, Captain, but I ain't got but one."

"What!" I exclaimed, "have you had an escape?"

"No, not 'zactly. One of the fellers hung hisself t'other day, when he heard you was comin'."

The unfortunate man had committed suicide in his cell. I took the remaining prisoner and drove away. We arrived at Marianna without incident, and I picked up two more, all negroes. It was my intention to pass the night at a little place called Greenwood, and before I left Marianna, the sheriff

12

approached me with a serious air and drew me to one side.

"Captain," he said, "I think it my duty to warn you that there is a Ku-klux society at Greenwood, and they have declared that they would take all offenses by negroes into their own hands. I wouldn't be surprised if they made an attempt to capture your prisoners."

"For what purpose?"

"Oh, I guess they'd lynch them, of course."

"Are they strong enough to make an attack right in town, do you think?"

"No, hardly. It is more likely to be an ambuscade. They may not trouble you at all, but if I were you, I would keep my eyes open."

I thanked him for the warning and determined to follow his advice. We arrived in the village at about dusk, and there being no jail, I deposited my prisoners in a vacant house and hired a guard to watch them for the night. Then I strolled back to the hotel where I found a crowd had assembled, attracted by the news of our presence. They followed me into the dining-room when I went to get supper and annoyed me with all manner of questions, the general drift of which was to discover my plans for the night. I gave evasive replies, but this in connection with the sheriff's warning, made me very uneasy, and after I had gone to bed I could not sleep. The more I thought about the matter the more I felt that I was not fulfilling my duty to my prisoners in leaving them until morning. At last I jumped up and hastily dressing, ordered the team, paid my bill, and drove to the improvised jail. I took out the three men, told them to get in, and gave the driver the word to whip up.

At that hour the little town was pretty well deserted and our exit did not appear to attract any attention. Our objective point was the Chattahoochee River, which we intended to cross at a place called Neal's Landing. All went well until we were about midway between there and the town, when I heard the muffled sound of hoofs behind us, up the road. In a few moments a party of horsemen galloped past, closely followed by a second detachment, at an interval of a few hundred yards. They went by so quickly and the darkness was so extreme that I could not make out their faces or even determine their number exactly, but there were a dozen or so of them, and broken fragments of a most disquieting conversation reached my ears through the night.

"That's them, sure!" exclaimed one voice.

"Where shall it be?" said another, and then came a murmur in which I several times distinguished the words—"Neal's Landing." There was no room for doubt but we were heading straight for a Kuklux ambuscade.

My prisoners and my driver both took in the situation at once. The latter was also a darky, and no doubt supposing that he might be included in the lynching festivities on general principles, his teeth chattered as he pulled up the horses. My inclination was to stop and prepare to defend the party, but the driver informed me that he knew of another road, somewhat longer, but leading by a circuitous route to the ferry. I ordered him to take it and make the very best time possible, so as to arrive ahead of our pursuers. He did not spare the lash, and we dashed through the forest at break-neck speed, escaping accident a dozen times by the merest luck. At one o'clock in the morning we emerged on the bank of the river.

There was a profound hush everywhere and not a sign of Ku-klux, but I felt instinctively that there was not an instant to lose and hastened to put into execution a plan that I had formulated on the way.

The river at this point was crossed by a flat-boat that plied back and forth in answer to the hails of passengers. It was moored at the ferryman's shanty on the other side at the time, and getting down with my prisoners, I told the driver to shout over and cross as quickly as he could. I particularly cautioned him to instruct the ferryman to say that the buggy had passed over, in case any one afterward inquired. He was to await us at the other side, and as soon as I saw him well away I took my three prisoners a couple of hundred yards up the river bank to where the current had washed out a tiny cove or bay, well sheltered by high banks. We scrambled down and I made my men sit on one side

while I took up my position on the other and watched and waited.

In about an hour the delegation that had passed
us on the road came galloping up to the landing.
I cast an anxious glance at my charges, fearful lest
in their excitement they would inadvertently make
some sound that would betray us, but they were
sleeping peacefully, their heads on each other's
shoulders. The Ku klux reined up at the bank and
gave a loud halloo. Presently the ferryman came
drifting across on his cumbersome craft.

"Have you seen a buggy pass here?" shouted the
spokesman.

"Yes, it went over about an hour ago," replied
the boatman, speaking literally the truth.

"Curse it all!" exclaimed the Ku-klux; "what
shall we do, boys?"

They had a general consultation and finally decided that I had too much start for them to hope to
overtake me, and that they had best abandon the
chase. Little they thought that the game lay then
within gun-shot, and at last, with a feeling of indescribable relief, I heard their horses' foot-falls die
away in the distance. I devoted the balance of the
night to closely watching my prisoners, and in the
morning called over the boat and resumed our journey, which ended without further adventure, at the
camp.

CHAPTER XII

In my account of our experiences at Camp Sing Sing, I have mentioned the escape of Alec. Lige and Nathan Shell, the latter of whom was not recaptured. Shell was one of those negro outlaws, occasionally encountered in the South, whose desperation partakes of the nature of insanity; who on the impulse of the moment will dare anything, do anything, and take any chances without apparent regard for their own life or the possibilities of success. A couple of years passed after his escape, and, although we had reason to believe he was in Florida, he could not be definitely located. At last he was recognized at the town of Enterprise, on the St. Johns River, and arrested.

The jail there was a two-story wooden structure, the lower floor of which was used as an office for the deputy in charge. When Shell was brought into this building, he seized an opportunity to rush over the guard, leap out of the window and run. He was immediately fired upon and before he could gain cover three balls struck him. One pierced his shoulder, another passed through his thigh, and the third wounded him in the calf of the leg. He staggered at the shock of each bullet but did not fall and did not cease to run, and when the smoke

cleared away, he was out of sight. His wounds
were bleeding profusely and he was in a condition
that would have prostrated an ordinary man, but
he gained the margin of a little lake that lies upon
the outskirts of the town and unhesitatingly plunged
in. By an almost superhuman effort he managed
to swim across, and drew himself out, half dead,
upon the other side.

He was too exhausted to continue his flight and
he crawled into a clump of underbrush where he
succeeded in partially stanching his wounds. For
hours he lay hidden in this spot while search was
prosecuted in every other direction. Nobody for a
moment dreamed that a wounded man could swim
the lake, and consequently nobody looked in the
right place.

At last pain and hunger drove him out. He
dragged himself to a cabin not far away and begged
for food and help. The people who lived there
seized him and brought him back to jail.

This was the situation when we were notified of
his presence there. The authorities requested that
we come and take him away as soon as possible and
I was sent upon the errand. There were some
doubts as to the man really being Shell, but these
were dissipated as soon as I laid eyes upon him.
He was alone in the jail proper, at the time, and
professed great gratification that I had been sent
after him, instead of some stranger being intrusted
with the business. His wounds were giving him

intense pain, and he was hardly able to move; in fact, he seemed to be anything but a dangerous character.

I had arrived in the evening and intended to take the St. Johns River steamer next day. When I retired, at the hotel, I found that by chance my room faces the jail, and I had a clear view of it from my window. At about midnight I was awakened by a cry of fire, and jumping up, I saw at once that the conflagration was at the jail. Dense volumes of smoke were pouring from the roof, and the window on my side was a square of lurid red against which the bars stood in black and checkered relief. I hurried on some clothes and ran at the top of my speed for the scene. When I got there a bucket brigade was hard at work and the upper story apparently a mass of flames. I hastily inquired after my convict.

"He is up there," said the jailer; "I was afaid to open the door for fear he might run."

"Come with me!" I shouted, and rushed up an outside stairway that led to the upper story.

I peered through the grated door as the jailer nervously fumbled with the lock, and distinguished Shell, lying prone on his face. At last the door was opened, and we were immediately enveloped in a cloud of smoke. I groped my way in, half-suffocated and dazed by the roar and crackle of the flames, but managed to lay hold of him, and dragged him to the stairs. He was unconscious, and

seemed at first to be dead, but he recovered his
senses in the fresh air. He was not burned in any
particular place, but the heat and smoke seemed to
have fairly dried him up—no other words describes
his condition. The color of his skin was changed,
his face was shriveled into a thousand wrinkles, and
I would not have recognized the man had I seen
him on the street. He looked twenty years older.

Some idea of the terrific heat to which he had
been subjected may be formed from the fact that
the soles of my own feet were blistered through
the heavy shoes I wore, and I was not in the cell
to exceed fifteen seconds.

No one but a southern darky, inured to the ver-
tical sun of the tropics, could have endured that ordeal and lived.

The fire originated in a curious effort on his part
to escape. He had broken a heavy wooden bunk to
splinters and built a fire with them in the center of
the cell floor, intending to burn his way through to
liberty.

There was a large jug of water in the cell, and
he kept a circle dampened to prevent the flames
from spreading. In time the heavy flooring was
burned completely through, but here an unforseen
accident occurred. Between the floor and the ceiling below there was a space into which the flames
instantly entered and spread beyond control of the
prisoner.

When he saw that he was about to be burned

alive he gave the alarm, and a close call he had of it.

I naturally concluded that when a man was shot almost to pieces and then half-roasted he would give me no further trouble, except to attend to his injuries; but I was deceived. When we took the steamer next day, I dressed his wounds and turned my back on him for a few moments, and in that brief interval he crawled to the side and attempted to jump overboard. I was finally obliged to chain him to a stanchion, and in that condition he made the balance of the trip.

He served out his unexpired term of sentence, but never ceased his endeavors to get away. When he was at work on the railroad one day he made some excuse to step aside, and climbing down an embankment, began to crawl over a large brush heap. The guard saw him when he was on top of the brush and fired four loads of buckshot without hitting him. By that time he had gained the open beyond, and was running at good speed, but another guard, seeing that he was about to escape, also fired on him and one buckshot hit him in the back. He fell over, and before he could regain his feet, a trusty had overtaken and seized him. I do not know what became of this desperado. He is probably dead or in some other prison.

I have frequently pondered over the motives which induce men to escape and the impulses that nerve them to the act. To an outsider it

seems a very simple matter, namely: that liberty is
sweet and that one will dare much or little for it,
according to his personal courage. But there is a
great deal more to the question than that. A man
who has any hopes at all of regaining his liberty,
either by expiration of sentence or pardon, usually
prefers that method to becoming a fugitive, yet
there appear to be times when the craving for pardon grows so strong that it is irresistible, and a
prisoner will forfeit then and there the most certain
prospects of clemency, and throw away all the ben-
eficial consequences of years of good conduct, when
a little patience would insure legitimate delivery.
For that reason I do not regard a convict as at all
times exactly responsible for what he does, and be·
lieve that he should always be watched, like a luna-
tic, for the appearance of these morbid impulses.

To illustrate, I once had a convict known as
"Number 102." I forget his right name, but at any
rate he had commenced his sentence amidst the
horrors of the old penitentiary at Chattahoochee,
had worked on steady through the terrible times
that followed, never violating a rule, until he had
largely won the confidence of all the officers with
whom he came in contact. At last his time was
drawing near a close. He had lived it through, and
all his years of toil and suffering lay behind him,
like a dream. He was to be released next day. I
had received his discharge papers, giving him the
benefit of the commutation won by his faithful serv-

ice, and on the morrow he was to go into the world, a new man so to speak, to begin life over again.

That morning he was one of a squad working out of doors, and I had occasion to use a barrel which had been left over the brow of a little hill, near by. I saw no one else to send and called up "102."

"Do you think you could come back," I said, half joking, "if I send you over that hill for a barrel?"

He laughed back at me.

"Why of course I could, Captain," he replied. "I've had a hundred chances to escape and I will be a free man to-morrow."

"Go ahead," I said.

He started over the hill, and in a little while I saw him coming back with the barrel. Then I turned to direct some work and when I looked again he was gone. I was thunderstruck, but called immediately to one of the guards to get the dogs and pursue him. The chase was a short one. The man had run for about a mile and then sat down and began to hammer off his irons, but before he accomplished it he was recaptured. He appeared to be half-dazed when he was brought back, and the only explanation he could offer was that he "just couldn't help it."

The act cost him punishment, the loss of many privileges, and servitude for months of "gain time" that he would otherwise have been granted.

Another prisoner was more honest with me. He

also had nearly served out his sentence, and common sense should have counseled him against attempting to escape, at the risk of life, when he would be a free man anyhow in a few days more. I had some errand that I wanted done which would take a man temporarily out of range of the guard's gun; and I called him to me.

"Do you think it would be safe for me to send you over there?" I asked.

A singular expression overspread the man's face, and in a sudden burst of candor the truth came out.

"Captain," he said, "you'd better not send me. If I got that far away, I couldn't come back if I wanted to."

I let some one else do the errand. This man was named Horace Stalsworth. He came from Pensacola, and was subsequently murdered by Smith Oliver, whom I have mentioned elsewhere.

And so I might cite instances by the dozen. Men have been made trusties and in this capacity have gone miles from camp, have had abundant and excellent opportunities to leave, and then at some moment when the odds were perhaps all against them, have suddenly levanted. At another camp a cook who had the entire freedom of the place, and who was up and about before day-break every morning was seized with the impulse of flight just as he struck a match to light the kitchen fire. He carefully blew out the match, laid it on the edge of the stove, went into the guard's quarters, picked up a Winchester rifle and a handful of cartridges, and took his departure. Men who were afterward recaptured have told me that the craving for freedom would come upon them without warning while in the middle of a conversation, while eating, or when they awoke at night-time, and that it was absolutely impossible to resist its promptings.

But to resume the thread of my story: When I took my prisoners from the Marianna jail, I left a white man named Jackson Cox who was under ten years' sentence for felonious assault upon his daughter, but who had obtained a stay pending a hearing in the upper court. His sentence was shortly after confirmed, and I made the trip after him. I was in a hurry and essayed to make the drive to Bainbridge, a distance of forty miles, in one day, but night overtook us on the road and we were obliged to stop at a farm-house until morning. Both to spare the feelings of my prisoner and to insure our reception I removed his handcuffs and agreed to represent him as simply a traveling companion.

None of the family suspected the ruse, although I dare say they thought I was very much attached to my friend, for I never took my eyes off him, and after a pleasant evening we retired to the "spare room." There was only one bed, and after handcuffing Cox, I told him to occupy the rear, and that if I felt sleepy I would lie down in front. In the course of the night I did so, with my arms back of my head and my revolver in my hand.

I closed my eyes and was pondering over the fact that misfortune makes strange bed-fellows, when I became aware that Cox was watching me. He rose softly to his elbow, surveyed me once or twice and then gently touched me. I simulated sleep, and then very quietly and gradually he began to lift himself out of bed. He was half over me when I suddenly threw him back and thrust the pistol into his face. He crouched for an instant glaring at me, and then tremulously begged me not to kill him. I reminded him rather sternly of my efforts to save him mortification and the advantage he had taken of them, and spent the balance of the night watching him, weapon in hand. In the morning, irons off and smiling, he reappeared in the role of traveling companion, and the whole family followed us out to say good-bye, little dreaming of the somewhat dramatic scene that had taken place under their roof a few hours before. Cox served four years of his sentence and died in prison.

This brings me to an event which made a considerable change in my fortunes. I had obtained a fifteen days' leave of absence to visit my family at Live Oak, but on the first evening I received a telegram from Mr. Haines, the agent of the railroad, to report at Jacksonville at once. I found him greatly perturbed.

"You must assume charge of the camp immediately," he said; "things are going to the deuce there. Ten men escaped in a body yesterday."

I inquired the particulars and learned that a plot had been formed among some of the more desperate of the convicts, and when the construction train was coming in, ten of them leaped from different points on one of the cars. Such a wholesale delivery threw the guards into confusion and they fired almost at random. The result was that nobody was hit, and all escaped to the woods. The company had been for some time dissatisfied with the management, and this incident capped the climax, but I was most reluctant to accept the responsibilities of the position. However, at the urgent request of Mr. Haines, I agreed to take charge and went back to camp, armed with an order to Captain Forrester to turn over the keys and effects to me. When he read this document he drew a bunch of keys from his pocket, and exclaiming, "There they are!" flung them down and instantly left the premises. In this manner I was placed once more at the head of the lease system.

This terminated my duties as prison agent, although, as will subsequently be seen, I was frequently called upon to act in special cases. During the year that followed I had exactly two escapes.

Our work on the Jacksonville & Waycross road was meantime approaching completion, and six months more wound it up. Everything in that time passed off smoothly with one exception, which occurred in this wise: I had gone out to inspect some road work and one of the foremen complained

STRANGE BEDFELLOWS.

Siberia, Page 218.

to me that a convict named Joseph Williams had refused to obey orders and made threats. The malcontent was a burly fellow, a new arrival, who had made up his mind not to work, and determined to have it out on the spot. I spoke to Williams, and as he answered me very sullenly and reiterated his determination to do nothing, I ordered him to get down for a whipping, at the same time stepping up quite close to him.

"No, by heaven!" he shouted, and sprang upon me.

I had a pistol in my pocket with the handle slightly protruding, and he made a violent effort to seize it, but I got my hand upon it first, and snatching it out, fired point-blank at him. The bullet plowed a furrow across his back, and the pain and shock brought him to his knees. He instantly gave up the fight, but if ever a man had murder in his face, he had. I knew that he would kill me unhesitatingly if ever an opportunity afforded, but he was kept "under the gun," as the saying goes in camp, and never had a chance for further mischief.

Very shortly before we left Camp Hillyard, Dick Evans, the ex-sheriff of Pensacola, whose sensational attempt to escape I have detailed elsewhere, tried his luck again and learned with tolerable certainty that fate was against him. He had been once more placed in charge of the hospital, and while I was out with the men upon the road one afternoon he managed to slip away from the yard,

13

undetected by any of the guards. In some manner
he had secured a suit of citizen's clothes during
the morning and carried them to the rear of the
cell-house in a wheelbarrow full of rubbish. In his
flight he stopped long enough to secure the bundle.
He then cut across the fields and down a little
road, making for the woods at the top of his speed.

This happened late in the afternoon and a few
moments before I had disembarked the squads at
the railroad track. Instead of coming in by my
usual route, which would have taken me entirely
out of the path of the runaway and which I had
never before varied, I obeyed a sudden impulse
which seems next door to a premonition, and took
another way back. This led me into the road which
Evans had struck, and we almost collided as he
came dashing down, bundle in hand. He stopped
thunderstruck and smiled a sickly smile. He was
too heart broken to resist, and I simply turned him
right-about-face and led him back to camp.

Our work on the short line was now drawing to a
close. The road was built as usual, from both
terminals; we started the construction north from
Jacksonville and another force pushed it south from
Waycross, Ga. This latter labor was done by
Georgian convicts, but as under the law they could
not be worked out of their own state, it was planned
that we meet at the St. Mary's river, which forms
the northern boundary of Florida at that place.
However, the Georgian party arrived at the river

first, leaving a radius of about twelve miles on our side, over which the grading had been completed, leaving the ties and iron yet to be laid down.

Thereupon the company put a force of about two hundred free laborers, mainly negroes, at work at the St. Mary's to push down to us, and an exciting race began. The civil engineers drove a stake midway between both gangs, and they pressed for it as if life itself depended upon who arrived there first. I had only eighty available men, but they were all infected with the general enthusiasm, largely due to the fact that they also were principally negroes. It was really a race of a race. No driving was necessary, but on the contrary I was obliged several times to slacken their pace to keep the force in condition. One might have supposed that every convict was a stockholder from the way the ties went on the road-bed and the heavy rails assumed position. We averaged a mile and a fourth of track a day, while the best the other party did was three-fourths of a mile, and there was a howl of triumph when two men passed the half-way post before the others were in sight.

We were two miles on the other side when we encountered them, and I shall never forget that day. The free laborers came over the brow of a hill, and such deafening cheers and acclamations rose from both sides that it was impossible to hear one's self speak. Upwards of forty railroad officials were present when the last rail was laid. The final tie was made of magnolia wood, and a solid silver spike completed the work. We all had a hand in driving it in, and had not each official been limited to one light blow, a spike a yard long would have scarcely sufficed for the ceremony. It was subsequently replaced by one of brass, and the silver spike made into a cup for H. S. Haines, present general manager of the S. F. & W. It was a unique piece of work. The sides were engraved with a view of a squad of convicts, track-laying, with "Post Boy," as our construction engine was called, in the background. This engine had, by the way, some interesting associations for me. In earlier years it had been in service in Georgia, and one of my earliest recollections was riding behind it to school, when a boy. I never saw the little locomotive without feeling that it was an old friend, and many a day when sick, tired and harassed I have wished that I could jump upon its foot-board and ride back through time and care, to school again.

When the work on the short line ended, I made immediate preparations to move the convicts to Live Oak, from which point the Plant Investment Company proposed to construct what was called the Live Oak & Rollins Bluff Railroad, afterward known as the Savannah, Florida & Western. There was difficulty in securing transportation over the Florida Central, the direct line from Jacksonvllle to Live Oak, which was in the hands of a rival company, and it was decided to take a roundabout route by

way of Waycross and Dupont, Georgia, and thence
south to our destination. When we arrived at the
first railroad camp, a little less than a year before,
we came in four freight cars; it required eight to
remove the men and equipments. We embarked
at Camp Hillyard; the best engineer of the railroad
was sent down from Savannah and we had the right
of way for the journey. Some apprehension of
trouble had been felt by the railroad officials, owing
to the prevalent idea, which I have once before
alluded to, that the prisoners of one state could not
be legally carried through another. They were
afraid that this mistaken impression would gain
ground among the convicts, and that when we were
once over the state line, they would attempt a
revolt. But no such difficulty occurred. We took
the cars very early in the morning in the midst of a
dense fog and ran the distance at top speed and in
safety, without making a stop between Jacksonville
and Waycross, and only one or two afterward. When
we reached Live Oak, we found the approaches to
the depot thronged with people. Not only the
townsfolk were out in force, but settlers had flocked
in from the country, so eager to witness the disem-
barkation of the convicts. We pushed with difficulty through the throng and took up the line of
march to the new camp, which was two miles distant. Wagons conveyed the sick, and we arrived in
pretty good order. The buildings at the camp had
been commenced by free labor, but were not nearly

completed. The roof was not on the cell-house, no stockade was erected, and there was altogether work enough to occupy a large squad for a considerable length of time.

The balance of the convicts were put to work at once on the line of the road, grading back to Live Oak; but before anything was done I took a shovel and turned the first earth in the new enterprise. The surveyors had fixed the lines, and this two miles of roadway was constructed without much difficulty and with only one special incident that clings to my memory. About midway, between the camp and the town, an old fellow, one of the original settlers of the county, had a small farm, in the midst of which was a pond of water. He set great store by this little lakelet, and when he learned that the line of survey ran directly through it, his indignation knew no bounds.

"Plague gone these new-fangled steam railroads!" he said; "I'll shoot a hole right inter the fust man that comes fooling round my pond!"

He took down his old rifle and stood guard, but we paid no attention to him and built an eighteen foot embankment right through the middle of his cherished water-supply. During the construction, he stood in his yard, shaking his gun at us and invoking every curse known to crackerdom upon our heads, but in the course of time he resigned himself to fate, and found the railroad a very handy thing to ride to town over.

This calls to mind another odd episode of a somewhat similar character. The railroad purchased the
right of way through Live Oak, through the medium
of Ivy Brothers, merchants, who owned considerable property there themselves. They perfected
title to all the land needed, and turned over the
deeds in good order, but there was one obstinate old
man named Bill Harrison, who claimed that he must
be settled with before the road could pass on. He
kept a small store in a shanty upon a piece of property that he held by what is called "squatter's
title," supplemented by force of arms. His title
was very shadowy, but he was a belligerent old fellow, capable of using his long-barreled deer rifle at
the drop of a hat, and the force of arms part was
extremely real.

The property in question was at the outskirts of
town and directly upon the right of way. The railroad company held a valid title from the real owner,
but they desired to avoid all trouble with citizens
and made Harrison a number of friendly overtures,
all of which he repulsed. They offered to move his
store out of the way and send wagons and men to
cart his goods. He replied that he would kill the
first person who laid his hands upon the premises
for the purpose of disturbing them. I did not
care to assume too much authority and finally had
the track constructed up to one side of the shanty
and commenced again at the other. An engine,
coming along, would have run right through it.

Affairs were in this attitude when the superintendent sent me most positive orders to have the place moved. I sent Harrison notice for two or three days, but as he paid no attention, I determined to take the bull by the horns, and put in an appearance one morning with all my men. Harrison and his clerk had barricaded themselves inside, and we could see them, guns in hand, through the open door. Their supposition was that I would begin operations by attempting to remove the goods. I stepped up to the threshold and notified the old man for the last time that he would have to move.

"I'll kill the first man that pokes his head in!" roared the store-keeper.

"Very well, Mr. Harrison," I replied, and ordered a cordon of guards to surround the premises and fire inside, the moment he pulled trigger. Then I had some skids adjusted, ropes passed around the shanty, and gave the word to the convicts to lay hold. They obeyed with a will; there was a tremendous creaking of timbers and snapping of supports and the old house started on her journey. Harrison and his clerk stood it until the house had advanced about ten feet. Then some loose boards on the ceiling fell, covering them with grime; and fully convinced that the whole structure was about to tumble about their ears, they fled precipitately.

"Dog gone you fellers!" shouted Harrison, shaking his rifle at us. "I believe you would tear a man's house down right over his head!"

We moved the shanty the requisite distance, nailed on the loose boards, and a company building now stands on its site.

CHAPTER XIII

Things had settled down into first-rate working order, and I was beginning to hope for a little respite from the troubles and dangers that so continually beset us at the other camp, when a curious story reached my ears, that eventually sent me upon an exciting chase into distant wilds. It came about thus: In the evening the guards off duty frequently lounged into my office and chatted around the fire over their experiences. While such a conversation was in progress I happened to mention my pursuit of Thomas Nix, the escaped convict who vanished in the woods of the St. Mary's, wearing his hat of tree-moss. One of the guards, a young Georgian named Hardy Hays, listened to me attentively and when I concluded remarked:

"That's an odd story, Captain, and the fellow in it reminds me of an old chap who moved into our neighborhood about that time. What did you say his name was?"

"Thomas Nix," I replied.

"By George! you don't say so!" exclaimed Hays; "why, my man is named Thomas Nix, too."

He then proceeded to relate to me how a woman with one grown daughter and a family of little ones had moved into Randolph County, Georgia, and

settled upon a small piece of land. · They were natives of the state, although they came immediately
from Florida; and the woman said that her husband
was detained there by a lawsuit but would join the
family before long. In time he put in an appearance, and upon his arrival the eldest daughter went
away. It may be remembered that the complainant against Nix at his trial was his own daughter,
and all things taken together, including the simi-
larity of names and coincidence of dates, I became
satisfied that the long lost fugitive was at last located. This episode shows upon what slender threads
the safety of a man, who is once "wanted," hangs.
He may be ever so far and the past apparently as
dead as Cæsar, when some chance word or trifle
light as air, knocks over the whole fabric of his
security like a house of cards. In this case, Hays
happened to stroll in among a party of story-tellers,
and the consequence was that a man at that moment
eating his supper in fancied safety, far away in another state, lost his liberty and died in chains.

But I anticipate. We moved as cautiously as
possible in the matter, quietly applying for a requisition upon the Governor of Georgia for a fugitive
from justice. In due time the document arrived,
and I was named in it as state agent to make the
arrest. Hays gave me all the directions he could
and supplemented them with a letter of introduction
to his father, who lived quite close to Nix's house.

The nearest stopping point on the railroad was

a little town called Ward's Station, and arriving there, I went at once to the Hays' place. I was kindly received, and after I learned the lay of the land, I determined to stop over night and make the capture just at day-break. I adopted this plan because I knew Nix to be a desperate man, who under the circumstances would be likely to resist to the bitter end. So I determined to take him by surprise, if possible.

One of the Hays boys volunteered to act as my guide, and while it was yet dark we drove close to Nix's house and awaited light enough for action. As dawn broke I discerned a primitive, two-room log-house, standing in a small yard, surrounded by a low rail fence. All was as yet still and there were no signs of life; but in an hour or so I was warned by a thin wreath of smoke that curled up from the stick-and-dirt chimney that the family were stirring, and I told Hays to drive to the fence.

He did so, and we had barely reached it when a woman came to the door, evidently attracted by the sound of wheels. She scrutinized us for a moment and called shrilly over her shoulder:

"Thomas! oh, Thomas! thar's some strangers out here."

That brought matters to a sudden crisis. It had to be now or never, so I leaped from the buggy, cleared the log fence at a bound, and ran straight into the house. Nix was coming out of the rear room, pulling his suspenders over his shoulders, and we encountered face to face. He recoiled violently, for he recognized me on the instant and turned a ghastly yellow—the color of dirty tallow.

"Hello, Nix, old man!" I cried, holding out my hand to him; "how are you?"

He did not reply, but backed away a pace, keeping his corpse-like visage turned on me.

"Don't you know me, Nix?" I said.

The blood rushed into his face as though some one had smitten him, and he found his voice.

"Yes, by God!" he replied hoarsely; "I do know you! Get out of my house, or I'll cut your throat from ear to ear!"

As he spoke, he whipped a huge dirk from the waistband of his pants and whirled up his arm, with a lightning gesture, to strike; but I was prepared for something of the sort, and before the blow could fall I had a frontier Colt six-shooter in line with his heart. We stood in this position for perhaps a minute, looking each other in the eye— he with his blade raised, I with my finger on the trigger. Then I said to him:

"Nix, you know my business. I am here to take you and if necessary I will take you dead. Drop that knife or I will drop you!"

"You'll never take me alive!" he answered fiercely. "Get out of here or I'll kill you as sure as you are a man!"

"That is a two-handed game," I said, keeping him covered.

I knew that we were balancing upon a deadly climax point, where a breath either way would turn the scale. The whole soul of the outlaw seemed in his eyes—wild, dilated, fastened upon me with the quivering eagerness of a panther waiting to spring, and had I flinched for one instant, the dirk would certainly have been in my vitals. I did not want to kill the man, although it looked very much as if I would have to in order to emerge alive. Meantime his wife began to cry and scream. "Don't kill him here! Don't kill him here!" she kept repeating. "Take him away if you are going to kill him! I don't want to see it! Oh, Thomas! you told me it was all settled!"

Throughout this tumult we stood motionless—as strange a tableau as can well be fancied. At length I tried again.

"Nix," I said, "we can't stand this way all day. Will you drop the knife or will I have to shoot you?"

"I'll die before I go!" he screamed.

Upon that I pulled out my watch with my left hand and held it up so as to bring the dial within my range of vision.

"Very well," I said; "I will give you half a minute to decide whether you want to live or die. Suit yourself, my man, but don't think for a moment that I'm trifling. If you don't drop that knife when the time's up, you're a dead man."

"Curse you! Kill me then!" he replied.

I cast a sidelong glance at the little second-hand, and as it neared the thirty mark, I began to pull the trigger. The revolver was self-cocking, and I saw Nix's haggard eyes riveted upon the hammer as it rose until it was on the point of falling and his life hung absolutely by a hair. Then a sudden and deadly contraction crossed his face and he cried out: "Stop! Don't shoot me, Captain! I'll give the knife to my wife!"

"Throw it down!" I answered, holding the hammer suspended above the shell.

His fingers slowly unclasped, and the blade fell clattering to the floor.

"Now then," I said, still keeping him under the muzzle of the pistol, while I returned my watch to my pocket and drew out a pair of hand-cuffs, "we are getting down to business. I'll trouble you to slip on these bracelets."

He caught the manacles and clasped them on his wrists, but he had evidently not yet resigned himself to his fate, and he fastened them so loosely that I was sure his hands could be easily drawn out. I told him several times to tighten them, and then, watching my opportunity, rushed in and pushed them up to the last notch. At that I saw a glance of swift intelligence pass between him and his wife and she immediately moved toward the rear room. I followed her with my eyes and saw a rifle leaning in one corner, but before she could reach it I called her back.

"So you too mean murder," I said. "I know what to look for now, and if you stir out of this room I will kill you just as quickly as I would your husband."

She protested that she meant no harm, but the expression of her face convicted her. Thereupon neither made any further attempts at resistance, but when Nix's excitement had passed away he became deathly sick, and after that paroxysm was over he was the hungriest man I ever saw. He implored me to allow him to breakfast, and I marveled at the singular effect of emotion in that section as I watched him store away a huge kettle of "greens," bacon enough to feed a family, and a pot of coffee almost as large as a water pail.

On our way to the station Nix tried another tack. He told me that he had an orange grove of two hundred bearing trees in Florida and that he would deed it to me if I would permit him to escape. I heard him through and then told him that I was not in the market and he had best abandon hope in that direction, which I presume he did, for we made the trip back without further overtures from him. He served four years of his eighteen years sentence and then died of pneumonia. One of his last acts, while he was lying at death's door, was to attempt to slip off the building-chain and escape from the hospital.

Nix came of a family with a history, but it was a history so strange and infamous that there is no

ARREST OF JOHN NIX.

language in which it may be told. There were many of them and there may have been a strain of insanity in the blood, but at any rate their methods of life were those of the beasts of the field, and they peopled the wilderness where they lived with idiots and hideous human monstrosities. The tales told of them do not bear repeating. In time they were systematically hunted out, like wild animals, and fled to the south, where they disappeared in the trackless regions of tropical Florida. Some of them stopped over night, during this migration, in a shed near where I lived. There were two horrible hags in the party, that ran on the ground on all fours and had faces like things seen in a nightmare. They were a sister and an aunt of Thomas Nix.

The two escapes which I have mentioned as occurring during the first year of my administration, took place shortly after my return from my trip from Georgia, and were of a decidedly unusual character. Two of our white convicts were men named James McDaniels and John Kelly. The latter was a thief sent to prison from St. Augustine, a rather ordinary character, although he had plenty of nerve. McDaniels was a professional crook from Washington, D. C., a man of quick wit, ready resources and great determination. He was big-framed, with a sinister face and a look of such ferocity when angered that he had almost the entire camp, guards included, intimidated. His crime

14

was a sensational one. He had shot a policeman at Jacksonville, and when pursued rushed to the St. Johns River and jumped in near the market house. He had on all of his clothes, but swam, against tide, among the wharves and shipping, confusing the chase and emerging above the Florida Central depot. Not one in a thousand could have done this and lived, and the general impression was that he was drowned.

When he gained terra-firma, he started off, without resting, in the direction of Baldwin, and crawled into a freight-car that stood upon a siding near that place. He had hopes that the car would be attached to some train, but such was not the case, and he lay in it for two days and nights, when at last he called to a passing negro and attempted to hire him to bring him something to eat. The negro proved his undoing, for he went straight into Baldwin and reported that there was a suspicious stranger hiding in a box-car. A crowd sallied out to investigate, and when McDaniels saw them coming, he leaped from his hiding place and ran. He was pursued into the woods where he was captured, and subsequently taken to Jacksonville and tried. He received a fifteen year sentence.

This was his history, and he was a man I usually kept my eye upon; but one day he and Kelly remained in camp on a plea of sickness, while I took the squads out to work. There was a commissary-man on the premises, an armed guard at each of

the four corners of the yard, and everything was
considered secure.

In the course of the morning the two convicts
managed to secure an ax from the yard and struck
off their leg-irons. McDaniels immediately ran
into the officer's quarters, burst in the door of my
private room, and forced the lock of my trunk. He
hurriedly threw the contents upon the floor, select-
ing two suits of clothes, a box of cartridges and a
large Colt's revolver, the same weapon with which
I had brought Thomas Nix to bay, made them into
a bundle and rushed back into the hall. It so happened that my son Sam, a little fellow then of about
six years, had run away from home at Live Oak that
day and came out to camp to see me. He was in the
hall when McDaniels emerged with his plunder, and
at once began to give the alarm at the top of his
voice.

"McDaniels has papa's pistol!" he shouted, until
the whole place rang.

The desperate convict turned, weapon in hand,
but when he saw his tiny antagonist, he broke into
smiles and hurried on, without harming the boy.

He was rejoined in the yard by Kelly. The commissary-man had heard the uproar, and, when he
caught sight of the pair, he very promptly ran to
his quarters and locked himself in. This left the
coast clear, and they deliberately walked out between two of the guards. Such was the terror that
McDaniels inspired, that they were not fired upon,

the guards afterward claiming in excuse that both were armed, Kelly with a Winchester rifle. My boy, who gave the alarm, said that Kelly had nothing but a stick, and, as no guns were missing, he was very likely correct. Only one guard, Sol Phillips by name, made any attempt at pursuit. He started after them, as they pushed their way toward the woods, and when they reached the margin of the timber, McDaniels turned on him and said:

"Phillips, I have always liked you. You are a good fellow. I don't want to kill you. Now, take my advice; go back to camp as quick as you can trot, for if you don't, I will surely put the contents of this six-shooter into your head."

He said this coolly, calmly—like a man offering a friendly suggestion. Phillips looked into the muzzle of the pistol for an instant and acted on the hint.

I did not return until toward evening, and my boy, who ran down to the train to meet me, was the first to tell me the news. Directly I learned of the delivery I prepared to give chase, but I could persuade none of my guards, except young Mills, to accompany me. The best of them firmly declined, and we rode off alone with the dogs. Although the trail was cold, it was struck without much difficulty, and we followed it through the intervening woods until the railroad was reached. By that time night had fallen, and, as we forged ahead toward Live Oak, the darkness grew intense. Road, woods, and everything was swallowed up in the profound gloom.

But, fortunately for us, a trained horse finds his footing by a sort of sixth sense, and we dropped our reins on our animals' necks and allowed them to follow the baying of the hounds after their own fashion.

We realized fully that a fight was morally certain to follow an encounter, and between pursuers and pursued the advantages were certainly all on the side of the latter. For we made an unearthly tumult as we swept along, and were helpless targets for a shot from the way-side. The dogs were our only reliance, and they kept the trail steadily, still holding to the direction of the town. When near Live Oak, they made a detour and ran around it, keeping straight on at the other side for several miles, when they struck a cross-trail and plunged at a tangent into the woods.

The scent was evidently so fresh, that it seemed probable they had taken it at a point where the fugitives had rested and then changed their route; and we looked for some speedy developments. Those who have gone pleasuring on the saddle, through only daylight forests, can form no conception of a dash into them by night. Everything is magnified. The little inequalities of the ground seem like hills and valleys; there is constant danger of being swept off by unseen boughs, or dashed into collision with tree-trunks; for all one knows, the next bound may send him plunging down some sink-hole, and the impossibility of guarding against these perils brings on a sense of helplessness that no nerves are proof against. The man who first described death as a leap into the dark, selected a good comparison.

To return: the baying sounded directly ahead of us, and by a certain tenor of its note, that to prac- ticed ears is unmistakable, we were satisfied that the hounds were close upon some one. A few mo- ments later a darker patch of gloom, that we knew to be a man, flitted through the trees, and Mills, after calling upon him to halt, opened fire with his revolver.

He sent a couple of bullets in that direction, and we heard the dogs baying around their game. Our disappointment and disgust may be imagined when we found a scared negro huddled up on the ground, and begging for mercy as fast as he could wag his tongue. He lived somewhere in the woods, and was on his way home when the dogs took his trail. There was nothing to do but retrace our route, and we called off the dogs and made for the railroad, where, after some hard riding, the old and cold trail was resumed.

It led us to the town of Ellaville, but there it was effaced in the general passage of travel, and, while we felt certain that our men were somewhere in the vicinity, we were unable to unearth them. How they made their way out, nobody knows, but make it they did, and were never heard of again. We rode wearily back to camp, with nothing for our risks and pains.

CHAPTER XIV

Several curious things happened in toleraby rapid succession at about this period. We had three cooks named Hewett, Fennison and Green. Hewett was a white man and the other two were colored, Fennison being the trusty who has already figured to some extent in these pages. One morning, when I had most of the men at work on the road, these three started off, stating that they were going to a neighboring house to get some eggs. In the evening, when I returned, I went to the kitchen to order in supper and was surprised to find the place dark and deserted. I asked the commissary-man, who had had charge of the premises during the day, where the cooks were. He did not know, and in brief, they had not come back yet. The trail was too cold for the dogs, and prisoners never made an easier or more leisurely escape.

Not a great while after, I prevented, by a mere accident, what would otherwise have been a wholesale delivery of our most desperate convicts. I had quite a large squad at work in a cut, and among the number were half a dozen or so who were acknowledged to be dangerous outlaws. In the party were Nathan Shell, to whom I have already devoted considerable space; "Doc" Montague, a life-convict, wanted for murder in two other states; Jim **Ota,** the desperado whom I brought from Pensacola; Frank Manning, an outlaw who had once before attempted escape and been shot down by the guard; Hardy Todd, one of the coolest and most formidable fellows who ever wore stripes, and Alexander Gadsen, Henry Williams and Samuel Johnson, all men with "records." Taken altogether it was as fine a galaxy of prison talent as could well be brought together; and I made it a practice to scrutinize the squad with more than ordinary vigilance whenever I passed that way.

One evening, shortly before time for quitting work, I arrived at the cut on my usual rounds, and seated myself at one side, where I could watch the progress of excavation. While so employed, Frank Manning passed me, trundling a wheelbarrow of dirt, and instinctively eying his stride-chain I was startled to observe that one of the links had been cut and the two loose ends tied together with a bit of string.

"What's the matter with your chain?" I asked.

He changed countenance instantly but did not reply, and I walked over to him and saw that the links had been fastened in such a manner that a slight pull would break the string and leave him free to run. I told him, in a low voice, to stand to one side and not to move or I would shoot him down. He obeyed mechanically, and the rest of the squad, who were eying us furtively, redoubled their work, and I burst into loud song, apparently unconcerned.

It was necessary for them to pass, one at a time, before where I sat, to empty their wheelbarrows, and it was not long before I espied another chain, cut and tied exactly as Manning's. This time it was Doc. Montague, and I had him also step to one side. Presently I bunched, in this manner, all the desperadoes whom I have named and enough more to make an even dozen. The balance of the men were all right.

When I made sure that I had all who had tampered with their manacles, I called for a "squad-chain," and strung the conspirators upon it, passing the chain between the shackle-iron and ankle of each of them. This done, I hurried them aboard the construction train and went back to camp, where I made a searching investigation, and the whole plot came to the surface. The men had planned to revolt in a body just at the hour for knocking off work, and the chain-cutting had been most ingeniously done, right uner the eyes of the guards. It was accomplished by driving a pick-point into the links, and even the men who were at work at the side of the plotters were unaware of what was going on.

Some time after we went into camp on the new road, Dick Evans came to the surface again as the principal in a very sensational conspiracy. It was discovered by so mere a chance, that it seemed from my stand-point to be providential.

Among the teamsters who plied between the

camp and Live Oak was a negro, a free man, who slept in the loft of the barn in the yard. I was always on the lookout for plots, and one morning it occurred to me to go to the barn and inspect this man's sleeping quarters. I did so, and the first thing that met my eyes was a letter lying upon his blankets. It was sealed and addressed to the negress who had figured as Evans' quondam wife in Pensacola. Here was evidently surreptitious mail, and as such is contraband in prison, I tore it open and read it.

The contents astounded me. It was from Evans to his mistress and it began by detailing a number of barbarities, for which he had drawn upon his imagination. He told her that when a new prisoner arrived it was my habit to strike him one hundred lashes, merely to see how he would take punishment, and that the convicts I had murdered with the strap would stock a cemetery. He then went on to say that I had become so embittered against him, owing to his attempts to escape, that his life was in momentary danger, but that he had succeeded in enlisting ample and powerful aid that would soon result in his delivery. My commissary-man, the prison physician, and another official in a position of responsibility. were named as those who had consented to assist him; and the fact that these three were prominent masons, as was also Evans himself, was affirmed to be the lever he had used upon them.

He concluded by urging the woman to stand in readiness to furnish assistance at her end of the line, as soon as things were ripe for action, and cautioned her to forward all her letters to him under cover to any one of the trio he had named.

He did not describe in terms the character of the projected escape, but the inference was that they would stop at nothing; and the thought that, if what he wrote was true, I was surrounded by traitors among my own corps, startled me beyond measure. I acted immediately upon such a possibility and went to the commissary-man with the letter in my hand. He was visibly perturbed, but he positively denied all knowledge of the affair, and I next interrogated Evans, who at first refused to talk, but under the lash made a confession, in which he said that the men named had certainly formed a plot to liberate him, and that he had given the letter to the commissary-man on the previous evening to be mailed.

When the teamster came in, he was badly scared at the developments, and stoutly insisted that he had been handed the letter by the official in question, but that in going off in a hurry in the morning, he had forgotten it and left it on his bed.

I will not aver that Evans told the truth. He was a bad man and capable of anything, but I have given the facts as far as I know them and leave conclusions to others. The commissary-man was discharged and there the matter dropped, which, had it not been for my accidental visit to the stable, might very easily have involved the entire lease system in a very ugly scandal.

The railroad lease had as yet about a year to run. Our objective point in construction was Rollins Bluff, a little river station named after a Mr. Rollins, an old settler, but subsequently called New Branford and now an important railroad point in North Florida. We pressed on and in time reached the village of McAlpin, which is associated in my mind with something remarkable in the way of railroad casualties. A siding had been constructed there, and it was my habit to run a few flat-cars upon it to carry the convicts back to camp at the conclusion of the day's work. While this was in progress, early one evening, Jesse Simpkins, the one-armed trusty who figured in the bloody tragedy on the Suwanee River, described some chapters back, had taken his stand on the end of the first flat-car, pin in hand, ready to make a coupling when an engine, which had just entered the siding, approached close enough. He was holding some oranges, and being crippled, his attention was somewhat divided between his duty and the safety of the fruit.

The engine was not backing in, but coming pilot first, and when the coupling-bar struck the socket, the shock threw Simpkins off his feet and the men were horrified to see him fall in between. Before the engine could be stopped, the pilot

struck the trusty, doubled him together and ran up
over his body, lifting the truck wheels clear off the
track.   I rushed to the spot and found him wedged
into a ball, sustaining the whole enormous weight,
and the pilot canted over him at an angle of forty-
five degrees.

I supposed the man dead, of course, and it was
more to get out the corpse, than with any notion of
saving him, that I yelled to the convicts to pry up
the engine at once.   They ran at the word.   Beams
were thrust under, and in less time than it takes to
tell it, the great mass of metal was raised by main
force and Simpkins pulled out.   To my amazement,
he stretched himself, felt his limbs and body,
slowly regained his feet, and said:

"Whar's my oranges?"

I almost hesitate to tell this story, for I am well
aware that it seems incredible that any one could
survive such an experience, but it is true to the
letter.

Simpkins suffered from lame back for a few days,
but was afterward none the worse for his squeezing,
and is a free man to-day, and as sound as a dollar.

When I speak of villages throughout this country,
I use the word for lack of a better term, for in nine
cases out of ten, they were the smallest imaginable
focus of the scattering settlement, and usually one
general store embraced the sum total of business enterprise.   There the natives came at intervals to trade for coffee, tobacco, and the few other

necessities that the woods and waters did not provide them with. Alligators' hide's and teeth, bird plumes and various kinds of pelts were the medium of barter. They were curious people, and there are plenty of them there yet, born and bred to the forest and as ignorant of the affairs of every-day life outside of their domain, as are the bears and deer upon which they mainly subsist. A man who would venture to tell them that the earth moved instead of the sun, or that there was a device by which a message could be flashed for leagues across a wire, would run the risk of being lynched, as too dangerous a liar to be at large.

There are scores of these folks who have never seen a train of cars, and only heard of such things as a vague rumor of doubtful reliability. It is not surprising, therefore, that as our work progressed, there were plenty of natives who came out of the woods and marveled at such strange proceedings; and I will anticipate the course of my narrative far enough to detail an incident that will illustrate the point.

We had completed the line to a spot near Rollins Bluff, at which place the track made about a three-degree curve, partly masked by the walls of a cut. I was directing some work there when a backwoods family approached. They consisted of a tall, gaunt cracker, carrying a baby in his arms and closely followed by several women, all evidently from the interior.

"Cap'n," said the man, when I was pointed out to him, "we all have hearn a right smart about the railroad, and we've come to see it."

I pointed out the track and told them to feast their eyes upon it to their hearts' content. They stared for a while at the iron highway in childish glee, admired the regularity of the ties, and evenness of the track, and then one of them said:

"Where is the engine?"

The engine and construction train were away on some errand, a short distance up the road, and I told them to sit down and wait for a few moments. They did so, and presently the whistle sounded around the curve. They shrank a little closer together, and I could see their color come and go as they waited anxiously for the appearance of the strange machine. It so happened that the engine was pushing a long line of flat-cars, and, as they began to come around the curve, the amazement of my visitors knew no bounds.

"Sakes alive! What's movin' them little houses with wheels onto 'em?" screamed one of the women, and it seemed marvelous to them that the wheels kept the curve instead of going ahead in a straight line. When the engine finally appeared, the whole party sprang to their feet, the women seized the man by the coat-tails, and he nearly dropped the baby in his alarm. I thought for a moment that they meditated a dash for the woods.

One experience of the sort was clearly enough for them, as they never put in a second appearance.

On one occasion, a native of these wilds, a venerable, white-bearded settler, by the name of Hays, was subpœnaed as a witness in an illicit whisky case, on trial at Jacksonville. Had he been left to his own devices he would as soon have thought of going to the planet Mars to appear as a witness against the Man in the Moon, but a United States marshal came after him and he had to go. He had hopes that he would be allowed to walk, and when he was informed that the trip would be made by rail, he was filled with consternation. He had never ridden on a car in his life, and to venture aboard one seemed to him to be wantonly tempting a violent death. He had to be fairly dragged up the steps and forced inside.

When the train started, he burst into tears. He explained, between his sobs, that he was no coward; he had faced destruction a thousand times in the woods and killed more bears than could be packed into that passenger coach, but the idea that he would never see his wife and family again filled him with sorrow.

"Don't be alarmed, Mr. Hays," said the United States marshal; "there is not a particle of danger."

At that instant another car was coupled on with the usual jolt. Hays leaped from his seat as though he had been shot.

"Thar, she's struck a stump!" he yelled, "just as

THE FIRST SIGHT OF THE CARS.

Siberia, Page 253.

I knowed she would! Lord a-mighty! I'll never
see Betsey agin!"

I brought many a man to prison who made his
first, and for that matter his last, railroad ride under those circumstances; and cases of the sort are
by no means infrequent, even at the present day.

Although, as I have said, the duties of recruiting
agent were now out of my province, the contractors
continued to call upon me, from time to time, to
bring in men who were considered especially dangerous. Such a case was that of George Ball or
Balf (it appears both ways on the prison records),
an outlaw of Pensacola. Ball had been a convict
under me before, and I had discharged him at the
expiration of his sentence, very glad to get rid of
him, for he was constantly in trouble of one sort
or another. He was perfectly desperate, cared
nothing for punishment, and was, in short, one of
those characters who have the worst possible influence upon their fellow-prisoners.

It was not long before he was in trouble again,
tried and sentenced to two years imprisonment.
I went to Pensacola after him.

I remember the trip chiefly because I happened
to arrive there on Sunday, a day which was in those
times dedicated to the wildest sort of debauchery
along the harbor front. Palafox street, the principal thoroughfare in that section, was lined from
end to end with dives and dens where sailors off
duty were lured and robbed by every device known
15

to crime. Jack ashore is proverbially an easy victim, and on the day I was there, 111 schooners lay
in the harbor, and the crews of most of them were
carousing in the neighborhood. There was no pretense of concealment. Drunken mobs of men and
women went howling from door to door, every bar
was doing a roaring trade, the faro banks were in
full blast, and fighting, drinking and gambling were
the order of the day.

Sailors were in demand that season, and "shang-
haiing," or even stealing whole ship's crews bodily,
was a common offense of the land-sharks who
masqueraded as boarding-house "runners," and for
which they were paid round prices by captains of
belated ships, unable to leave for lack of hands.
A case of that kind was reported to the sheriff,
while I was talking to him. The entire crew of a
Norwegian bark had been kidnaped while drunk
ashore, and there was evidence to show that they
had been delivered to a vessel lying some distance
out and which was known to be short-handed.

The sheriff promised to look after the matter, and
later in the day he invited me to accompany him
to the United States Navy Yard, where he wished to
secure a prisoner in another case. We started
across the bay in a little sail-boat, and when we
were well under way saw a similar craft approaching us from the direction of the vessel suspected
of having received the abducted sailors. It contained the very "runner" who was thought to have

conducted the affair, and it was highly probable that he was returning with the pay for his villainy. He was a practical looking fellow, one of the most dangerous and notorious men in the business, and no doubt supposing that the sheriff was after him, he sailed on such a tack as to circle around us and close in from the rear. It was evident that he intended to make a fight of it, and not knowing at what moment he might open hostilities, I covered him with my revolver and ordered him to stand off. That was as good a thing as he wanted, and he sailed away in short order. The episode shows how exceedingly bold and desperate this class of outlaws were in those times, and the fact was that most of them lived in constant defiance of law and arrest.

I took Ball to prison, and while there was nothing peculiarly sensational about it, our experience with him was a constant struggle—more or less a repetition of his first term. On the night following his discharge, on expiration of sentence, the ruling passion was too strong for him, and he secreted himself in the house of one of the guards, a married man, who lived near the camp. He was on duty, and his wife, who had retired, heard a noise and started to get up to investigate. Instantly the burly convict leaped clear over her, but she dodged out the door and ran for the cell-house, Ball in hot pursuit with a bludgeon in his hand. She was in her night-clothes, bare-footed and badly frightened, but she fairly outran the fellow, who, seeing him-self distanced, broke for the woods and escaped.

The subsequent career and fate of this man is interesting, and as it has nothing to do with my story proper, I will narrate it here. He was not long at liberty when he was again arrested and sent back to prison. Major C. K. Dutton was the lessee at the time, and Ball was sent to work on a turpen-tine farm at a camp called "Passum Trot." The captain was Charles P. Jolly, an officer subsequent-ly well known in connection with the lease system, and more or less trouble was experienced in keep-ing up the commissary department. It was said, how truthfully I can not personally affirm, that sweet potatoes were sometimes the only food of the prisoners, and that even they could not always be obtained. At any rate some of the bolder of the prisoners, with Ball at their head, determined to revolt unless they were better fed.

An opportunity was offered one morning, when a provision wagon was said to be delayed and no breakfast given the men. Captain Jolly entered the cell-house, explained the situation, and told them that they would have breakfast in the woods, sometime during the morning. Upon that, Ball and a number of others flatly declared that they could not and would not go to work without food.

At this point conflicting stories are told. Some say that Ball, who was undoubtedly still linked to the building-chain, atttempted to strike T. J.

Leverett, a commissary-man formerly with me, and all that is positive is that in the midst of the confusion a shot was fired and the convict fell dead in the arms of the next man chained by his side. No one has made any particular effort to claim the act. But the tragedy ended the food riot, and the scared men ceased resistance and went to work on empty stomachs. Ball's corpse was drawn off the heavy building-chain, buried in the little camp graveyard, and so ended his history.

CHAPTER XV

It was when the road was rapidly approaching New Branford that a crime of a peculiarly cold-blooded character was committed near the town of Troy in La Fayette County. William Bryant and Daniel Bass were two horse-traders who followed their calling in the place whenever opportunity afforded, and the former had purchased an animal of a young Georgian named Moore, out on a trading trip. The price agreed upon was $100, and Bryant paid a part down, giving his note for the balance.

Moore was a free-handed fellow, and the impression prevailed that he carried a large amount of money on his person. Acting on this supposition and for the further purpose of getting back the purchase money paid for the horse, and the promissory note, Bryant and Bass formed a deliberate plot to decoy him into the woods and murder him.

Toward the close of the day the two miscreants invited the unsuspicious Georgian to accompany them a little way on the road to their home. Moore accepted and went, laughing and joking, to his death.

The road took them toward the Suwanee river, into a neighborhood where the timber is thick, the underbrush dense, and the way very lonely and little traveled. In this desolate spot Bass suddenly seized Moore and held him while Bryant coolly and deliberately shot him to death. They at once possessed themselves of what money the trader had upon him, which was very little, and leaving the body where it fell, went on their way home. Both murderers were soon arrested, and on trial all of the facts came out, although each stoutly denied his individual guilt. Bryant was sentenced to death, and Bass to imprisonment for life.

I was ordered to Troy after Bass, and popular feeling ran so high at the time that on the day of my arrival, the other prisoner was removed to the Madison County jail for safe keeping. He did not stay there long, but escaped under peculiar circumstances, right under the nose of the guard. It was said that he was armed, but the only weapon he was known to possess was a hundred-dollar bill. At all events he got away, gained the gulf-swamps and there became the nucleus of a band of forest robbers and desperadoes with whom I had something, later on, to do.

But to return to Bass: I found him in an extraordinary jail. I doubt if its equal exists in the United States. It was a tall, square, two-story tower, built of enormous logs. The upper section was used as a living-room for the guard and entered by an outside stairs. A trap-door, bristling with bolts and bars, opened through the middle of the floor, into the lower compartment, which had no window, and was as dark as midnight. When a prisoner was received, a ladder was lowered and raised again after he descended, leaving him in a veritable dungeon into which neither light nor sound could penetrate. The floor was dirt; there was no ventilation, no drainage; it was the Black Hole of Calcutta on a small scale. A man immured in this horrible place would have nothing to do but stumble back and forth in the darkness until he was tired, and then stretch himself on the dirt. He might shriek and howl; not a murmur would pass through the ponderous log walls; he would not know whether it was day or night, and the stench in that confined space would soon grow almost unbearable. Without knowing it, these backwoodsmen had constructed a very formidable torture-chamber.

Bass was the only inmate of this dungeon and had been there for some time. He crawled out gladly enough, through the trap-door, and without any delay, I started back with him. On the way he showed himself to be indeed a hardened wretch. Our route happened to be the same as that taken by the three men on the evening of the murder, and some sympathetic friend had placed a little tablet at the spot where Moore was shot. When we reached it, Bass gave the slab a careless kick.

"Here's where we did that fellow up," he said.

"What do you mean?" I asked,

"Why, we killed Moore here," he replied with an idiotic laugh.

"So you admit it," I said in unconcealed disgust at his brutality.

"I might as well. I didn't do the shooting, but I had hold of him to keep him from kicking."

He afterward told me the whole story, claiming that he was drunk at the time of the tragedy. He conducted himself pretty well for a long period in prison, until he ultimately figured in a plot long to be remembered and which I will describe further on.

An escape of some importance took place shortly after Bass' arrival. As a matter of convenience, we had constructed a side-camp at New Branford, a temporary affair, at which a squad stayed during the week, returning to the main camp on Saturday evening. One Friday I was taken suddenly ill and forced to return to my home at Live Oak. Late the following evening, Mr. Phillips, one of my guards, came rushing in and reported that when the count was made a short time before at the main camp, it was one short, but that they were unable to determine who it was that was gone. They had not yet thought of calling the roll, and after thinking for a moment, I asked whether Jim Ota was there. Phillips slapped his thigh and rushed out. I had guessed correctly; it was Ota, the Pensacola outlaw, who was missing. I knew the cool, desperate character of the man, and was not surprised in the least; but the question was how he had managed to so cleverly effect his escape as to avoid all notice until so late an hour. We afterward learned that he had managed it very simply. When the men were called out of the cell-house at the side-camp, to go to headquarters, there was always more or less of bustle and rush, and in the confusion he had hidden under a bunk. He was not missed among so many and had plenty of time to get away at leisure. It was useless to think about pursuit, for by the time the facts were discovered the trail was too cold for the dogs.

All we could do was to send out descriptions, but these intercepted his flight, and he was arrested as he left a St. Augustine steamer at Jacksonville. I went after him and he remained under me until, in changes of management, he finally passed out of my hands.

A Nemesis seemed to pursue this man, and although he repeatedly made his escape in after years, he was invariably recaptured, and is at this writing a convict under me. Some of his dashes for liberty were thrilling in the extreme. While under Captain Jolly at "Passum Trot" camp in the turpentine woods, he rushed right from under the guns of the guards and was on the verge of making good his escape, when a load of buckshot struck him full in the back and stretched him on the earth. The distance saved his life, but he lay for a considerable time in a precarious condition and will carry the scars to his grave. When he recovered he tried another plan. The trusties were called from the cell-house some time before the other men and while the morning was yet quite dark. Ota noticed this fact and acted upon it. One night he filed his chain in two, and when the trusties were called out he fell into line with them and passed out of the cell-house undetected. As he went down the aisle, he picked up a bludgeon, from a stack of fire-wood, and when he passed the night-guard at the door he suddenly wheeled and dealt him a crushing blow over the head and stretched him senseless on the ground. Ota picked up the rifle that had fallen from his hand and rushed off in the darkness.

An alarm was instantly given, and the guard carried to his quarters, bleeding at the mouth and ears, and apparently dead. After hovering for two weeks between life and death he finally recovered and Ota, meanwhile, was arrested while pushing north, and returned to prison.

On another occasion, while still in Captain Jolly's charge, Ota and five others ran directly from under the guns of the guards in the turpentine woods. He was slightly in the rear of the rest of the runaways, and the fire, which was opened immediately, was mainly concentrated upon him. For two or three perilous minutes he well deserved the trite description of bearing a charmed life. Bullets whizzed all around him, cutting the bushes as he pushed them aside, piercing his clothing and mowing the grass between his feet, but none touched him. There was a narrow strip of thinly wooded ground to cross, and then a hill, all in easy range. When he reached the crest of the eminence he was a splendid target against the sky, and it was fairly raining lead; but he stopped, turned around deliberately, and raising his hat waved the guards a polite farewell. Then he vanished on the further side.

The whole surrounding country was aroused, and after three weeks chase an armed party ran upon him by the merest accident while he was crossing a little bridge in the dead of night. They halted him at the muzzle of their guns and brought him in. The other five, who were not to be compared to Ota for either nerve or fertility of recourse, made good their escape.

Shortly after Ota's escape from our side-camp, the Plant Investment Company decided to put a line of steamers on the Suwanee river to ply from New Branford to Cedar Keys, and from thence on to Cuba. A corps of engineers were sent down the river to determine the draught of the boats, and word was sent that a party of leading railroad officials, including young Mr. Plant, son of the president of the company, and himself a chief manager, would pay us a visit. The day before Mr. Plant and his immediate party were due to arrive, several of the magnates put in an appearance, bringing

with them a beautiful yacht carried in a casing
on two freight cars. She was probably the most
luxurious craft of the kind and size ever built in
the United States. Her name was "The May," and
her entire hull, from stem to stern, was constructed
of solid mahogany, producing a rich effect, perfectly
indescribable in words. A tiny engine, that was
as daintily fashioned as a watch, moved a propeller blade about the size of a shark's tail, and the
interior finish was of fine, carved, natural wood, nick-
el and hammered brass. Although strong, stanch
and entirely serviceable, she seemed more like some
curious toy for a velvet case than an actual vessel
to do duty in the water.

It was the intention to take a pleasure-trip upon
her, but it was a serious question how to accomplish
the launching without damaging the costly hull, on
which a pin would make an unsightly mark. I
turned a force of men over to the visitors, to do
the work, and one of the superintendents labored
all morning at the job. He brought all his knowledge of engineering to bear, but "The May" stub-
bornly refused to budge an inch. In the afternoon
he washed his hands of the matter and turned it
over to me. I did not know anything about engineering, but I knew a plain, every-day way of making an incline, and I proceeded to put it into exe
cution. I had a number of pens of logs, constantly
diminishing in height, built between the track and
the river, and over these I lashed a pair of skids,

so as to form a tolerably smooth roadway. I then had the yacht, just as she lay, inclosed in a frame so as not to mar her timbers. This enabled us to handle her with impunity, and I had my whole force of about two hundred hands push her, by main force, upon the skids. Once on, it required all of them to hold her back and ease her passage down.

The upshot of it was that she was launched in safety, and I turned my attention to the removal of the frame, which still surrounded the hull. It was cut away by a man in a row-boat with a large bridge-saw, and by evening "The May" rested on the water as lightly as a duck.

Next morning a special car brought in our distinguished visitors. I had considerable curiosity to see Mr. Plant, not only because he was one of my employers but on account of his great wealth and the prominent position he occupied in the management of the powerful company that bore his family name. I had never seen a millionaire before, and I confess that my fancy had pictured an individual decked with diamonds and attired in purple and fine linen, unapproachable by the common herd. When the party arrived I saw nobody who filled this ideal until a tall young man, elegantly dressed, gloved and surmounted by a silk hat, stepped from the platform. He lit a cigarette, assumed a languid attitude near the platform, and I promptly made up my mind that this was Mr. Plant. While I was eying him furtively a man of perhaps thirty, dressed in a very ordinary blue suit and wearing a black slouch hat, walked up to me and asked for Captain Powell.

"That's my name," I said.

"My name is Plant," he replied.

I was never more surprised in my life. The young gentleman by the car turned out to be his clerk. Mr. Plant proved to be as affable as he was unassuming, and he insisted on my accompanying the yatching party. He would not take no for an answer, and we had royal good time. There was no ceremony on board "The May," and as servants' room was limited, every man took a hand at the work. Mr. Plant was wood-chopper, Mr. E. D. Owens, a New York general manager, "toted" water, and Captain Fitzgerald was cook. The rest of us played the role of assistants. We went as far up the river as Troy and back again, past New Branford to the mouth of the Santa Fe River, a total trip of about fifty miles, through magnificent tropical scenery. My work called me back, but the balance of the party subsequently made a journey to Tampa in their stanch little craft.

This episode calls to mind another notable visit. One day two distinguished looking strangers alighted from the passenger train, and made their way to my office at the camp. One was a young man and the other rather elderly. They were followed by a couple of colored men, loaded down with valises, guns, bags and various luggage, mainly of a sporting character, and a pair of fine dogs brought up the rear of the procession.

The two visitors proved to be a young English lord and a commander in the British navy. They had created a social furore in other parts of the country and had determined to give a novel finish to a pleasure trip, by taking a look at a southern convict camp and incidentally killing some game. The railroad superintendent had given them a letter to me, in which I was instructed to show them all the attention possible, and to detail whichever of my guards was the best hunter, to accompany them in the field. They were the first specimens of British aristocracy I had ever seen, and I eyed them pretty curiously while I did the honors of the camp. They were both very polished and affable gentlemen and were filled with interest over the novelty of their surroundings. The equipments they brought were simply princely, and must have cost a small fortune. Their guns in particular, which were magnificently mounted and inlaid with precious metals, excited the admiring envy of all my men.

It was about supper-time and presently I invited them to the table. Here an embarrassing contretemps occurred. The commodore had no sooner seated himself than he began to exclaim: "Where is Jack? Poor Jack! I fear he must be lost." I supposed Jack was one of their dogs, but he continued with

DISTINGUISHED HUNTERS.

Siberia, Page 271.

an air of relief: "Ah, here he is! Is there no plate laid for him? No matter. He can sit here by me."

I looked around in amazement and saw Jack. He was a big and very black southern plantation darky, whom they had picked up, partly as a valet and partly as a curiosity, and who was evidently much embarrassed at this unexpected condescension.

Hospitality has sacred laws, but this was carrying the joke too far, and I informed the commodore that among us the negroes ate apart from the whites, and that I did not fancy Jack's company at my table. Instantly the courtly old gentleman was all confusion and apology. He told me that in England no color line is drawn, and that negroes are practically unknown there. In brief, the episode passed off harmlessly, although it seemed strange enough to southern eyes, and Jack gorged himself to his heart's content in the kitchen.

Our visitors stayed with us for two days and shot away many a pound of powder. They stood upon great ceremony in the field, and the right to the first shot was determined by a code of etiquette, which they would discuss at length, while the bird flew away. But no harm was done, for neither one could hit a barn at twenty yards, and despite their beautiful breech-loaders, their elegant hunting suits, and imported dogs, they killed nothing but one sparrow and a black-snake. The guard who guided them, a raw-boned backwoodsman who had been raised with a rifle in his hand and who could knock

16

over a running deer almost as he could see it, could scarcely conceal his amazement and disgust; but I was sorry to see the pair leave, for they were capital company, and their stay formed a pleasant variation of the routine of camp-life. They took the sparrow and black-snake with them.

CHAPTER XVI

The lease of the Plant Company expired with the year 1882. We had completed the railroad by that time to a point seven miles beyond New Branford, and when bidding for convict labor again took place, the contract was awarded to Major C. K. Dutton, the turpentine operator. I was invited to retain my position, and finally accepted, after hesitating for some time between that and an offer from the railroad company.

I at once made preparations to move the men. Major Dutton proposed to work them entirely upon his extensive turpentine property, in the vicinity of Live Oak; and a camp, afterward called "Newburn," was planned, about seven miles from town; but as the securing of the lease had been a matter of extreme uncertainty, no buildings were erected beforehand. Consequently I first took only a part of the men to the spot, and, leaving the balance at the old railway camp, I proceeded to put things in order. The first thing on the program was a cell-house, and its construction received a curious interruption. We had erected the frame of the building, put on the roof, and, in fact, almost finished it throughout, when Mr. Hildreth of Live Oak, Major Dutton's local representative, concluded that a huge pine tree, growing by the side of one of the walls, ought to be cut down. The tree was a perfect giant and inclined slightly toward the building, and I told him that it could not be felled without failing upon the roof. He insisted that I was mistaken, and, at last, I washed my hands of the affair and told him to go ahead if he thought he could get it down in safety. Some choppers were sent for, and, while they were at work, I stepped quietly inside of the building and had some sick men removed and placed under guard outside. Mr. Hildreth had props wedged against the trunk, and the chips flew merrily. At last the monster began to crack, and swayed directly toward the cell-house. The next instant it was in full fall, and he shouted for the convicts to hold the props; but they very prudently paid no attention to his orders and ran. As I expected, the tree crashed straight across the roof, and the entire structure came to the ground in ruin. Mr. Hildreth surveyed the wreck ruefully for a moment, ordered his horse, and drove away. With the exception of this mishap, all progressed smoothly, and in due time I sent for the balance of the men and resumed in earnest the old work in the turpentine woods.

Soon after this, our first death in the new camp occurred. The man was Dick Evans, frequently mentioned in these pages, and the circumstances of his end were these: It may be remembered that he had but five years to serve, and although he was constantly plotting delivery, the sentence was mean-time slipping away, and at last four years passed, leaving but a very short time to serve. A little while before the situation assumed this shape, I was at Pensacola, and happened to see the negress who had formerly been his mistress and business partner, and with whom he had maintained a constant, and on his part, very loving correspondence. She was a thick-lipped, repulsive harridan, and coolly remarked that Evans had caused her trouble enough, and that she had another lover. That news was shortly conveyed to him by letter, and thereafter this strong and desperate man, who had been at all times willing to do and dare anything, pined away like a baby and died, when liberty was right at hand. He babbled about his "Ellee," as he called this wretch, and opened to me a depth of depravity and vicious fascination that I had never dreamed of. We buried him in the woods, by the side of the tram-road, and built a pen of logs over the grave to protect it from the invasion of wild beasts. In this spot he lies to-day.

Three convicts were shot during our stay at Newburn, and the circumstances gave rise both at the time and afterward, to a great deal of comment. I will detail them in the order in which they occurred.

The first case was that of Henry Simmons. He was one of the convicts in a "chip" squad, and for some time had been quietly looking for a good chance to run in the woods. One day, when his guard, whose name was Henry Howell, was looking in another direction, he dropped his tools and took to his heels.

He had a pretty good start before he was seen, and was about one hundred and fifty yards away when Howell, after vainly calling on him to halt, opened fire with his repeating rifle. One of the big bullets struck the fugitive in the middle of the back, tearing a hole clear through him and just grazing the left of the spine. Simmons sprang into the air and fell head foremost to the ground.

A little while afterward, a trusty dashed into camp all out of breath, and told me of the affair. I sprang into the saddle and rode immediately to the spot, where I found the squad bunched together, and the guard holding them under the muzzle of his gun. Simmons lay some distance away, where he fell, weltering in a pool of blood, and to all appearances dead. The ball had passed straight through one of his lungs, and the hole where it emerged was as large as a silver dollar. I put my finger on his pulse, and, finding it still fluttering, lost no time in improvising a litter and having him carried back to camp. As soon as Dr. Hankins, the prison physician, laid eyes upon him, he declared that it was useless to attempt to treat a wound that would prove fatal in an hour or two at furthest, and he did nothing at all. I had more faith in Simmons' vitality, and had him placed upon his back in such a way that the wound would drain without being pressed, and then detailed another prisoner to keep it saturated with cold water. Next day the man was still alive, and the next, and, to cut a long story short, he recovered under this simple treatment, and eventually went back into his squad, apparently none the worse.

Not long afterward another prisoner decided to risk hot lead for liberty. His name was Charles Jourdan, and his guard was a very good-natured young man named Arthur Gleaton. The dash, as in the case of Simmons, took place in the woods, and Gleaton, not wishing to shoot a man if he could possibly avoid it, gave chase. Jourdan was double-shackled, and so handicapped by his stride-chain that he could not run, but went off at a strange hopping gait, like a kangaroo. The guard on the other hand, found that he had too much superfluous flesh for good sprinting. Thus their impediments were about equal, and it was said to be a tolerably even race for some time; but at length the fugitive began to out-distance his pursuer, and the gap between them widened out. The guard tried in vain to spurt, and then realizing himself beaten, stopped, panting and blowing, and brought his rifle to his shoulder for a farewell shot.

By that time Jourdan was fully four hundred yards away, and it was almost an impossible shot, but Gleaton rested his gun against the trunk of a tree and fired. To his surprise the man tumbled over. The bullet, aimed at the middle of the back, had dropped almost spent, and struck in the hollow of the knee, shattering the joint—literally tearing it into a pulp of flesh and bone. When we reached him, he had seated himself upon the ground, ripped open his trousers leg and was coolly scrutinizing the wound, which presented a ghastly appearance.

"I wish you would take this leg off for me, Captain," was the first thing he said.

"Well; we'll see about that when we get you in," I replied.

"No," he insisted earnestly, "do it now, with whatever knife you have. I believe that that is the only thing that will save my life."

When we brought him to the camp, he still insisted upon immediate amputation; but the physician regarded such an operation as necessarily fatal, and would not perform it. But the man's fate was sealed in any event. A short time afterward gangrene set in, and, after suffering untold agony for weeks, he died.

I shot the third man myself. He was one of two northern professional burglars received at prison under the names of Will Dare and Charles Kelly. They were sentenced at Pensacola and came for one year each. Kelly was a stupid, spiritless fellow, with not enough energy to work and not enough determination to say point-blank that he would not, and he shuffled through his sentence without more trouble than such characters usually encounter; but

Dare was of another type. He was a desperate man, murderous when aroused, and rebelled from the first against the prison yoke.

During the period of his sentence we had established a side-camp, where a certain number of prisoners stayed during the week, joining the main body at Newburn every Saturday. Dare was in the side-camp squad.

One morning one of the guards, detailed for duty there, sent me word to come into the woods to discipline Dare. The night before he came within an ace of making his escape. He had broken a hole through the cell-house wall, then cut his chain and started to crawl out. The watchman caught sight of him when he was half-way through, and covering him with his rifle, told him to come back or he would fire. Dare hesitated between two minds for quite a while, but at last he decided not to risk it and returned to his bunk, sullen and breathing vengeance. In the morning he repeated his threats, and such was the situation when I reached the woods. I inquired into the matter, and as the man showed clearly by his manner that he was unsubdued, I walked over to him and told him to get down to be whipped. He cast a furious look at me.

"Never!" he exclaimed. "I'll let no man beat upon me!"

Again I ordered him to get down.

"I tell you no!" he answered. "You'll have me to kill first."

"I don't want to kill you," I said; "but even that might be done, if necessary to enforce the rules."

"Come on, then!" he shouted; "I'll see if I can't get you first, anyhow!"

The squad were scraping gum at the time, from the faces of the boxes. The work is performed with a short-handled tool, terminating in a sharp, square blade, and it makes a formidable weapon, if used as such. As Dare spoke he rushed at me with his scraper raised in the air. I closed in and shot him through the chest with my pistol before the blow could descend.

The bullet struck him near the right nipple, passing through his lungs and lodging under the skin of his back. He turned livid as death, dropped the scrape-iron and clapped both hands over the wound.

"You've killed me!" he gurgled through a bloody foam that came upon his lips.

I saw that he was about to fall and caught him by both shoulders so as to ease him to the ground.

He lay there gasping, each respiration sending a jet of blood and air hissing from the wound, and from the expression on his face it was evident that he was trying to gather his strength for some communication. Finally he beckoned to me and I knelt close to him.

"Will you do me a favor?" he said with difficulty.

"Of course I will, Dare," I replied.

"Then write to my mother," he gasped. "She

lives at Nashville and her name is Mrs. Mary Porter. My right name is William Porter."

That exhausted him, and he was carried as speedily as possible back to camp. The prison physician happened to be there at the time, but the bullet was not removed until next day, as this case, like the others I have mentioned, was supposed to be hopeless. Nevertheless he recovered, to the surprise of everybody, and one of the first things he did, when he saw he was not going to die, was to ask me whether I had written to his home. When he learned that I had been waiting the result of his wound before sending the letter, he was very much relieved and told me not to write it at all. When I thought over the matter, however, I determined to drop a line privately to the chief of police at Nashville, to ascertain whether my prisoner might not be a fugitive from justice and wanted elsewhere. I described his personal appearance in my letter and repeated what he had told me in regard to his real name.

The reply I received startled me. It was from the mayor of Nashville, and after explaining that the letter had been handed him to answer, he said that Will Porter was his brother and the brother-in-law of the chief of police. The convict's uncle was the then Secretary of State, and my correspondent went on to say that the whole family were deeply distressed at the news I had sent them, and that I should draw upon them freely for any funds needed for medical treatment, or comforts of any character. The young man, he assured me, had always been a source of trouble to his relatives, but on account of the standing of the family they were willing to come to his assistance in any way possible. As I wrote simply to inquire after other charges and not to pry into family secrets, I dropped the matter then and there and did not answer the letter. Dare, or Porter, finally got well and served out the balance of his time without further trouble. I do not know what became of him.

It may be gathered from the foregoing that among the calls upon me was occasionally one to take a hand in surgery or medicine when emergency demanded it. Among so many men there are sure to be times when prompt surgical assistance was demanded, and to hesitate was to be lost, as far as the patient was concerned. I encountered the most remarkable case in my amateur practice a short time after Dare was shot. We had received a tall, athletic negro from west Florida, and for two or three months he worked steadily in the woods, never making any complaints. Then he came to me one morning and said that a swelling had suddenly appeared in his chest and gave him a good deal of pain.

I examined him and found a lump near the left nipple. It seemed to need lancing and in the course of the morning I laid it open. To my surprise my blade encountered a hard substance, too firmly imbedded for me to remove, and apparently a piece

of metal. Thereupon I questioned the negro closely
and elicited the fact that upward of eighteen months
before, he had got into a fight and was stabbed
in the back, near the left shoulder-blade. The
point of the knife, so he said, was broken off and
left in the wound. He had never experienced any
trouble from it, except an occasional pain in the
chest, and the swelling I have described was his first
real notification of the presence of the steel in his
body.

I did not make any further attempt to extract it,
but when the doctor arrived on his weekly visit, I
called his attention to the case and explained the
circumstances as I had heard them. Supposing the
foreign body, whatever it was, to be very small,
the doctor seized it with his forceps and gave a
smart jerk. He drew out a large knife blade between three and four inches long, and to say that he
was surprised would be to put it very mildly.
There was a ragged fracture at the lower end,
showing where it had been broken off, and the edge
was honey-combed with minute holes, like a piece of
metal that has lain in acid. The same corrosive
power that had pierced these holes had almost
erased three deeply etched letters—"IXL"—upon
the side of the blade, showing plainly that the
man's system had been gradually absorbing the
solid steel. A scar on his shoulder substantiated
the story of the stabbing, and the fact was that in
receiving the blow as he did, from behind, the ne-

gro had no idea how much of the blade had really been left in his flesh. How such a weapon had passed in its journey right through his chest and escaped severing the branching arteries of his heart, among which it certainly must have threaded, is a problem that I leave to surgeons.

We had no lack of odd characters at Newburn, and among them was an eccentric old stone-cutter from Cork by the name of John McCarty. There was nothing very bad about McCarty, but he had a vein of slyness in his composition, and he was fully determined not to tarry with us any longer than possible. In brief, he took the first good opportunity that presented to slip away, and was soon after reported to me as gone. I did not trouble myself about the usual chase but adopted simpler and more effective methods. McCarty was no woodsman, and I was morally certain that he would never dare to venture into the forest. He had lived all his life in cities, and under the circumstances such a man would gravitate to a railroad as surely as the needle finds the pole; so I dispatched three of my guards in different directions by rail, instructing one to go toward Jacksonville, one toward Tallahassee and one toward Dupont, Georgia, and all of them to get off, after riding for some distance, and walk back on the track. I particularly cautioned them not to show themselves at the car windows, and rested assured that one of them would encounter the missing McCarty.

It turned out that I was right. One of the guards, Tom Harley, went to a place called Baker's Mill, where he left the train and took his way back, counting ties. He had gone but a short distance when he bumped against a man in the darkness.

"Who's that?" asked the voice of McCarty.

"It is Harley," replied the guard, collaring him.

"And is it you, Misther Harley?" said the runaway, not the least disconcerted in the world and producing a quart bottle of whisky, "Faith an' I'm glad to see ye. And won't ye have a wee drap of whisky to warm ye some?"

Harley brought in his convivial prisoner and he never made a second attempt. He is with me now on a more recent sentence (his third), but trouble and old age have broken him and he is no longer the jolly Irishman that he was.

A pitiable case lingers in my memory of this period and calls up a picture of suffering not to be forgotten. It shows how little the outside world knows of the miseries that crime and misfortune entail.

I had gone to Gainesville after some prisoners, and while the preliminaries were being arranged I strolled through the jail and stopped before the grated door of a cell in the upper story. It was in December, 1881, and the air was bitterly raw and cold. The cell was a bare, unfurnished stone room, lighted by a large barred window without glass or covering of any kind, and the wind rushed freely through, burdened with a penetrating chill. In this wretched place a young white woman, blue-lipped, haggard and evidently sick, was crouching and seeking in vain to shelter herself from the cold. Her clothes were mean and threadbare and she was pitifully thin.

I stopped to question her, and she turned a pair of hollow eyes upon me, with a miserable, appealing look. It appeared that her name was Handsome Keene; she was a poor enough parody on it then, and she was charged with infanticide. Her teeth chattered as she told me that she had been in this cell and had no bed or bed-clothing of any kind. She slept at night on the stone floor and had no money to enable her to better her condition.

The spectacle moved me so that I did not care to trust myself to talk with her, but I handed her some money to buy a blanket. I suppose it was the first sympathy she had received for so long that she stared at the money for a moment and then burst suddenly into tears. I turned away hurriedly and rejoined my prisoners.

This woman was subsequently sentenced to prison for life, but after remaining for a time at the convict camp, she received a pardon.

CHAPTER XVII

An extraordinary incident, altogether unparalelled in my prison experience, took place near the close of our stay at Newburn. We received notice that a female prisoner was waiting transportation at Lake Butler, and I sent Mr. Wilder, our then convict-runner, after her. He appeared in due time with a rather voluptuous young negress, tricked out in gaudy finery, her hair banged over her forehead and, to all appearances, an African belle. She gave her name as Marietta Williams and was consigned to the women's quarters.

Next day she went to the commissary department after a thimble, and on her return something peculiar in her contour struck my eye. Her shoulders seemed to me inordinately broad, her hips very narrow, and her feet were certainly of abnormal proportions. The more I turned the matter over in my mind the more I was convinced that we had a masquerader, and that evening I called my assistant, Mr. Hillman, and went to the female quarters to investigate.

I ordered the other women into an adjoining room, and told Marietta of my suspicions. She whimpered and protested, but to no avail, and proved, as I supposed, a young negro man dressed in female attire. After the discovery of the ruse, he told a very curious story, which I subsequently found to be true in every particular. He was a member of an organized gang of thieves who operated in the larger towns of northern Florida. Three or four would visit a place together, and in day time would stroll around, dressed as women, and locate favorable spots for depredation at night. This not only enabled them to do all of a burglar's preliminary work with comparative safety, but it made them almost secure from identification afterward. My prisoner happened to get into a difficulty with some man while he had on skirts and was arrested before he could remove the disguise. Seeing no way out of it, he determined to carry out the deception and did so with perfect success, both at the jail and in the court-room. He pointed out several members of the same gang who were already convicts, and when questioned they corroborated his statement. They were all smooth-faced, slight fellows, well adapted to carry out a female disguise successfully.

Even when he was in the proper attire of his sex, Williams was a strange, incomprehensible fellow, who conveyed in a manner that I cannot describe that there was something abnormal about him. His history bore this out to the end. After serving a portion of his sentence, he took sick with some malady that baffled treatment, languished a long time, and at last died. That is to say his heart stopped beating and he ceased to breathe, but his body did not stiffen or lose its warmth. To all appearances he might have been asleep, and although none of the usual tests indicated life, we were afraid to bury him in that condition. Three days passed, and at the end of that time the body was as warm and flexible as in life. I took a lance and thrust it into one of the arms. Blood and foam came from the wound. I was completely nonplussed, but the physician had no doubts as to the man being already dead, and on the fourth day the body was buried. I learned afterward that in the course of his career as a double-sex thief he had hired as a servant-girl in the family of a well-known doctor at Live Oak, for the purpose, I suppose, of familiarizing himself with the premises. He gave great satisfaction in the family, and after he left they frequently spoke of him as an exceptionally good girl. When they afterward learned by accident of his secret, they were horrified.

About this time an amusing incident occurred, through which I fortunately, although unwittingly, rid the state of a notorious negro desperado named Edward Bell. He had served a term in prison, and as he was an idle, worthless fellow, I was obliged to punish him frequently. Upon his release, he went to Live Oak, Gainesville, and Jacksonville, and at all of these places declared that it was his intention to kill me on sight. He said that he proposed to have no words with me but simply shoot me down, and those who heard him were so impressed that he meant exactly what he said that many of them lost no time in putting me on my guard. However, other matters had almost crowded the matter out of my mind, when one day, happening to be in Jacksonville, I encountered Bell face to face upon the street.

"Why, hello, Bell!" I exclaimed.

"Howdy, Cap'n," he replied in considerable surprise; "I 'clar to goodness I'se glad to see you."

"I suppose you are, Bell," I said. "From what I hear you have been very anxious to see me for some time. They say you intend to shoot me on sight."

"Now who tole you such a lie as dat?" he answered with all the sorrow and indignation that a wily African can assume. "'Fore Gaud, I wouldn't tech a hair on yo' head."

"Never mind about that," I returned; "if you want to shoot, go ahead and we'll both shoot; but if not, I want to run this story down. Suppose we go to the chief of police; he is one of the parties that told me."

"I face anybody in dat lie," he replied stoutly, and we started off together. On the way, Bell suddenly remembered that he had a message to deliver in a neighboring saloon, and left me waiting for him on the pavement. I gave him time enough to get out of the back door, which I surmised was what he wanted, and then went in. Of course he was not there, and from that day to this no human being has ever laid eyes upon him in this state. He disappeared, utterly and entirely, never to return.

But not all of our prisoners left the camp in a savage frame of mind, and a female convict named Alice Franklin furnished an amusing instance of the other extreme. She came on a six months sentence, and when her discharge papers arrived I was surprised to see her burst into tears. She protested, between her sobs, that she didn't want to go, and finally I had to threaten her with severe punishment before she could be driven from the place. I had supposed that any term in a convict camp would be sufficient to satisfy a rational creature for the time being, but that night Alice returned and begged to be taken again into the fold. Again we had to drive her away, and when last seen she was slowly departing, lamenting as she went.

While affairs at camp were progressing with the vicissitudes I have endeavored to describe, a desperate man was waiting on the hope of pardon, with the firm determination to break for liberty if clemency was refused. He was Dainel Bass, the man who so narrowly escaped the gallows in 1882, for the murder of the horse-trader Moore. His partner Bryant, it will be remembered, escaped to the wilderness, and it is highly probable, although I do not know it as a fact, that he found some means of communicating his whereabouts to the prisoner.

Meantime two years had passed away, and some-what to my surprise, Bass had given me no trouble whatever. But he was a renegade by nature, in-stinct and education, and I regarded him as I would some wild animal who shows docility for a period, but is never tamed. This view proved to be cor-rect, and on November 20, 1884, he escaped under circumstances which have never fully been explained, and which were thoroughly sensational in their character.

Some little time before, his brother, who had very persistently worked for his pardon, decided that it was useless to make any further effort in that direction, and on the evening of November 19 he paid a visit to the camp ostensibly to obtain my signature to a petition, but really to in-form the prisoner that there was no longer any hope of the Governor interfering, and that a plot had been formed for his release. I was suspicious of the man, and as it was moreover positively against my orders for citizens to talk with convicts, I in-structed the guards to prevent a second occurrence of the kind.

The following morning Bass was sent with eight other prisoners to work on a tram-road some little distance from the camp. Several others in the squad were life-time convicts, and they were un-der a guard named Lenier. They had been on the tram-road but a very short time when Bass' brother again put in an appearance, and against my instructions the guard permitted the two to talk together. This visit was repeated later on, and in the afternoon, shortly before the hour for quitting work, the visitor again appeared. They chatted a few moments, apparently on general topics, and the brother, cordially bidding all good-bye, went up the road and disappeared over the brow of a little hill.

Directly he was out of sight, the crack of a revolver sounded in the air. It was a signal, and Bass, who was standing on one of the stringers of the tram-way, raised his ax at the sound and severed his chains with a single blow.

"Well, Mr. Lenier," he said, turning to the guard, with a polite bow, "I guess I'll have to be going. Good-bye, sir."

Thereupon he started off in a jog-trot in the direction his brother had taken.

"Halt!" shouted Lenier, throwing his rifle to his shoulder, "halt, there, or I'll fire!"

"Blaze away," retorted Bass, over his shoulder. The guard pulled the trigger; there was a snap and nothing more. The cartridge had failed to explode, and Lenier hurriedly pumped in another shell from the magazine. The result was the same; the gun missed fire. This was repeated until it was evident that the weapon had been tampered with, and the fugitive disappeared over the hill. At this juncture the situation was decidedly critical.

The entire squad were witnesses of the episode, and knew full well that they could make a dash without the slightest danger of being shot, and the worst of it was that Lenier was completely demoralized.

"What shall we do, boys?" he exclaimed wildly.

A life prisoner named Silas B. Carter, who has since been pardoned, saved the situation.

"Let us go back to camp at once," he said, and the balance of the gang, who were so surprised that they probably did not fully realize their opportunity, acted upon the suggestion and fell into line without a word.

When they reached the camp, Lenier was still pretty badly confused and told a curious story. He claimed that he had discovered his gun was out of order shortly after he started out with the squad, but although all of the guards had explicit instructions to come in immediately in such a contingency, he went on, trusting to luck, he said, that the squad would not discover the condition of the weapon. The rifle had been "doctored," in a peculiar fashion. The pin on the hammer, which explodes the cap, had been hammered upwards at such an angle that it just missed touching. This left the weapon perfectly useless; yet to all appearances its mechanism would be in first-class working order.

The peculiar part of the matter was that all the guards carried guns exactly alike, so that an outsider certainly could not distinguish one from the other. They were stacked together when not in use, and I was skeptical of the ability of a confederate of Bass', to pick out the right rifle to manipulate. This, coupled with the fact that Lenier had twice deliberately violated my rules according to his own admission, placed matters in so equivocal a light that I had no hesitancy in discharging him at once. I then turned my attention to pursuit.

I was sick at the time and barely able to take the saddle, but nevertheless Mr. Mills and I started with the dogs and in a short time struck the trail. I could not conceal from myself that the chances for a fight were very much better than the chances of success, for it was morally certain that Bass had been joined by a crowd of relatives and sympathizers, and that all would be armed and prepared to resist to the last ditch. We had no difficulty in finding the first traces of the flight. Bass had stopped for a moment on the other side of the hill, where he mounted a horse that his brother had in waiting, and the two rode off in an easterly direction, eventually taking the course of the Suwanee River.

The trail led first from the hill to a settler's house some distance away, where they were evidently joined by a large party. The hounds followed the scent through the house and out beyond, where it led into a field overgrown with a peculiar, prickly variety of weed know as "sand-spurs." Their needles cruelly lacerated the feet of the dogs, and we were obliged to stop and spend some time in extracting them. It was obviously impossible to follow the trail over such ground, and consequently we made a detour, striking scent again on the further side of the sand-spur field and from thence taking to the woods.

When I say that it was a long, thrilling and perilous night ride, I describe it in general terms. Words hardly do justice to the details. We were in a wilderness, expecting momentarily to be attacked by superior numbers and had not the least idea in the world where the chase would lead us. To cut the matter short, we eventually lost the trail and were obliged, most reluctantly, to turn back; but before we had proceeded any great way, the dogs struck a new track which crosses at right angles and was so hot and fresh that we felt positive it was made by the fugitive and his friends. The woods were so thinly settled and night journeys in them so unusual that we were justified in this supposition, but it proved an odd blunder. After running a while, the hounds came to bay and we rode up upon a much-excited resident, who in pursuing his homeward way had suddenly heard the note of the pack and taken to a stump. There he was perched, the dogs leaping frantically around, he waving them off, swearing the while in good set terms, and altogether a picture for an artist. We called off the besieging forces and reached home without further delay but badly disappointed.

Bass made good his escape, and penetrating the fastnesses of Taylor and Lafayette counties,

lying along the wild coast of the Gulf of Mexico,
was joined by Bryant and Columbus See, the latter
the outlaw who had led the wholesale delivery
from Hillman at camp Sing Sing. Robin Hood
and his merry men were never more typical forest
robbers and outlaws than this trio and the band
they collected about them became. They would
disappear for months in the coast jungles, living by
rod and gun, and then suddenly emerge at some
isolated country store, clad in skins, their hair
down to the middle of their backs and loaded
with forest plunder to trade for powder, shot and
tobacco. When they wanted fresh beef they put
a bullet through the first steer they encountered,
and the owner knew that it would be suicide to
make the slightest protest. People were intimidated, cabins robbed, and a mere list of their depre-
dations would fill many pages of this volume.

On one occasion they emerged from their retreat
to commit a crime of a horrid character.

Bass was at daggers' points with a brother-in-law
who lived in Jefferson County, not far from the location of the present state convict camp. He was
a farmer and lived in a little place near the public
road. Bass went to his house and called him out,
saying that he desired to have a private conversation with him. The farmer unsuspectingly complied, and the two were standing together by the
road when Bass suddenly knocked him down. Before he could rise the desperado sprang upon his

body and literally beat his brains out with a rail. He left the bloody corpse on the ground, and rejoining his companions, they went back to their hiding-place.   After this murder they were more chary of showing themselves, but it was well known where they were.   Nevertheless no officer was ever able to assemble a posse that would hazard attempting their arrest, and they are still as free as air.

CHAPTER XVIII

Some of the peculiar features of Bass' escape were duplicated not long after in a daring break made by two convicts named Wiliam Tyner and John Anderson, both white men, under short sentences. They worked in a wood-squad and were guarded by a man named Reed. One morning while in thick timber, they signaled to one another and then dropped their tools and ran. Reed called on them to stop and then began to fire. At the first shot he brought down Anderson, with a bullet through his hip, but when he pulled the trigger on Tyner he stepped upon a fallen branch and lurched forward sufficiently to throw his gun out of line and missed his man. The bullet however came so close to the fugitive that it cut a hole through his clothes, but he did not stop, and succeeded in getting away.

The wounded man lay bleeding where he fell in the bushes, and when they picked him up he glared fiercely at Reed.

"You infernal scoundrel!" he exclaimed; "why didn't you keep your promise?"

"I don't know what you mean," replied the guard.

"I mean," said Anderson bitterly, "that you bar_

gained to let us go and then shot me down like a dog."

Reed protested his innocence of any such an arrangement, and Anderson was brought into camp, where he repeated his accusation and told his story in detail. It was that he and Tyner had been promised by Reed that when they ran he would not shoot to hit but merely fire a few shots at random, to save appearances and give them plenty of chance to get away. The consideration was an order for one hundred dollars upon Anderson's brother. This story may of course have been a pure fabrication, but I am bound to say that Reed himself gave it some color by not facing the music, but leaving the camp. We nursed the wounded man and he eventually got well, always sticking to his story of a violated bargain. I took unusual interest in the matter, because some of the very ugliest rumors of prison life have their origin in affairs of the kind. I have no doubt but there have been cases probably many of them, where convicts have purchased the consent of guards to their escape and were afterward deliberately led into a death-trap. If I had any man capable of such dastardly business about me, I wanted to know it.

Six months passed, and the affair was well nigh forgotten, when I was told, one morning, that a stranger wished to see me privately. I went out and found a rudely-clad, wild-looking backwoodsman, who introduced himself as the brother-in-law of William Tyner.

"Bill is tired of hiding," he said, "and he wants to come back and serve out his sentence."

"Well, let him come," I replied, greatly surprised.

"But there's a leetle pint to be settled first," said the backwoodsman, cunningly. "You see Bill mortally hates the idea of being whipped. Now, if you'll agree not to strap him for running, he'll come back and give you no more trouble."

This novel compromise struck me favorably, and I told the man I would consent to it. He took his departure, but reappeared next day looking a trifle foolish.

"Well, what are you back for?" I said; "where is Tyner?"

"Cap'n," he replied, scratching his head, "Bill is almighty skeery of that thar whip and—"

"Yes, yes," I exclaimed impatiently, "I know all about that, but I've sent him word that I wouldn't whip him."

"I know you did, Cap'n, but Bill is such an all-fired suspicious cuss that he won't believe me—kinder thinks it's too good to be true."

"Oh, pshaw!" I said; "I'm tired of this fooling. What on earth does the man want?"

"He wants to see it in your own handwrite."

I went back into my office and drew up a formal promise not to strap William Tyner in consideration of his delivering himself up to justice. It was probably the most singular document that ever emanated from a penitentiary, and the messenger departed with it in his hand.

I was about to go into the woods the following morning when I descried Tyner coming down the road. He had on a belt stuck full of cartridges, and an immense pistol hung in easy reach of each hand.

"Good morning, Captain," he said, with a sheepish grin.

"Good morning, Tyner;" I replied, "did you receive my note?"

"Yes, sir," he said, unbuckling his pistol belt and handing it to me, weapons and all; "I guess I have no further use for this."

I took the arms and sent him to put on the stripes. He came back presently to be ironed, but I looked him in the eye and told him that I thought I could trust him without shackles and that he might consider himself a trusty. I never had occasion to regret putting this man upon his honor, and he served out his sentence without violating the parole. He corroborated Anderson's story as to the arrangement they had entered into with the guard, and claimed that they had been assured that the firing would be only a make-believe. He was employed as a guard at the expiration of his sentence, and I believe he is still working in that capacity at one of the sub-camps.

My guards were recruited almost entirely from young men of the vicinity, and not only gave me trouble constantly of a petty character, but treated me, while at Newburn, to an experience that came near being very serious. I had hired a new man, and on his first evening in camp, he requested the commissary man to take charge of fifty dollars for him. He was referred to me, as there was no safe in the commissary department, and at that moment several of the guards entered, and began drawing lots for cigars at the counter. In the midst of this, the new man discovered that he had lost his money, which he last remembered thrusting into his vest pocket. I was sent for, and to prevent a scandal, I suggested that everybody be searched. Meantime a heavy rain came up, but passed over before I ceased speaking, and just then one of the men discovered the money lying in the yard. The bills were dry, showing conclusively that they had been thrown out since the rain, and I did not hesitate to say that some one in the party had committed the theft and thrown the money away to prevent discovery upon search. This created a general outburst. The most hot-headed construed my remarks as a personal accusation, and all of them notified me that they proposed to strike, and that I need not look for any further service from them after that night. Such a step would have left me alone with all the convicts on my hands, at a long distance from help, and in a decidedly ugly position, but I decided to bring matters to an immediate crisis, and, walking over to the stockade gate, threw it wide open.

18

"All who wish to strike," I said, "will put down their guns and leave now. There is the gate—pass out."

At this they hurriedly consulted among themselves. In the parlance of poker, I had raised them out of the game, and they had no idea of being immediately taken at their word. At last they concluded to think it over and retired to their quarters. Next morning I rang the bell as usual for duty and every man filed out and took his post. The strike had died a natural death, and the subject was never alluded to again.

One of the trusties at Newburn was a colored man named Allen Davis, a very reliable fellow, although he was in for life. My sympathies were enlisted in his case and I had a movement under way to secure him a pardon, and would probably have succeeded had not Allen fallen from grace.

There was a woman at the bottom of it. We had a buxom negress as a convict, and upon the expiration of her sentence, she hired out to a family not far from the camp. She had become much enamored of Davis, and when his duties took him near her new home, she pursued a somewhat vigorous courtship that resulted in her persuading him to run away. He was acting as cook, and one morning got up early, built a fire, and disappeared.

His dusky mistress fled with him, and as the dogs, for some reason or other, refused to follow the trail, we gave the pair up for lost.

Thus matters stood for upwards of a year, when I received a letter from a gentleman named Rayford, who lived in Georgia, above Valdasta. He inquired whether a convict named Allen Davis had escaped from our camp, and stated that a man of that name had settled in his neighborhood, was said to be a fugitive, and defied arrest. The story, as I subsequently heard it in detail, was a peculiar one. Davis and the woman had gone direct to Georgia and took up quarters in a little cabin, representing themselves as man and wife. Eventually the woman became a little too gay, excited Davis' jealousy, and he administered a sound flogging to her. To revenge herself she revealed his identity, and he thereupon boldly avowed that he was a prison runaway, but swore that he would kill the first officer who attempted his arrest. As he armed himself with a double-barreled shotgun and a revolver, and was never seen without both, it seemed very probable that he would put his threat into execution, and his neighbors feared to have so dangerous a character in their proximity; hence Mr. Rayford's letter.

We made requisition upon the Governor of Georgia and procured a state warrant, in which I was delegated as agent to make the arrest. I went to Valdasta and drove nineteen miles into the country, to Mr. Rayford's house. He consented to show me the cabin of the runaway, and we proceeded thither together. I did not care to enter the house, where I would be at every disadvantage, and sent Rayford to decoy him out with the story that he wished to hire him to do some work about his place. Meantime I concealed myself among some high weeds that grew by the road-side and awaited developments.

In a short time I saw the pair emerge. Davis, his pistol at his side, his shotgun over his shoulder, and they advanced slowly toward me, engaged in conversation. When they were only a dozen or so yards away Rayford called his attention to something on a distant hill, and when he turned his head to look, I rose up, pistol in hand. The next instant Davis faced about and our eyes met.

"Uh—oh!" he exclaimed, "I won't move, 'case I knows you."

"Drop your gun, Allen," I said.

He unclasped his hand and the weapon slid off his shoulder and fell into the grass. I then ordered him to unfasten his belt, which he did, and I threw him a pair of hand-cuffs. They proved to be broken and I was obliged to take him along without them. The damsel who had caused this catastrophe was absent from home at the time, and my prisoner said that he had no yearning to stay to bid her farewell. So we started off for the station. I made him sit in the bottom of the buggy, his back to the dash-board and his legs sticking under the seat, and in this fashion, so I could look him in the face, I drove the distance. We arrived at camp without trouble, and he has been a good prisoner ever since. He said, like our original forefather, that the woman tempted him, and he became a confirmed hater of the sex.

This case calls to my mind another episode. A young man, whose name, in the absence of proper records, has escaped me, became much smitten with the pretty daughter of a settler, and, after trying in vain to ingratiate himself with the old folks, he stole the girl away one night. If he had confined himself to that, matters would probably have ended in the usual way with a parental blessing, for the young lady was a willing victim; but he stole a horse to carry out the elopement. The pair were traced, riding double, up into Georgia where sheriff Sessions of Live Oak followed them and put the honeymoon into eclipse. The girl was sent home, and her lover deposited in my charge for three years for horse-stealing. Thus ended their romance.

One other odd affair, in the way of escapes, is part of my recollection of Newburn. The principal in it was a man named Charles Springer, sent to prison for life for rape. He always protested his innocence and brooded not a little over his situation. One morning when the squad in which he was lined themselves for work in the woods, he dropped his hack and ran for it. The guard fired repeatedly, but he succeeded in getting away unhurt. This was at about 6 o'clock in the morning.

As soon as possible word was carried to the camp, and taking my two old dogs, Loud and Music, I galloped off in pursuit. We struck the trail which led toward Live Oak, and it was evident that the fugitive was making for the line of the Live Oak & Rollins Bluff Railroad. Wher he reached it, however, he feared to take along the track but ran through the underbrush and woods at the side. The two dogs never once hesitated, and we forged steadily ahead, my only fear being that Springer would reach the Suwanee River first and thus break the trail. Mile after mile reeled off behind us when we reached a place where several families did their washing at a little pool. There Springer had paused long enough to steal a woman's dress which had been hung out to dry, and the way the hounds traced his exact movement was a beautiful and wonderful thing to see. They swerved from the track, ran to the edge of the water, then to the place upon the line where the dress had hung, and then back again. It was at that time the intention of the fugitive to disguise himself, and he did put on the dress and wear it some little distance to a spot where he put a curious ruse into execution. There was a high rail fence inclosing a field at the spot, and he leaped over, ran a few yards, then jumped back, going a little distance more and repeating the process perhaps twenty times. His object was to delay the dogs, while they crossed and recrossed recovering the broken ends of the trail, but he underestimated their intelligence. When we reached the fence, Loud took one side and Music the other, and in this order they doubled down to where Springer took to the open again. In the fence-corner I found the stolen skirts, which had proven too cumbersome and which he had thrown away.

By this time we were close upon the river and I urged both dogs and horse to their utmost. At last we were rewarded by a glimpse of the runaway rushing up a little hill some distance ahead, and I gave a loud shout, upon which he dropped into a clump of underbrush. There was no escaping us now, and the dogs in their eagerness ran clear over where he lay. When I came up I pulled out my watch and saw that it was exactly noon. I had started at eight o'clock and covered thirty-five miles of trail in four hours.

In order to give the man a little punishment for all the pains he had caused me, I told him that since he had run that far he might as well run back. He started in a slow trot but soon begged to be allowed to rest, and when he essayed to get up, found himself unable to do so, for sheer stiffness and exhaustion. I dismounted, helped him into the saddle and fastened him there by passing a bridle rein from shackle to shackle under the horse's belly. Then I took the end of the other rein and we started again.

I pursued a somewhat shorter way back, through the woods, hiring a native for a guide, and we arrived at camp at about midnight. Springer served in all about eight years of his sentence, which terminated in a manner that furnishes food for reflection to juries who are inclined to form a hasty conclusion as to a man's guilt. The woman who had accused him of outrage fell sick of a mortal malady, and when she knew that death was close at hand she sent for the authorities and confessed that she had perjured herself, and that he was entirely innocent. Upon that the Board of Pardons lost no time in restoring him to liberty, but it was beyond the power of tardy justice to give back the years that had been carved out of his life.

CHAPTER XVIII

In the latter part of our stay at Newburn a case occurred involving a mystery that has never yet been solved and probably never will be. I think it took place during our second year in camp. One of our prisoners was a man named Sol Simons, sent for life. He was a burly, powerful fellow, with a face not calculated to inspire confidence. One day while at work with his squad, he leaped a fence, bounding an adjacent field, and darted into a patch of well-grown corn. This masked his escape, and the guard, despairing of obtaining a shot at him, put one of my dogs, that happened to be there, on the track and told his trusty to follow behind. This trusty was a boy of not more than fifteen, small for his age and known in the camp as Archie. I never learned anything of his history.

In a moment the trusty also had disappeared, entering the chase with all the reckless enthusiasm of a boy, and the guard sent word for me. I came soon afterward and took the track which led through thickly-wooded and swampy country, toward the river. Some miles out I was astonished to see the dog coming slowly back, alone. If ever distress and perplexity were written upon an animal's face it was on his, but he turned about upon catching sight of me and led the way to a place upon the river bank where I had no doubt but the runaway had plunged in and broken the trail. It was useless to attempt to track him farther, and the main question then was: What had become of Archie? The boy was nowhere to be found, the inference was, of course, that he had joined the fugitive in his flight.

Some days passed and several curious things came to light. A family, living near the river, had seen Simons a short time before I took up the chase. He was in the act of climbing a fence, and they remembered that he looked around and made a menacing gesture at some one. The next moment the boy and dog appeared and also climbed the fence. They were about two hundred yards behind and in this order all disappeared in the direction of the river. This story certainly did not corroborate the theory that Simons had persuaded the boy to accompany him, and still later we heard of the fugitive passing through different sections of the country, but always alone.

A few weeks later Simons was apprehended in South Florida and returned to prison. Naturally the first question that was asked him was in reference to the boy, Archie. He quailed visibly and told a rambling story to the effect that they had agreed to run away together, and that he had left him in Gainesville. I immediately communicated with the authorites of that place but could get no trace of the missing trusty. However, I learned enough to make it positive that many of the little details of Simons' story were false, and I never had any confidence in it as a whole. We made a most rigorous search in the vicinity where he took the water; we dragged the deeper places, probed the shallows and thoroughly beat the brush, but found no trace of Archie and have not to this day. Simons is still a prisoner and at this writing is under me. He sticks tenaciously to his original story, but he does not like the subject. I suspect he smells blood when he hears it mentioned.

A short time after the events narrated I severed my connection with the convict camp in consequence of a disagreement touching a division of the labor between my own and a side camp. The details of the matter would not interest the general reader and have not affected my cordial sentiments toward my old employers. Suffice it that I felt it impossible to do myself justice or do the camp justice under the arrangements proposed, and resigned. I left the camp in charge of my assistant, W. T. Hillman, who was subsequently confirmed as captain. The side-camp was under C. P. Jolly, whom I have had occasion to allude to before. I went into Jefferson County and engaged at different times in farming and mercantile business.

Although my connection with the system at this time ended as described above, the events which I am about to narrate came more or less under my personal observation and are properly part of this memoir. Among the prisoners during my regime was a young mulatto boy named John Evans. I had received him two years before, and he was about sixteen when he entered the camp. He conducted himself well, and when I left he was a trusty accompanying one of the squads into the woods. This liberty proved his undoing, for one Saturday afternoon, about a week after my departure, he was guilty of an abominable crime. He had been sent after water to the house of an old lady named Mrs. Redding, who lived in a rather isolated place and happened to be alone. Evans entered the house and made an assault upon her. There was no doubt as to his intent, and she screamed for help. As good fortune would have it, there was a large dog on the premises, and he rushed to the rescue and eventually drove the convict off. Evans took his water pail and returned to the squad.

When the news of the attempted outrage spread, the whole country-side was aroused, and arrangements were quickly made to take summary revenge. A lynching party was formed, and on the following day a visit was privately paid to my house, and I was urged to head the movement. Of course I declined to have anything to do with it, but I saw that the participants meant business, and was not surprised at the news that subsequently came in.

The mob, if a deliberate and systematic gathering including many of the leading citizens of the country could be termed a mob, put in an appearance at the camp early in the morning. It was impossible to estimate the number, but it was very large; all were armed with some sort of weapon, and they were grimly determined to put down all resistance. Some rumors of the affair had, of course, preceded them, and Captain Hillman was in a painful quandary. To make a stand would involve bloodshed, and he could not consistently turn the boy over to any one except the proper authorities. Finally he adopted a compromise. He sent the boy away in charge of a guard named Rodgers, with instructions to hide him somewhere in the woods until the storm blew over. Rodgers, with another guard, took him to a deep sink-hole a few miles from camp, secreted him in the bottom, and concealed themselves in the bushes near by.

This was done a short time before the lynchers appeared, and they were convinced that Evans was somewhere on the premises. The captain met them at the gate and a brief but pointed colloquy ensued.

"We want that convict," said the spokesman, "and if you don't give him up voluntarily, we are prepared to take him at any cost."

"He is not here," said Captain Hillman.

"Then where is he?"

"I don't know. He has gone, somewhere."

The mob hooted at this statement and insisted on searching the camp. "Very well," replied Captain Hillman;" go ahead and search."

The prisoners were on the building-chain in the cell-house, greatly alarmed, for while they knew that some sinister movement was in progress, they were unaware of is exact nature. Many a man questioned his conscience to see whether it was not he whom the vigilantes wanted, and some prepared to defend themselves. A party of the lynchers entered the building and went rapidly up and down the chain. Several of their number knew Evans, so they soon concluded that at any rate he was not about the cell. Then they gave the premises a quick but systematic search, and not finding their man came to the immediate and correct conclusion that he had been spirited away and hidden in the woods.

Upon that they divided into small parties and entered the timber. An hour or so later a party of fifteen discovered the guard Rodgers. He sprang up and presented his rifle. "Bring out Evans!" they shouted. "There aren't enough of you to take him," he replied, rapidly surveying the group. One of them laughed. "Will a hundred be enough?" he asked, and blew a small whistle. Immediately men began to pour in from all quarters of the woods and surrounded the sink-hole. They covered the guards with their rifles and took Evans out. He made no resistance and was perfectly cool. They carried him first to Mrs. Redding's house, where she identified him as her assailant, and then took him into the woods again.

They stopped where a couple of saplings, with

forked tops, grew close together and threw a pole across. A rope was attached to this improvised gallows and a horse led underneath. Evans was then placed in a standing position upon the horse's back, and the noose adjusted around his neck. Some one hit the animal a blow with a switch and the boy swung round and round in the air, where he strangled to death.

After the deed was done, the lynchers immediately dispersed, leaving the body where it hung.

There it remained, undisturbed until the following morning, when at an early hour some settlers cut it down and brought it into camp. An interesting feature of the affair was that when the mob demanded the boy of Rodgers, a squad of chippers happened to be working in the vicinity. Their guard heard the tumult, and suspecting the cause, ordered his men to lie down in the underbrush. From this point they witnessed the whole affair, unseen themselves, and could no doubt give some valuable testimony in the matter. But no notice was ever taken of it by the courts, and all I can positively affirm is that whoever prepared the noose was a seafaring man, for it was fastened with a difficult knot that no one but an experienced sailor would understand.

A few weeks after this affair the entire camp fell under a very serious difficulty which resulted in the total suspension of work for four or five days, and a great deal of trouble for everybody. The appointment of Captain Hillman created a great deal of dissatisfaction among the guards, and things did not progress smoothly under his management from the very start. Charges of mismanagement were made against him, and dissatisfaction finally culminated one day when a guard reported his trusty for punishment, and Hillman, after investigating the case, refused to administer it. Upon that the guards gave notice in a body that they would not work under him until the matter was referred to the lessee and passed upon by him. Mr. Woods and Mr. Hildreth, Major Dutton's managers, were sent for, and a searching investigation ensued, in which all the charges were advanced and probed to the bottom; they ended by sustaining the captain. That night all the guards struck.

There was nobody to send out with the squads and the prisoners were left in the cell-house upon the chain for four days. Meantime all the guards were discharged, and Captain Hillman picked up new ones wherever he could among the young men of the neighborhood. Ultimately he filled all the places, and things went on as before.

It was at or about this time that a very faithful servant of the lease system met a tragic death. I allude to my old dog Loud, who participated in so many thrilling chases, detailed in these pages. He died in harness. An escaped convict, named Jack Baker, had made his way to Jefferson County and hung about a settlement called "Lickskillet," in the country vernacular, and known by the more decorous name of Lamont upon the map. His mother lived on the outskirts of the town hard by a dense swamp, miles in extent. Baker established himself in the swamp and made incursions into the settlement, terrorizing everybody, until the settlers finally applied to the authorities to come and take him out.

The prison authorities applied to me to undertake the job. I was living not far off, knew the country well, and was considered an expert trailer. I accepted their offer and went to the spot, taking with me my old dog Loud, the best of the pack. I put up at the house of a neighbor and spent several days hunting my man. I got on his trail a number of times, but he was always so wary that I was unable to corner him. I was satisfied that he could survey the entire vicinity from his hiding-place in the swamp, and finally I made preparations as if to leave, and loudly blowing my horn galloped away. I stopped back of a hill, and after waiting about an hour I rode back just in time to see Baker dash from his mother's house and rush for the swamp. He was out of gunshot and disappeared in the rank undergrowth in safety, but Loud was hard on his track and plunged in right after him. It was impossible to follow through the morass, but I could hear the hound baying distinctly. This continued for some moments and then suddenly ceased. I waited for several hours and went as far in as I dared, but the dog never came out, and Baker per-

19

manently disappeared. I suppose that he threaded the swamp to some distant spot and then left the country. There is no doubt but that the dog ran upon him in his flight and was dispatched then and there.

Another incident overlapping the old regime into the new: One of my prisoners was a man named Andrews, an ingenious fellow, who was always tinkering at something about the shop or the yard. One day he called me over and exhibited two slabs of white hickory wood on each of which the impression of a coin was sunk, in intaglio. He explained that he had made it by putting a silver half-dollar between the slabs, screwing them together in a vise and from time to time tightening the pressure until the metal had buried itself completely in the wood. "How easy it would be," he went on to say, "to take this mold and make as many half-dollars as one wanted." I was astonished at the distinctness of the impression in the hickory; stars, eagle, goddess of liberty and all were there, down to the minutest line, but I did not encourage the enterprise, and he dropped the subject.

After Captain Hillman assumed charge he resumed experiments in secret, and finally produced an extraordinarily perfect mold. It was made by boring a hole in two pieces of wood, half the thickness of a half-dollar, and putting a disk of copper at the bottom of each. Then he repeated the old operation in the vise, and the result was that all the configuration of the coin was exactly impressed upon the copper. He then cut a minute channel to connect with the mold, and fastening the boards together, poured in an alloy of babbitt-metal, silver and powdered glass. This combination produced a splendid imitation of silver, and the coins he turned out were almost fac-similes of the genuine. The babbitt-metal he procured in the shop, where some had been used in repairs for an engine; he melted up an old spoon for the silver, and the powdered glass, which was part of the alloy, gave the true metallic ring. The only thing that the counterfeits lacked when they came out of the mold was "milling," as the minute notches around the edge are technically termed. This he remedied with a file, and the result was as near perfect as such work can well be.

He made quite a number of the spurious coins without any one suspecting the existence of his private mint, when his supply of babbitt-metal ran out and he was brought to a stand-still. Finally he resorted to an ingenious ruse. He knew that one of the wheels of Captain Hillman's buggy hung loose on the axle, and he volunteered to cast a new box. "If you will just get me a little babbitt-metal," he said to the captain, "I will make it as good as new." Captain Hillman unsuspectingly sent for a supply of the article, and it is needless to say that the box was cast very thin. Most of the metal went into half-dollars. He stole all the forks and spoons he could lay his hands on for his supply of silver.

There were two ways in which he could dispose of his counterfeits. One was at the commissary department where a supply of staple groceries, canned goods, etc., were on sale, and the other by sending to Live Oak for similar articles, which the prisoners were permitted to do. He worked both for all they were worth, and fairly flooded that section of the county, all without the least suspicion being aroused; for so many small purchases were made by convicts that the fact of any one of them possessing money attracted no attention. He was ultimately pardoned out for "exemplary conduct," which was quite a fine satire in its way, and I have lost sight of him; but I dare say he is still in his old line of business if not in some United States prison. The secret would probably never have leaked out, for none of his coins were ever returned, but in the hurry of departure, he neglected to destroy his molds, and they were discovered, long afterward, in the shop. I believe that this is the only instance on record of successful counterfeiting in a prison.

I have had frequent occasion, in the course of this narrative, to allude to the wild regions of Taylor and La fayette Counties, abutting the Gulf of Mexico and forming a favorite haunt for fugitives from justice, outlaws and desperadoes from this and adjacent states. A condition of things difficult to describe or credit exists in this section. It is literally a jungle, as wild, as desolate, and almost as impenetrable as any of interior Africa. Palmettos

and other tropical trees grow there with rank lux-
uriance, and are interlaced by gigantic creepers into a
solid mass of vegetation. As the coast is approached,
the earth becomes swampy and is finally nothing
but a vast quagmire that even the sure-footed pan-
thers cannot cross with safety. San Peter's Bay,
so called, is indicated on the map as a harbor on
the coast line of Taylor County. It is really no bay
at all, but a formidable morass, created by the en-
croachment of the sea, and extending miles inland.
To the eye it is a forest, dense, vividly green, and
carpeted with moss, but all this growth is enrooted
in a quivering stratum of slimy soil, filming the
bosom of a lagoon. To tread there is to disappear.
The treacherous moss, inviting sure foothold and
promising solidity, opens like a trap in a theater
and closes over the victim it engulfs. The ooze
beneath is full of the skeletons of animals.

Those who live in this region have learned by
long experience, and at the cost of many lives, that
there are certain paths by which the quagmire may
be traversed. San Peter's Bay is full of islands. A
stranger could not distinguish them, for the surface
presents no indications of their existence, yet some
of these areas of solid land are hundreds of acres
in extent, and they are the home and haunt of every
beast of sub-tropical America. Deer abound; black
bear smaller than the cinnamon and less savage than
the grizzly; catamounts, American tigers measuring
often eight feet from tip to tip; wild hogs; foxes,

red, black and silver; wolves; and such smaller game as rabbit, coon and "possum" swarm in the wilderness. There is generally some route, often devious as the winding of a snake, connecting these islands, and thus egress to the gulf is obtained.

It is by no means surprising that such a natural stronghold should be chosen by those who have had occasion to fly from the law or avoid their fellow-men. The huge lagoon is a nest of outlaws. There are some good people among the settlers, of course, but the bulk of them are escaped prisoners from everywhere, army deserters, and those who are hiding from the consequences of crime. They are perfectly secure. No officer ever dares venture into the lagoon, for if he escaped the quagmire, a bullet would be almost morally certain to be his fate. I have never known a single warrant to be served in that part of the country.

This outlaw population live in the rudest possible manner. A log-hut with a dirt floor and a skin bed in the corner is the usual habitation. The wilderness furnishes them with nearly everything they need, but occasionally they are obliged to emerge to purchase powder and shot and other necessaries. Most of them obtain what they need by trading on the coast. There is a considerable fishing population along the Gulf, who catch mullet, red-snapper, sea-trout, gooper and sheeps-head, and carry them to Cedar Keys, bringing back such articles as they can dispose of to profit. There are also sponge fisheries, extending all the way from Key West to Appalachicola, and constant intercourse is maintained between the outlaws and the divers. The former bring pelts and the latter augudente, Cuban liquors, ammunition, tobacco and clothing.

An inveterate hatred prevails against the negro in these sections. I do not suppose that there are over half a dozen colored families in Taylor County, and when a negro passes through he goes on a run. To illustrate; the natives had formerly a favorite amusement which consisted of organizing a bear-hunt and inviting one darky to accompany the party. He would invariably be missing when they returned, and they would report sorrowfully that he had gone into a swamp after a bear and that the beast had eaten him. Finally the appetite of Taylor County bears for negroes became so notorious that no black man would consent to join in sport of that character.

After I left the convict camp, I worked for a while near this territory, superintending turpentine culture for Ivy Brothers & Co. My hands were nearly all negroes, and I had the greatest difficulty persuading them to cross the line into Taylor County. One day I sent one of them out to "blaze" the trees around the margin of the tract in which we were working, and he lost himself in a swamp. He wandered around all night, and in the morning his cries attracted the attention of a couple of natives who were out hunting. They covered the negro with their rifles and asked him what business he had in that county.

He was too frightened to reply, and they took him into the road and told him to "git." He got. It happened that he was facing in the wrong direction when he started, and it was two days before he arrived in camp. Then he demanded his wages, and went home as straight as his legs could carry him.

On another occasion while in the same employ, I sent a negro to a settler's house to grind an ax. The darky was perfectly inoffensive and went on his way whistling. As he neared the house, the backwoodsman threw open a shutter, and not having any other pretext, shouted out: "What do you mean by whistling in my yard, you black scoundrel?" At the same time he reached for his rifle, but the negro fled in time to escape a shot, and could never after be induced to leave his squad alone.

Although homicide, theft, and every sort of outrage are very common affairs in the counties I have named, there is never any effort made to execute the law. Taylor, Lafayette, Suwanee, Columbia, Hamilton and Madison counties comprise the judicial district. Perry Court House, a straggling village, is the seat of Taylor County, but its very name is a farce. In unusually troublous times, when lawlessness of every variety was rampant, I have known the district judge to go there, open court on Monday and adjourn on Tuesday without a single case on the docket. We never had but one prisoner from Taylor County, a colored boy convicted of horse stealing. Things are almost as bad in Lafayette, but in the other counties the population is as a rule peaceful, quiet and law-abiding. It goes without saying that where the local officials, when they exist at all, have no authority, the federal officers are very unpopular characters. In the domain I have described, it would be regarded as a pious act to kill a United States marshal, and none have ever been foolhardy enough to take a warrant there. Whenever anybody wants government timber they simply help themselves, and that is the last of it.

I have spoken elsewhere of having knowledge that Daniel Bass, the desperado who escaped from prison during my administration by "doctoring" the guard's gun, was in Taylor County. I obtained my information in this way: Some time after my resignation I joined a party of friends in a hunting excursion on the gulf coast. While we were there encamped in a very wild place, a native put in an appearance, one evening, and drew me aside.

"Are you Captain Powell?" he asked.

"I am," I replied.

"Well sir," he continued, "I came from Daniel Bass. He understands that you are not now warden of the convict camp. Is it true?"

"It is perfectly true," I said; "I have nothing to do with the prison at present."

"Then he wishes to see you," said the messenger. "If you will come with me I will take you to him."

I turned this proposition over in my mind, doubtful whether it was a plot to assassinate me or an overture made in good faith. However, I could not conceive any possible business that Bass could have with me and finally I said:

"If he wants to see me, let him come here. He knows where I am, I presume, and if not, you can tell him."

The backwoodsman went away with this message, but the fugitive never appeared. I am still in doubt as to what his purpose was.

CHAPTER XIX

My memory of the year of prison management, which I have detailed in the foregoing chapters is thickly interspersed with incidents having no historical value and which I have purposely omitted from their proper chronological place, lest I might grow garrulous in my narrative. They may however have interest to those who fancy the curious, the odd, the unusual, and to that end I have grouped some of them here, where they may be easily skipped or read, as the reader pleases.

They are detached, disjointed recollections, which I have jotted down under heads, just as they occurred to me.

CONVICT'S MAIL.—Next to attempting to escape, I have found that getting out surreptitious mail occupied the thoughts and engrossed the ingenuity of the average convict. Many were the plans devised. On one occasion a prisoner bribed one of my teamsters to post his letters, but the difficulty was to get them to him. Finally he arranged to inclose his letter between two pieces of pine bark, and drop it on the road as he went to work with the squad. This ruse was probably in operation for some time before it was discovered. It is surprising and pitiful to watch how a convict's mail dwindles. The rule is that friends, brothers, sisters, parents, and wife or husband cease to write regularly inside a year and cease altogether inside of two.

After that the convict is dead to the world, abandoned, forgotten. It is hard, but it is a fact.

PROPORTION OF WHITES AND BLACKS.—When I took charge of the Florida prison the proportion of whites to blacks was as one to twenty. At present nearly one third are white. I attribute the increase to several different causes. In the early days it was possible to send a negro to prison on almost any pretext, but difficult to get a white man there, unless he committed some very heinous crime. This has largely changed, and a few years will probably see even greater differences in the race proportions, in this and other Southern convict camps.

NAILS IN THE BOXES.—Several times, while the convicts were at turpentine work, the enmity of the settlers to the lease system manifested itself in damage to the timber. The favorite method was to drive nails in the "boxes" just above the place where they were last chipped. The first blow of the hack would then be almost certain to break the blade of the implement. I have known a dozen hack-blades to be thus broken in one day. We were never able to discover the perpetrators of this mischief, and Major Dutton, who was lessee at the time, was disposed to take the matter rather nonchalantly. He sent word that he could buy hacks as

long as they could buy nails. Another plan was to
fill the "boxes" with dirt, after throwing the gum
on the ground. Thousands of dollars worth of turpentine was no doubt lost, from first to last, by this
species of deviltry, and it still breaks out at intervals at the side-camps, where the woods are worked.

PRISON AND DIVORCE.—There is a prevalent idea
among the "crackers" and negroes of the state that
a sentence to prison operates as a divorce. This
probably springs from the fact that a conviction
for felony is a ground for divorce. However, act
ing upon the above theory, there have been an immense number of bigamous marriages all over the
state. I have frequently known wives to write to
husbands in prison, coolly informing them that they
had entered wedlock for the second time, under the
circumstances, and as far as I know, there have
never been any prosecutions in the matter.

"JACKS" AND BLACK-ART.—The southern darky is
proverbially superstitious. Voodooism flourishes in
South Florida, and charms, amulets, talismans,
evil-eyes, potions, witche's-brews and the like are
devoutly believed in as efficacious in sickness, love
and revenge. The left hind foot of a rabbit, shot
in the full of the moon while in the act of jumping
over a grave, is averred to confer good luck upon
its possessor. A piece of the back-bone of a black
cat, boiled between dark and dawn, beside running
water, has a reputation for similar properties. The
root of the scrub-oak is a charm forever; a cer-

tain pink-white stone found in the beds of creeks guards the wearer against snake-bites; a piece of bark tied with red flannel and buried, causes an enemy to languish as it decays; poke-root made into tea and stirred with a silver spoon, creates jealousy. In this category come "jacks." A jack is a talisman composed of a bunch of roots, bound mummy fashion, with strips of cloth, and subjected to an incantation pronounced by an adept at voodooism. It is supposed to discover hidden articles by vibrating on the end of a string when the right spot is approached, and is a guard against danger of any sort. An old-time negro is skeptical of anybody's ability to kill a man if he has a well-made jack on his person.

From time to time we had, of course, numerous professors of the black-art in prison. Most of them immediately made jacks, and they were much feared by their fellow-convicts. One of them did quite a brisk trade in jacks, which he sold for five dollars apiece, and warranted of the most deadly character. They still play quite a prominent part in the amenities of prison life.

STORY OF ONE PRISONER.—At this writing (1890) there is but one white woman in the Florida prison. She has served twelve years, and has been in my charge during most of the changes I have described. Her name is Georgiana Abbott, and she is a life-prisoner on a charge of infanticide. I suppose she has passed through every frame of mind common to unfortunates of her class, and, at any rate, she has settled down to a dull, apathetic condition, and a habit of contentment that is remarkable. She is perfectly trustworthy, and, not long ago, thinking to do her a kindness by removing her from the environment of the camp and the association of the negro female convicts, I took her to my house near by and put her to work there. In a few days I noticed that she was looking troubled, and inquired the cause.

"Well, Captain," she said, "it's terrible lonesome here."

So I took her back to camp, where she became at once contented again. There are generally from a dozen to twenty negresses serving out sentences in camp, and they treat her with great consideration. She goes by the name of "Mamma" among them.

A CLEVER FRAUD.—The public scrivener flourishes in a convict camp. Most of the negroes are unable to read or write, and those who can drive quite a trade on Sundays preparing letters for their less fortunate companions. On one occasion this was the vehicle of a clever fraud. One of the prisoners was exceedingly anxious to write a letter, but had no stationery or postage stamps. Another convict solicited his services in writing home. The first prisoner proceeded to write his own letter on the materials furnished him, and when he had concluded read from imagination the supposititious epistle he was supposed to have indited. As the other man could not read or write he did not detect the fraud, and after that furnished paper and stamps regularly for letters that his own friends never saw.

THE UGLIEST MAN.—When I was acting as prison agent I went to Ocala after a batch of prisoners. The sheriff was a Mr. Schwartz who resided out of town, and the business of his office was mainly transacted by his chief deputy whose name was Eminger. I had never seen this man, but went at once to the court-house and inquired of the county clerk where I would be apt to find him. "He is on the street and certain to be between two blocks," answered the clerk, describing a certain locality. "You can't possibly miss him."

"But I don't know the gentleman at all," I protested. "How am I going to identify him?"

"Well, I'll tell you," replied the clerk. "Just go ahead until you see the ugliest man you ever laid your eyes on. That's Eminger. There is only one of him in the United States."

I walked over to the street he mentioned and began scanning the passers-by. In a few moments I saw a man so phenomenally ugly that I was petrified with astonishment. To borrow an expression from Artemus Ward, the very pavement recoiled from the visage he wore. I hesitated no longer but approached and addressed him by name. He at once replied and asked in some surprise, how I knew him. Thereupon I explained, and he burst into a hearty laugh. "I pride myself," he said, "upon being the ugliest man in the United States, and I am delighted to know that you recognized me so readily. Let's irrigate." I can certainly recommend him to any enterprising dime museum manager in the country.

A TEAMSTER'S PLOT.—While we were in the railroad camp at Live Oak our hauling was done by free labor. One of the teamsters was a young mulatto who became quite intimate with one of the convicts. The consequence was that several of them, including one or two trusties, formed a plot with him for a wholesale delivery of the entire prison. They proposed to obtain duplicates of the keys for the building-chain padlocks, knock the night-guard on the head and turn all the prisoners loose. After unlocking the chains in the morning I was in the habit of hanging the locks upon the slatted front of the cell-house, and in a few days one of them was purloined according to program, and handed to the teamster. The act was seen by another who reported it to me, and without saying anything I watched developments. The teamster took the lock to Live Oak and had duplicate keys made which he brought back that evening and handed to a trusty. The latter was quietly detained outside and searched, but nothing was found. However, the locks were changed and in the morning we discovered the keys, where the trusty had dropped them at the first approach. Meantime the teamster took

20

the alarm and left the county. The company posted a large reward for him, but he was not located for years. I ran across him myself. I happened to be in Albany, Georgia, and dropping into a barber shop, recognized one of the workmen as our quondam teamster. The matter was old then, and I took no steps toward his arrest, but he slipped out of the shop at the first opportunity and left Albany.

PIGS AND PRISONERS.—The meat mainly served at all the convict camps was salt pork, and the consequence was that fresh meat was always in great demand. Many were the curious ruses resorted to to procure it. There were usually a good many pigs around the premises, and at one of the camps the cell-house was so loosely built that they could slip in through the cracks. One of the negro convicts acted upon this circumstance and caught every shoat that he could lay his hands on at night time. He would quietly kill, clean and cook it, and he and the others near him on the building-chain would enjoy a feast. This went on until he had not only thinned out our own drove but was rapidly killing off all those of the neighbors that happened to stray upon the yard. Finally I got wind of it, stopped up the cracks, punished the darky and discharged the night-guard. I suppose that upward of a hundred pigs were killed.

At another camp there was a huge negro named George Smith, who had an inordinate appetite for pork which he proceeded to gratify in a peculiar manner. He was employed in the cooper-shop and was always more or less under the eye of a guard. The question was how to catch and kill a pig without attracting attention. He would take an empty barrel, place it on its side and throw some cornbread near the bottom. When a pig went in after the bread he quickly set the barrel on end, making a prisoner of the animal. Then he ignited rags and thrust them under the edge. In a short time the pig would be asphyxiated. While this was in progress, Smith would be bustling about, making a pretense of work, and in order to drown the squeals of his victim he would vigorously hammer down hoops, making a most infernal noise. When the pig gave up the ghost he reversed the barrel, plunged half his body inside, as if putting in a "head" and proceeded to skin and clean it. In these close quarters and without exciting the suspicion of guards who were constantly moving all about the place, he would turn out as neat a piece of work as any butcher. When the pig was converted into pork he would roll the barrel containing it to one corner of the yard, and cooking would be the next thing in order. It was managed in an improvised oven over an open fire, and the result would not have discredited a professional cook. When the thing finally leaked out, Smith owned up that he had eaten fresh pork every day for three months, but the captain was so struck by his ingenuity that he stayed his hand and merely told him to go and sin no more.

CHAPTER XX

Major Dutton's lease ran, with renewals, to January 1, 1890. In the latter part of 1889 advertisements were made for bids, and the contract was awarded to Mr. E. B. Bailey, a capitalist of Monticello, Florida. This change was largely due to a widespread opinion that the turpentine work was too severe for the prisoners taken as a whole, and that agricultural labor, at which Mr. Bailey proposed to engage the bulk of them, was better adapted to make the system a success.

Mr. Bailey was the representative of a family of southern planters and owned a very large estate in Jefferson County, on which corn and cotton were cultivated upon an extensive scale. Here he proposed to locate the prison headquarters. He was given the privilege of sub-leasing, and made arrangements to hire a portion of the men to four other contractors. The quota fixed upon was as follows:

J. A. Crawford of Columbia County, seventy-five men; R. A. Williams of Suwanee County, twenty men; J. W. West of Hamilton County twenty-five men; and C. K. Dutton of Suwanee County, seventy-six men. All were turpentine farmers and Mr. Williams also conducted a saw-mill business. Major

Dutton proposed to continue his old works, partly with free and partly with convict labor.

The news of the change of lease was received with rejoicing by the prisoners at the turpentine camps. A convict is invariably anxious for a change of some sort, and is willing to take chances of getting out of the frying-pan into the fire. And the fact was that the work at the pine woods, particularly the chipping, had broken down most of the long-time men; they were eager to exchange the hack and dipper for the plow and hoe.

As soon as he was awarded his contract, Mr. Bailey made overtures to me to assume charge of his camp. We finally came to terms and on November first I went to his place in Jefferson County. Some weeks prior to this a squad of convicts had been sent to him by special arrangement, to erect the necessary buildings. I found the work in course of construction, and it was, in fact, long after all the men were formally turned over before everything was finished. A treble cell-house about 120 feet long was erected, similar in general construction to those I have already described. It was really three buildings in one, with four rows of inclined sleeping platforms and the central space left vacant. Women's quarters, a kitchen, a large cistern and other work was put under way, and at the last of the year I proceeded to Camp Seymour, Major Dutton's headquarters, four miles from McAlpin Station, to assist at the division of the men. By the terms of Mr.

Bailey's arrangement, the sub-contractors, Mr. Crawford and Major Dutton, were to assume control of their men at once; Messrs. West and Williams were to be supplied from headquarters later on.

I found Camp Seymour in an uproar. The prisoners were all excitement, and those at Cypress Lake, a side-camp under charge of Captain Jolly, had been sent for. They arrived at about noon and were greeted by prodigious cheering trom the Seymour convicts, many of whom had mounted on top of the buildings and sat astride the ridge-poles. The side-camp men filed into the yard and without much delay; all were strung out in a long line against the stockade. The process of selection was curious. It was agreed that Mr. Crawford's and Major Dutton's captains should pick seventy-five apiece, choosing alternately. Major Dutton's seventy-five were then to be returned to the balance, and his captain and I to alternate until the Dutton squad was again complete. All those left were to go to Mr. Bailey's. The object of all this circumlocution was to prevent any one squad from obtaining the bulk of the able-bodied men. Mr. Crawford's lease called for negroes only, as did that of Major Dutton, originally, but the latter eventually agreed to take some whites. As a matter of fact his squad numbered seventy-six instead of seventy-five as specified, the additional man being one W. W. Willingham who was left by special arrangement with him, for the reason that the turpentine camp was deemed more secure, and the man bore the name of a desperado. His case has attracted a good deal of attention in this state, and I may as well digress at this point to advert to it. Willingham was one of the cattle kings of South Florida and made a large fortune shipping beeves to Cuba. He was a man of violent passions, badly under control, and his word was law in his domain. In one of his numerous quarrels he killed a man named Rockner, and paid his lawyer $10,000 in Spanish gold to defend him. He was acquitted and was thereafter a greater terror than ever to his neighborhood. Finally he killed one McLaughlin, his brother-in-law, and was apprehended with the greatest difficulty. It was accomplished by decoying him on board a river steamer and tying him with ropes. He employed Judge E. K. Foster, a prominent Southern politician, to defend him and paid him also $10,000. But this time he did not escape so easily. In spite of one of the hardest fights in the history of the Floridian courts, he was convicted and sentenced to imprisonment for life. He was taken to the convict camp and proved thoroughly intractable. He feared nothing and was determined to escape at any cost. Several times he made the attempt, paying no more attention to the bullets sent after him than though they were chaff, but he was always overhauled and brought back. Meantime his lawyer and representatives made strenuous efforts to obtain a pardon. Nothing was spared, and in this way most of his money was absorbed, but without result. These failures embittered him, and when an attorney called at the camp one day and offered to guarantee a pardon for a fee of $5,000, he glared at him fiercely. "I won't pay it," he said, "but I'll tell you what I'll do. I'll give $5,000 cash for a Winchester rifle and fifty cartridges. I would clear this yard of guards in less than two minutes!"

He was finally sent to Cypress Lake where he again attempted to escape, running from the yard, right between two guards who fired four loads of buckshot after him, all missing. He was brought back, and a fifty-pound ball and chain riveted around his leg. He was then put to work at a force-pump and one day deliberately shouldered the huge ball and started to walk off the yard. A guard, named Rollin Hughs, called on him to stop and then fired, the Winchester bullet striking Willingham in the back, passing through his lungs and out, shattering his left arm from the elbow down. Strange to say the wound did not kill him. His soul seemed fairly pinned to his body, and he partially recovered, but remained a helpless cripple and was never able to get very far from the hospital. The shooting was very widely commented upon, and the state legislature, by joint resolution, recommended that Hughs be indicted for it. The grand jury of the county, however, never returned a true-bill. When I saw Willingham at Seymour he was weak, pallid, and wore his arm in a sling, but he looked every inch a desperate man. He has not made any recent attempt to escape and has probably resigned himself to his fate.

To return to the division, we went to work at once and the process of selection proved tediously long. It was concluded at dark, and before day-light next morning I started for Live Oak with our prisoners. They included all the sick, the decrepit and the women, and several wagons were used to carry those unable to walk and the baggage and camp equipments. It was a long line, patrolled by guards at each side, and moved slowly through the woods toward town. We found a large crowd waiting at Live Oak, where we took the train, but the embarkation was effected without any special trouble or difficulty. The prisoners were placed on the cars on squad-chains, and we pulled out for Drifton, the nearest railroad point to Mr. Bailey's plantation.

Early in the afternoon we reached the station where a number of four-mule wagons were waiting to convey the party to the camp, about twelve miles distant. The convicts were bundled in, the guards formed as before, and the procession started.

In order to appreciate the curious demonstration which followed us clear to our destination, it must be understood that the rich agricultural region in this part of the state is thickly settled by negroes, who live the most primitive of imaginable lives, and most of whom have never been out of Jefferson County. To these simple folks the spectacle that

we formed as we passed along was one of surpass-
ing interest. They flocked from far and wide and
lined the road-side. Almost as far as one could see
there was a vista of open mouths and uplifted
hands. At one point they brought out a gigantic
bass drum, and a darky musician beat the long-roll
as we hove in sight. The convicts caught the spirit
of the occasion and sang and yelled at the tops of
their voices. One of them thrummed a guitar, and
altogether it was like a nightmare of negro-min-
strelsy.

Our audience never left us as we wound among
the hills and valleys, until well after dark we
reached the camp. The cell-house was far enough
advanced for sleeping purposes and in an hour or
two we had everybody safely housed. The present
headquarters of the Florida prison are upon what
is known as the Gamble place. It has a history.
It is part of a vast tract of between forty and fifty
thousand acres owned by a planter prince of antebellum days, named Gamble. He was a Virginian,
and hearing of the great fertility of that portion of
Northern Florida he came into the country in the
incognito of a farm laborer. At that time ti was but
sparsely settled; the land was owned by the government, and it would have been dangerous, almost
suicidal, for a speculator to come openly among the
wild "squatters." Gamble remained for a year,
working first for one farmer and then for another,
meantime taking careful memoranda of the num-

ber and location of the most desirable property. Then he disappeared and a few months later the settlers were astonished to receive notification that he had entered the land at Washington, and that they must either pay rent or move. He did not come back for several years, but sent a small army of slaves and overseers, who did nothing toward cultivating but occupied themselves in simply clearing the land. In due time they had a magnificent virgin farm of almost unbounded extent, and the man who had last been seen as a ragged laborer reappeared as a Virginian aristocrat of the first water. He managed things with a high hand and with his family easily took the social lead in a society that was practically a planters' oligarchy. He entertained on a royal scale, built houses and little towns for his slaves, was the sole law and authority of his domain and lived like a prince of the blood. He raised enormous quantities of cotton, corn and cane, and put up among other improvements a huge sugar-mill of the model of those days. It is in ruins now, and not long ago, while riding the fields, I discovered one of the pieces of shafting rusting in the grass. It required an entire squad of convicts to lift it and carry it away. The rollers were ponderous, and twelve horses were used as motor power.

When Mr. Gamble died, his property was divided among his children and each set up separate establishments upon their share. That upon which the present camp is located fell to Edward Gamble, and he erected a house upon it in the best style of the day. Time has wrought havoc with it since, and it is now in the further stages of dilapidation, but its high ceilings, spacious halls and the general arrangement of the interior testify to its former pretensions. It was the scene of many a merry gathering, and the old inhabitants tell of long lines of carriages before its porch, obsequious slaves hurrying to and fro, and splendid fetes held under the huge red-oaks on its lawn. In time the family experienced reverses; the war came on and the property eventually passed out of their hands into those of the Bailey family. The present lessee controls about 5,000 acres of this historic ground, 1,600 of which are under cultivation at the headquarters camp, cotton and corn being the crops raised. A side-camp has also been established on what is known as the Scuffle place, about two miles distant, and the prisoners are divided between them. The women and the sick and disabled are kept at headquarters.

The Edward Gamble manor-house, which I have described has been somewhat repaired and is used as guards' quarters, commissary department and for office purposes. The other buildings do not differ in any essential from the stereotyped style I have mentioned in describing several of the former camps. Logs in the rough, reinforced with lumber, are the materials employed; building-chains are used in the cell-house, and the routine of searching and securing the convicts at night has not been changed. The larger part of the farm, 1,400 of the 1,600 acres, is in cotton, and the prisoners able to work are divided into hoe and plow squads. They are under the charge of guards, and weather permitting, remain in the field all day, taking their dinner there and returning at night. The number varies from week to week, with discharges and new acquisitions, but at the present writing there are about 175 prisoners at the headquarter's and Scuffle camps.

The farm work has proven much more satisfactory to the convicts themselves than any other at which they have ever been engaged. In point of severity it is not to be compared to turpentine culture, and the facilities for obtaining fresh vegetables on the farm is a matter of the first importance. There is a large and flourishing garden at headquarters in which cabbages, turnips, collards, sweet corn, peas, tomatoes, okra, cucumbers, potatoes (both Irish and sweet) and onions are raised. The women are partly employed in the field and partly in domestic work about the headquarters. They vary in number from a dozen to upwards of twenty, and are all negresses save one, to whose case I have alluded in the preceding chapter. Clothes for the prisoners are made upon the grounds. Striped cloth is purchased by the thousand yards, cut up by a convict tailor and made into garments by the women. Clean suits are given out once a week and the others washed by men detailed for that purpose.

The fact which would perhaps first strike a stranger in examining the records of the Florida prison is the extraordinary preponderance of murder cases. There are, in all, between forty and fifty life-prisoners upon that charge—about one sixth of the entire number of convicts. Aside from this there are no peculiarly distinguishing features in the roster of crimes.

The location of the camp is decidedly picturesque. It is surrounded by hills and vales, some of them heavily wooded, and a crystal-clear stream runs within half a mile of the cell-house. It is used to operate a mill, where corn-meal for camp use is ground, and the back-water from a dam has created a considerable pond, swarming with fish, and from which alligators are occasionally shot. There is good hunting in the immediate vicinity, and partridges are now and then scared up in the very prison yard.

The gulf coast is only eighteen miles away, as the crow flies, and an almost impenetrable swamp leads from the grounds to its margin. It bisects what is known as the "flat woods," a dreary, wild reach of land settled here and there by backwoodsmen and infested by deer, bear and other big game. Both swamp and flat-woods have played their part already in prison history. We have had some few escapes. One of them was a negro named Walker Banks, a trusty, who stole a horse from a settler and rode off toward the south, intending to strike the gulf coast and leave with some of the fishermen who cruise there. He fancied it would be a mat-

ter of no difficulty to cross the flat-woods, but when
he entered them he soon became bewildered by the
monotony of the scenery and lost his way. He rode
back and forth, often in a circle, occasionally hurrying from some settler's house that he would accidentally encounter, and night overtook him in the
labyrinth. Meantime we had started in pursuit and
notified the settlers, who quickly spread the news
and turned out in force, stimulated by the hope of
reward and enraged at the heinous crime of horse-
stealing, particularly by a negro. They tracked the
bewildered fugitive down, like Indians, and finally
pressed him so close that he abandoned his horse
and made on foot for a small river emptying into
the gulf. He reached it just ahead of his pursuers,
and although it was very cold and very dark he
plunged in unhesitatingly, and held to a little
branch, with nothing but his mouth above the
water. One of the settlers fired at random and
frightened him so badly that he came out. Had it
not been for the reward they would probably have
lynched him, but as it was, they brought him in
about midnight. The appearance of the posse was
rather intimidating. They were grim, raw-boned
hunters, clad in homespun and each man carrying a
long-barreled rifle over his shoulder. This experience has prevented any other convict from essaying
the flat-woods as an avenue of escape.

Sometime later three men escaped from the cell-
house where they were under hospital treatment.

They were Robert Rowley of Pensacola, a life-prisoner on charge of murder; Daniel Blackburn, serving one year for larceny; and "Jack" Treppard, a burglar from Louisville, under three years sentence. Of the three, Blackburn was decidedly the most dangerous. He was a man of about thirty, a Floridian, and a desperado by nature. He was arrested on a river boat and defied the posse who came to take him. They fired upon him, and it was not until he had sixteen balls in his body that he finally fell and was secured. When he arrived at prison he was greatly emaciated and suffering from the effects of his wounds, but his spirit was uncowed. Rowley and Treppard were both young men of magnificent physique. Treppard was single shackled, but the other two wore merely one chain.

The trio simply made a rush. We were after them in a few minutes, but they had time to gain the swamp, and to search for them there would be like looking for the traditional needle in a hay-stack. Two days later Treppard came out half-starved, and went to the house of a negro for food; he was captured and brought back to camp. It seemed, from his story, that the party had separated shortly after entering the swamp, he going his way, and Rowley and Blackburn keeping together. He had a terrible time among the snakes, alligators and mosquitos, and was really glad to be captured. The other two were not caught. We learned subsequently that Rowley had made his way to Pensacola where he saw his wife, remained for four or five days, and then shipped upon an outward-bound vessel.

Within view of the camp, under favorable atmospheric conditions, are the evidences of a mysterious natural phenomenon that has jealously kept its secret since the earliest known records. It is a strange vivid illumination which proceeds from the heart of the impenetrable morass about twenty miles to the southwest. By day nothing is distinguishable, but on certain nights a red glare lights the sky, as from some vast conflagration. There have been numberless theories as to its character. It is believed by some to be a volcano; by others to be a natural gas well of gigantic proportions; still others aver that the swamp is the haunt of a band of moonshiners and that the light proceeds from immense stills. This last hypothesis is absurd, for no still, however large, could cast a reflection visible at that distance. It was believed for years that a tribe of Seminole Indians had escaped the fate of their race by penetrating the recesses of the swamp, and the light proceeded from fires used in their religious ceremonies. A somewhat similar theory was that the negro priests of voodooism held their orgies there. Of late years, however, these views have been abandoned, and it is tolerably certain that the mysterious light has its origin in some great natural phenomenon.

The secret is well kept. Years ago a New York newspaper offered $10,000 reward for a solution of

21

the enigma, and an expedition made a determined effort to pierce the natural barrier of swamp and jungle. They had, in places, to literally cut their way with axes, and in others to construct pontoon bridges against the quaking lagoons. At short intervals they built look-out stations and endeavored to establish a chain of communication with the outside. Their progress was very slow and before they had penetrated many miles, the poisonous exhalations of the morass completed what the rank, tropical vegetation had begun. The explorers were stricken with swamp-fever, a terrible malady, in which the period of chills are real congestions, and the febrile intervals are delirium. This unseen sentry barred the way and drove them out. Some were lost on the way and perished miserably in the morass; others succumbed to the fever when they emerged, and their look-out posts are roosts for the bears to-day. No other systematic attempt was ever made to reach the light.

This brings me to a close of this desultory memoir, in the preparation of which I have, in the absence of records, drawn mainly upon my memory. Most of the events that I have narrated are not of a character readily forgotten by one who has been an actor in them, and I may say, I think, that they are reasonably free from inaccuracy of detail. It is the history of an institution that is rapidly passing away and as such may possess an interest outside of either matter or manner. At any event, I can assure the reader that it is at least a frank recital—I have suppressed nothing, extenuated nothing—it is the simple truth of fourteen years of one of the much-talked-of and little known convict camps of the South.

THE END

McVicker's Theatre

MARCH 30:

JEFFERSON and FLORENCE

THREE WEEKS.

APRIL 20:

LOTTA

In **REPERTOIRE**

TWO WEEKS

A WONDERFUL PAINTING.

NIAGARA FALLS PANORAMA

PHILIPPOTEAUX' MASTERPIECE.

Just come from London, and visited by Queen Victoria, Prince and Princess of Wales, Prince Albert Victor, King and Queen of Sweden, and all the crowned heads and nobility of Europe, and by nearly 3,000,000 people.

EVERYBODY IN CHICAGO SHOULD SEE IT.

The First and Greatest Attraction of the World's Fair.

S. E. COR. WABASH AV. AND HUBBARD CT.

Open Daily and Sundays 10 A. M. to 10 P. M.

THE LATEST AND GREATEST

—OF—

Josiah Allen's Wife's Books.

"Samantha Among the Brethren."

By JOSIAH ALLEN'S WIFE.

Square, 12mo., 452 pp., over 100 illustrations, cloth, elegantly and substantially bound.

PRICE, $2.50.

How the Canvassing Agent's Dream Came True in the Author's Work.

The Secret.

A Canvassing Agent's Bonanza.

SEE NEXT PAGE.

"SAMANTHA AMONG THE BRETHREN"

Is a Grand Book.

BISHOP JOHN P. NEWMAN says: "It is irresistibly humorous and truthful. The best of all that has come from the pen of Josiah Allen's Wife."

" Every night Josiah would tackle me on it."

The plot of this remarkable book has much to do with the last M. E. Conference in its relation to Miss Frances E. Willard and the other lay delegates who were refused seats in the Conference. The story touches at a thousand points the vital questions of the day. There are humor, sparkle and freshness on every page. And the reader is often carried into details.

"There wuz two or three old males in the meetin' house, too old to get mad and excited easy, that held firm, and two very pious old male brothers, but poor, very poor, had to be supported by the meetin' house, and lame. They stood firm, or as firm as they could on such legs as theirs wuz, inflammatory rheumatiz and white swellin's and such.

"But all the rest got their feelin's hurt, and got mad, etc., and wouldn't do a thing to help the meetin' along.

"Well, I tried every lawful, and mebby a little onlawful, way to break to this enterprise of theirs up—and, as I heern afterwards," * * * —*A bit of the book.*

AGENTS WANTED.   (SEE NEXT PAGE.)   **AGENTS WANTED.**

H. J. SMITH & CO.,

341-351 Dearborn St., Chicago, Ill.;   234-236 S. Eighth St., Philadelphia, Pa.

Exclusive general agents for the sale of this book in the United States.

THE REALIZATION OF AN AGENT'S DREAM.

The day dream of every active agent, engaged in supplying the people with books easy to sell and good to have, is always to secure a book that almost every intelligent person would desire to possess.

The books by "Josiah Allen's Wife" have the longed for merits. Everyone on first glance over the pages of any one of her books, wants to read it.

"Samantha Among the Brethren"

is her latest and greatest work. (See particulars on preceding page.) Many thousands of this, her new book, will soon be sold. Agents will simply coin money taking orders for it. Her books never fail.

WHAT IS THE SECRET?

It is that her works are full of—well, let others speak. Listen !

SERIOUS READERS become absorbed in her writings because of their quaint logic, telling arguments, good objects and decided power. HUMOROUS READERS are simply carried away with them—both sexes, all ages (the little ones laugh over the pictures)—all are captivated. The agent's day dream is realized in this—her books sell everywhere and to all kinds of people. "SAMANTHA AMONG THE BRETHREN " is considered her best work. It is also the latest.

SENATOR HENRY W. BLAIR says :

"I read everything from the pen of Josiah Allen's Wife just as soon as I can get it. I have often thought, when wearied out with grave and exhausting labors, that one great reason why I wanted to live, in fact, why I continue to live, is, that Miss Holley writes a book occasionally and that I read it, and keep on reading the old one until a new one comes. Her works are full of wit and humor, and yet are among the most logical, eloquent, pathetic and instructive productions of our time in the discussion of the great questions."

COMMERCIAL-GAZETTE, Cincinnati, says :

"'Josiah Allen's Wife' is a singular being. Given somewhat to phonetic orthography, she does not commit such wild extravagances in that way as the late 'Josh Billings,' but her wit is none the less pungent, her hits none the less telling. * * * The vein of humor running through the story will bring a smile through the tears; but there is not a funny incident which does not cover a barbed arrow directed against injustice which enters the soul, lacerating the feelings and checking the laugh with a sob. The hand of a pains-taking literary artist is everywhere apparent. * * * The author is master of the art that hides art. It seems so natural that 'Josiah Allen's Wife' should say just what she does say, under the circumstances, should view subjects just as she views them, and she is so candid, philosophic, upright as well as downright in her sentiments, that the reader is swayed sympathetically towards her conclusions, whether his former impressions harmonized with hers or not."

MISS FRANCES E. WILLARD says :

"Modern fiction has not furnished a more thoroughly individual character than 'Josiah Allen's Wife.' She will be remembered, honored, laughed and cried over when the purely 'artistic' novelist and his heroine have passed into oblivion. * * * She is a woman, wit, philanthropist and statesman all in one."

AGENTS WANTED.   (SEE PRECEDING PAGE.)   **AGENTS WANTED.**

H. J. SMITH & CO.,

341-351 Dearborn St., Chicago, Ill.;   234-236 S. Eighth St., Philadelphia. Pa.

Exclusive general agents for sale of this book in the United States.

CHICAGO OPERA HOUSE

FIREPROOF

DAVID HENDERSON, Manager

SUNDAY, APRIL 5

"THE LILIPUTIANS"

MONDAY, APRIL 13

McCAULL OPERA Co.

IN

"THE TAR AND THE TARTAR"

TWO WEEKS

MONDAY, APRIL 27

W. H. CRANE

IN

"THE SENATOR"

FOUR WEEKS

Columbia Theatre

Monroe and Dearborn Streets.

AL HAYMAN and WILL J. DAVIS, - - - - - - Proprietors.
ALFRED HAYMAN, Acting Manager.

MARCH 30,

DR. BILL

TWO WEEKS.

APRIL 13,

MEN and WOMEN

TWO WEEKS

THE PANORAMA OF THE BATTLE OF GETTYSBURG.

OPEN FROM 8 A. M.　　　　　　CORNER WABASH AV.
TILL 10:30 P. M.　　　　　　AND PANORAMA PLACE,

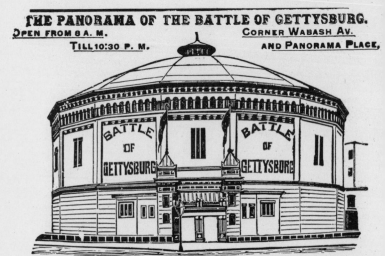

This Panorama is universally conceded by the two millions of people who have seen it to be the most extraordinary work of art ever seen in the United States. It must be seen in order to have an idea of its striking realistic effects. It took, at once, the first position and still holds it against all the competition in this country and is to-day the Standard Attraction of Chicago.

INDEXES

INDEX TO *THE AMERICAN SIBERIA*

INDEX TO THE INTRODUCTION